Reaching for the Invisible God

Also by Philip Yancey

The Jesus I Never Knew
What's So Amazing About Grace?
The Bible Jesus Read
Reaching for the Invisible God
Where Is God When It Hurts?
Disappointment with God
The Student Bible (with Tim Stafford)
Church: Why Bother?
Discovering God
Finding God in Unexpected Places
I Was Just Wondering

Books by Dr. Paul Brand and Philip Yancey

Fearfully and Wonderfully Made
In His Image
The Gift of Pain

Philip Yancey

Reaching for the Invisible God

what can we
expect to find?

ZondervanPublishingHouse
Grand Rapids, Michigan

A Division of HarperCollins*Publishers*

This is what the Lord says:
"Let not the wise man boast of his wisdom
or the strong man boast of his strength
or the rich man boast of his riches,
but let him who boasts boast about this:
that he understands and knows me...."

JEREMIAH 9:23–24

CONTENTS

PREFACE

IN ONE SENSE I have been writing this book since the first day I felt a hunger to know God. It seems rather basic, this hunger, but many of the recipes I have followed to fill it have not satisfied. Christians hold out the bright promise of "a personal relationship with God," as if to imply that knowing God works the way a relationship with a human person does. Yet one day a curtain descends, the curtain separating the invisible from the visible. How can I have a personal relationship with a being when I'm never quite sure he's there? Or is there a way I can be sure?

I have written the book in a progression from doubt toward faith, which recapitulates my own pilgrimage. For those leery of spirituality, or perhaps scarred by bad church experiences, I suggest reading as far as you can, then stopping. I plan a second book to address more practical issues of the relationship, such as communicating with God. In each case I am mindful of C. S. Lewis's comment that we need to be reminded more than instructed. I am, after all, taking up the oldest questions in the Christian experience, questions that no doubt troubled Christians in the first century as much as they trouble us in the twenty-first.

Because of certain sensitivities, I should also mention that occasionally I rely on the masculine pronoun for God. Obviously I know that God is invisible and has no body parts (the underlying reason for this book), and it's unfortunate that English has inadequate gender-neutral personal pronouns. I dislike all solutions that make God more of an abstraction and less personal. Because of the limitations of language, I fall back on the biblical solution of masculine pronouns.

My editor John Sloan accompanied me along an even more tortuous editorial path than usual. Somehow John manages to point out flaws that will require weeks of work to correct, but does so in a way that feels encouraging and hopeful. A good editor, I have learned, is part therapist or social worker. Bob Hudson and many others at Zondervan ushered the manuscript through later electronic stages. And my assistant, Melissa Nicholson, rendered much valuable service.

I sent an early draft of this book to a variety of readers to get feedback, and the marked-up manuscripts I received by return mail convinced me that a relationship with God is as subjective and varied as the persons on the other end. I wish to thank Mark Bodnarczuk, Doug Frank, David Graham, Kathy Helmers, Rob Muthiah, Catherine Pankey, Tim Stafford, Dale Suderman, and Jim Weaver for their valuable responses. They helped me not only with the content but also the structure and overall concept of the book. In early drafts I felt caught inside a maze; their shouted directions helped me find my way out.

One of these readers wrote back, "So be of good courage, my friend, and let this book be what every religious book is, an imperfect finger pointing with an indeterminable inaccuracy toward Someone we cannot by our pointing make present, but Someone from whom and toward whom we nonetheless feel permission to point, feebly, laughably, tenderly." To that, I say a hearty Amen.

PART ONE

Thirst

Our Longing for God

ONE

BORN AGAIN BREECH

*Oh God, I don't love you, I don't even want to love you,
but I want to want to love you!*

TERESA OF AVILA

ONE YEAR MY WIFE and I visited Peru, the country where Janet spent her childhood. We traveled to Cuzco and Machu Picchu to view relics of the grand Incan civilization that achieved so much without the benefit of an alphabet or knowledge of the wheel. On a grassy plateau outside Cuzco we stood next to a wall formed of towering gray stones that weighed as much as seventeen tons each.

"The stones you see were cut by hand and assembled in the wall without mortar — so precisely that you cannot insert a sheet of paper between them," our Peruvian guide boasted. "Not even modern lasers can cut so accurately. No one knows how the Incas did it. Which of course is why Erich von Daniken suggests in the book *Chariots of the Gods* that an advanced civilization from outer space must have visited the Incas."

Someone in our group asked about the engineering involved in transporting those massive stones over mountainous terrain without the use of wheels. The Incas left no written records, which prompts many such questions. Our guide stroked his chin thoughtfully and then leaned forward as if to divulge a major secret. "Well, it's like this . . ." The group grew quiet. Pronouncing each word with care, he said, "We know the tools . . . but we don't know the instruments." A look of satisfaction crossed his sunburned face.

As we all stared at him blankly, waiting for more, the guide turned and resumed the tour. For him this cryptic answer had solved the puzzle. Over the next few days, in response to other questions he repeated the phrase, which held some significance for him that eluded the rest of us. After we left Cuzco, it became a standing joke in our group. Whenever someone would ask, say, if it might rain that afternoon, another would reply in a Spanish accent, "Well . . . we know the tools, but we don't know the instruments."

That enigmatic phrase came to mind recently when I attended a reunion with several classmates from a Christian college. Though we had not seen each other for twenty years, we quickly moved past chitchat toward a deeper level of intimacy. All of us had struggled with faith, yet still gladly identified ourselves as Christians. All of us had known pain. We updated each other, telling first of children, careers, geographical moves, and graduate degrees. Then conversation turned darker: parents with Alzheimer's disease, divorced classmates, chronic illnesses, moral failures, children molested by church staff.

In the end we concluded that God is far more central to our lives now than during our college days. But as we recalled some of the language used to describe spiritual experience then, it seemed almost unintelligible. In theology classes twenty-five years before, we had studied Spirit-filled living, sin and the carnal nature, sanctification, the abundant life. None of these doctrines, however, had worked out in the way we anticipated. To explain a life of spiritual ecstasy to a person who spends all day taking care of a cranky, bedwetting Alzheimer's parent is like explaining Inca ruins by saying, "We know the tools, but we don't know the instruments." The language simply doesn't convey the meaning.

Words used in church tend to confuse people. The pastor proclaims that "Christ himself lives in you" and "we are more than conquerors," and although these words may stir up a wistful sense of longing, for many people they hardly apply to day-to-day experience. A sex addict hears them, prays for deliverance, and that night gives in yet again to an unsolicited message in his e-mail folder from someone named Candy or Heather who promises to fulfill his hottest fantasies. A woman sitting on the same pew thinks of her teenage son confined to a halfway house because of his drug abuse. She did the best she could as a parent, but God has not answered her prayers. Does God love her son less than she does?

Many others no longer make it to church, including some three million Americans who identify themselves as evangelical Christians yet never attend church. Perhaps they flamed briefly, in an InterVarsity or Campus Crusade group in college, then faded away and never reignited. As one of John Updike's characters remarked in *A Month of Sundays,* "I have no faith. Or, rather, I have faith but it doesn't seem to apply."

I listen to such people and receive letters from many more. They tell me the spiritual life did not make a lasting difference for them. What they experienced in person seemed of a different order than what they heard described so confidently from the pulpit. To my surprise, many do not blame the church or other Christians. They blame themselves. Consider this letter from a man in Iowa:

> I know there is a God: I believe He exists, *I just don't know what to believe of Him.* What do I expect from this God? Does He intervene upon request (often/seldom), or am I to accept His Son's sacrifice for my sins, count myself lucky and let the relationship go at that?
>
> I accept that I'm an immature believer: that my expectations of God are obviously not realistic. I guess I've been disappointed enough times that I simply pray for less and less in order not to be disappointed over and over.
>
> What is a relationship with God supposed to look like anyway? What should we expect from a God who says we are His friends?

That baffling question of relationship keeps cropping up in the letters. How do you sustain a relationship with a being so different from any other, imperceptible by the five senses? I hear from an inordinate number of people struggling with these questions—their letters prompted,

I suppose, by books I've written with titles like *Where Is God When It Hurts?* and *Disappointment with God*.

One correspondent wrote:

> I have been going through an enormously difficult couple of years — at times it seems I will crack beneath the pressure. All of this has shaken my faith in Jesus Christ and I am still trying to pick up the pieces of a once unshakable faith. I find myself asking the question not is God or Jesus for real, but is my faith and what is called a "personal relationship" truly authentic. I look back on all I've said and done in regards to Him and I wonder "did I really mean what I was saying?" I mean, how can I say I have faith in God when I constantly wonder if He is really there? I hear of people praying for things and that God told them this and that, but I find when I say those "spiritual" things I am only trying to impress someone or just being plain dishonest. It makes me sick to my stomach to think of it. I keep asking myself "when will I just get it? When will things click for me?" What is wrong with me?

Another reader wrote in a similarly downcast spirit, questioning whether the phrase "relationship with God" had any meaning whatsoever. He described his grandfather, a godly man who spends all day praying, reading the Bible and Christian books, and listening to sermons on tape. The old man can hardly walk or hear, and takes pills to relieve the pain in his arthritic hip. Since the death of his wife he has lived alone in a state of near-paranoia, anxious about heating bills and lights left on. "When I look at him," wrote his grandson, "I don't see a joyful saint in communion with God; I see a tired, lonely old man just sitting around waiting to go to heaven." He quoted a passage from Garrison Keillor about old Aunt Marie: "She knew that death was only a door to the kingdom where Jesus would welcome her, there would be no crying there, no suffering, but meanwhile she was fat, her heart hurt, and she lived alone with her ill-tempered little dogs, tottering around her dark little house full of Chinese figurines and old Sunday *Tribunes.*"

Yet another reader was more concise: "I wonder if in the born-again metaphor I was born breech."

———— ✿ ————

As AN EXERCISE ABOUT a decade ago, the members of a discussion group I belonged to agreed that we would each write an open letter to God and bring it to our next gathering. Going through some papers recently, I came across my own letter:

Dear God,

"You sure don't act as if God is alive" — that's the accusation one of Pattie's friends made to her, and it has haunted me ever since, as a question. Do I act as if you are alive?

Sometimes I treat you as a substance, a narcotic like alcohol or Valium, when I need a fix, to smooth over the harshness of reality, or to take it away. I can sometimes ease off from this world into an awareness of an invisible world; and most of the time I truly believe it exists, as real as this world of oxygen and grass and water. But how do I do the reverse, to let the reality of your world — of *you* — enter in and transform the numbing sameness of my daily life, and my daily self?

I see progress, I admit. I see you now as someone I respect, even reverence, rather than fear. Now your mercy and grace impress me more than your holiness and awe. Jesus has done that for me, I suppose. He has tamed you, at least enough so that we can live together in the same cage without me cowering in the corner all the time. He has made you appealing, love-able. And I tell myself he has made me appealing and love-able to you as well. That's not something I could ever come up with on my own; I have to take your word for it. Much of the time, I hardly believe it.

So how do I act as if you're alive? How do the cells of my body, the same ones that sweat and urinate and get depressed and toss and turn in bed at night — how do these cells carry around the splendor of the God of the universe in a way that leaks out for others to notice? How do I love even one person with the love you came to bring?

Occasionally I get caught up in your world, and love you, and I've learned to cope OK in this world, but how do I bring the two together? That's my prayer, I guess: to believe in the possibility of change. Living inside myself, change is hard to observe. So often it seems like learned behavior, like adaptations to an environment, as the scientists say. How do I let you change me in my essence, in my nature, to make me more like you? Or is that even possible?

Funny, I find it easier to believe in the impossible—to believe in the parting of the Red Sea, to believe in Easter—than to believe in what should seem more possible: the slow, steady dawning of your life in people like me and Janet and Dave and Mary and Bruce and Kerry and Janis and Paul. Help me to believe in the possible, God.

My friend Paul, I remember, was taken aback when I read my letter to the group. It seemed so impersonal, he said—so distant and tentative. What I described did not correspond at all to the closeness he felt with God. Recalling his response resurrects my self-doubt, making me pause and ask what qualifies me to write a book investigating a personal relationship with God. A publisher once asked me for a more "pastoral" book, and I could not deliver. I am not a pastor but a pilgrim, septic with doubt. I can offer only that perspective, an individual pilgrim's, reflecting what Frederick Buechner has described as "one who is on the way, though not necessarily very far along it, and who has at least some dim and half-baked idea of who to thank."

I have lived most of my life in the evangelical Protestant tradition, which emphasizes personal relationship, and I finally decided to write this book because I want to identify for myself how a relationship with God truly works, not how it is supposed to work. The stance of the evangelical tradition—one person seeking God alone, without priests, icons, or other mediators—peculiarly fits the temperament of a writer. Although I may consult other sources and interview wise people, in the end I must sort things out in solitude, introspectively, with blank sheets of paper on which to record my thoughts. This creates its own hazards, for the Christian life is not meant to be lived by a person sitting alone all day thinking about the Christian life.

When I begin a book, I take up a machete and start hacking my way through the jungle, not to clear a trail for others, rather to find a path through for myself. Will anyone follow? Have I lost my way? I never know the answers to those questions as I write; I just keep swinging the machete.

That image is not quite accurate, however. In carving my path I am following a map laid out by many others, the "great cloud of witnesses" who have preceded me. My struggles with faith have at least this in their favor: they come from a long, distinguished line. I find kindred expressions of doubt and confusion in the Bible itself. Sigmund Freud accused the church of teaching only questions that it can answer. Some churches may do that, but God surely does not. In books like Job, Ecclesiastes, and Habakkuk, the Bible poses blunt questions that have no answers.

As I investigate, I find that great saints also encountered many of the same roadblocks, detours, and dead ends that I experience and that my correspondents express. Modern churches tend to feature testimonies of spiritual successes, never failures, which only makes the strugglers in the pew feel worse. Books and videos likewise focus on the triumphs. Yet delve a bit deeper into church history and you will find a different story, of those who strain to swim upstream like spawning salmon.

In his *Confessions,* Saint Augustine describes in pinpoint detail his slow awakening. "I wished to be made just as certain of things that I could not see, as I was certain that seven and three make ten," he writes. He never found that certainty. This North African scholar in the fourth century contended with the same issues that plague Christians today: believing in the invisible and overcoming a nagging distrust of the church.

Hannah Whitall Smith, whose book *The Christian's Secret of a Happy Life* beckoned millions of Victorian-era readers upward to a higher plane of living, never found much happiness herself. Her husband, a famous evangelist, concocted a new formula for ecstasy that satisfied spiritual longings with sexual thrills. Later, he drifted into a pattern of serial adultery and denied the faith. Hannah stayed with him, growing disillusioned and embittered. None of her children kept the faith. One daughter married the philosopher Bertrand Russell and became an atheist like her husband. Russell's own depictions of his mother-in-law describe anything but a victorious woman.

Contemporary author Eugene Peterson attended in his adolescence a religious conference where people met by a lake each summer. They had fiery spiritual intensity and used phrases like "deeper life" and "second blessing." As he watched these people's lives, however, he noticed little continuity between the exuberance at the conference grounds and everyday life in town. "The mothers of our friends who were bitchy before were bitchy still. Mr. Billington, our history teacher, held in such veneration at the center, never relinquished his position in the high school as the most mean-spirited of all our teachers."

I mention these failures not to dampen anyone's faith but to add a dose of realism to spiritual propaganda that promises more than it can deliver. In an odd way the very failures of the church prove its doctrine. Grace, like water, flows to the lowest part. We in the church have humility and contrition to offer the world, not a formula for success. Almost alone in our success-oriented society, we admit that we have failed, are failing, and always will fail. The church in A.D. 3000 will be as rife with problems as the church in A.D. 2000 or 1000. That is why we turn to God so desperately.

"The Christian has a great advantage over other men," said C. S. Lewis, "not by being less fallen than they, nor less doomed to live in fallen world, but by knowing that he is a fallen man in a fallen world." That recognition forms my starting point in undertaking a journey to know God.

———— ✿ ————

As I began this book, I went to friends whom I respect as Christians. Some are leaders in their churches and a few have national renown. Others are ordinary citizens in the working world who take their faith seriously. I asked this question: "If a seeking person came to you and asked how your life as a Christian differs from hers as a moral non-Christian, what would you tell her?" I wanted to hear if their faith offered something besides the failures and unrealized dreams, perhaps some hope for transformation. If not, why even bother?

Some people mentioned specific changes. "Because of God, I haven't given up on my marriage, despite huge unresolved issues," said one. "And my use of money is very affected, too—I look for ways to help the poor rather than just thinking of my own desires."

A woman who had survived a scary bout with breast surgery spoke of her anxieties. "I can't help worrying. I worried about the cancer, I worry about my kids going astray. I know worrying doesn't help, but I do it anyway. Still, I have a kind of baseline confidence in God. Though it may seem deluded, I believe at a very deep level that God is in control. Some people call it a crutch, I call it my faith. For a crippled person there is one thing worse than a crutch, after all—no crutch."

Another spoke of sensing God's presence, a feeling of not being alone: "I have to incline my ear and strain to hear God speak; sometimes he speaks best through silence, but he does speak." One man said he could only detect spiritual progress by looking backward. "I know if my house caught fire, I would rush to save my journal. It's my most valuable possession, a record of my relationship with God. There have been few dramatic moments, but there have been intimate moments. As I read my journal now, in retrospect, I can see the hand of God in my life."

A nurse in a hospice described the results of faith evident at the bedside of dying patients. "I see a difference in how families with faith handle death. They mourn, of course, and cry; but they also hug each other and pray and sing hymns. There's less terror. For those without faith, death is final; it ends everything. They stand around and talk about the past. Christians remind each other there will also be a future."

Perhaps the most poignant response came from a friend whose name is well known in Christian circles. He hosts a national radio program and dispenses solid biblical advice on a weekly basis. Yet his own faith has been shaken in recent years, especially after an illness that almost killed him. Because of his radio training, my friend often responds to questions in sound bites, as if answering a listener on the air. This time, however, he thought for some time before responding, and then said this:

I have no trouble believing God is good. My question is more, What good is he? I heard awhile back that Billy Graham's daughter was undergoing marriage problems, so the Grahams and the in-laws all flew to Europe to meet with them and pray for the couple. They ended up getting divorced anyway. If Billy Graham's prayers don't get answered, what's the use of my praying? I look at my life—the health problems, my own daughter's struggles, my marriage. I cry out to God for help, and it's hard to know just how he answers. Really, what can we count on God for?

That final question struck me like a bullet and has stayed lodged inside me. I know theologians who would snort at such a phrase as one more mark of self-centered faith. Yet I believe it lies at the heart of much disillusionment with God. In all our personal relationships—with parents, children, store clerks, gas station attendants, pastors, neighbors—we have some idea what to expect. What about God? What can we count on from a personal relationship with him?

———— ✧ ————

M Y ROOMMATE FOR TWO years at a Christian college was a German named Reiner. Returning to Germany after graduation, Reiner taught at a camp for the disabled where, relying on college notes, he gave a stirring speech on the Victorious Christian Life. "Regardless of the wheelchair you are sitting in, you can have victory, a full life. God lives within you!" he told his audience of paraplegics, cerebral palsy patients, and the mentally challenged. He found it disconcerting to address people with poor muscle control. Their heads wobbled, they slumped in their chairs, they drooled.

The campers found listening to Reiner equally disconcerting. Some of them went to Gerta, director of the camp, and complained that they could not make sense of what he was saying. "Well then, tell him!" said Gerta.

One brave woman screwed up her courage and confronted Reiner. "It's like you're talking about the sun, and we're in a dark room with no windows," she said. "We can't understand anything you say. You talk about solutions, about the flowers outside, about overcoming and victory. These things don't apply to us in our lives."

My friend Reiner was crushed. To him, the message seemed so clear. He was quoting directly from Paul's epistles, was he not? His pride wounded, he thought about coming at them with a kind of spiritual bludgeon: *There's something wrong with you people. You need to grow in the Lord. You need to triumph over adversity.*

Instead, after a night of prayer, Reiner returned with a different message. "I don't know what to say," he told them the next morning. "I'm confused. Without the message of victory, I don't know what to say." He stayed silent and hung his head.

> C oncepts create idols, only wonder grasps anything.
>
> GREGORY OF NYSSA

The woman who had confronted him finally spoke up from the room full of disabled people. "Now we understand you," she said. "Now we are ready to listen."

Two

THIRSTING AT THE FOUNTAINSIDE

The human comedy doesn't attract me enough. I am not entirely of this world.... I am from elsewhere. And it is worth finding this elsewhere beyond the walls. But where is it?

—EUGENE IONESCO

ON A VISIT TO Russia in 1991 I attended my first Orthodox church service, which is designed to express sensually the mystery and majesty of worship. Ensconced candles lent a soft, eerie glow to the cathedral, as if the stucco walls were the source of light rather than its reflection. The air hummed with the throaty, bass-clef harmony of the Russian liturgy, a cell-vibrating sound that seemed to come from under the floor. A service lasts three to four hours, with worshipers entering and leaving at will. No one invites congregants to "pass the peace" or "greet the folks around you with a smile." They stand—there are no chairs or pews—and watch the professionals, who after a thousand years of unchanged liturgy are very professional indeed.

Later that same day, accompanied by a priest and a representative from Prison Fellowship, I visited a chapel in the basement of a nearby prison.

In an act of remarkable boldness, a communist functionary in the formerly atheistic nation had allowed its construction. Located on the lowest sub-terranean level, the chapel was an oasis of beauty in an otherwise grim dungeon. Prisoners had cleaned out a seventy-year accumulation of filth from the room, installed a marble floor, and mounted finely wrought brass sconces on the walls. They took pride in their chapel, at that time the only prison chapel in all of Russia. Each week priests traveled from a monastery to conduct a service there, and for this occasion the warden allowed pris-oners out of their cells, which naturally guaranteed good attendance.

We spent a few minutes admiring the handiwork that went into the room, and Brother Bonifato pointed to the icon for the prison chapel, "Our Lady Who Takes Away Sadness." Ron Nikkel of Prison Fellowship commented that there must be much sadness within these walls, then turned to Brother Bonifato and asked if he would say a prayer for the pris-oners. Brother Bonifato looked puzzled and Ron repeated, "Could you say a prayer for the prisoners?"

"A prayer? You want a prayer?" Brother Bonifato asked, and we nod-ded. He disappeared behind the altar at the end of the room. He brought out another icon of the Lady Who Takes Away Sadness, which he propped up on a stand. Then he retrieved two candle holders and two incense bowls, which he laboriously hung in place and lit. Their sweet fragrance instantly filled the room. He removed his headpiece and outer vestments, and laced shiny gold cuffs over his black sleeves. He placed a droopy gold stole around his neck, and then a gold crucifix. He carefully fitted a different, more formal headpiece on his head. Before each action, he paused to kiss the cross or genuflect. Finally, he was ready to pray.

Prayer involved a whole new series of formalities. Brother Bonifato did not say prayers; he sang them, following the score from a liturgy book propped on another stand. Finally, twenty minutes after Ron had requested a prayer for the prisoners, Brother Bonifato said "Amen," and we exited the prison into the bracing fresh air outside.

Elsewhere in Russia I met Western Christians who sharply criticized the Orthodox Church. Reverence, submission, awe—the Orthodox con-vey these qualities superbly in worship, they admitted, but their God remains faraway, approachable only after much preparation and only through intermediaries such as priests and icons. Yet I came away with the conviction that we have something to learn from the Orthodox. Under a Communist regime that had no place for God, that made human beings the measure of all things, the Russian church continued to place God at the center and survived the most determined atheistic assault in history.

I knew that Brother Bonifato was no otherworldly mystic, for I had seen his service among criminals in a place that could only be called a dungeon. His tradition had taught him, though, that you do not approach the Other as you would approach your own kind. The ritual helped him move from a spirit of urgency and immediacy — the demands of the prison ministry — to a place of calm whose rhythms were the rhythms of eternity.

If you find God with great ease, suggested Thomas Merton, perhaps it is not God that you have found.

THE PHYSICIST JOHN POLKINGHORNE, who resigned his post at Cambridge to seek ordination as an Anglican priest, points out a major difference between knowing science and knowing theology. Science progressively accumulates knowledge: first Ptolemy, then Galileo, Copernicus, Newton, and Einstein. Each of these scientists built on the foundation of those who preceded him, so that an ordinary scientist today has a more accurate conception of the physical world than was ever possible for Sir Isaac Newton. Knowledge of God proceeds in an entirely different manner. Every encounter is unique and individual, just like any meeting between two persons, so that a fifth-century mystic or an illiterate immigrant may have a deeper knowledge of God than a twentieth-century theologian.

With the hubris of a medieval cosmologist, Carl Sagan used to pronounce what he could not possibly know: "The cosmos is all there is and all there ever will be." Yet not even Sagan stayed immune from the desire to connect with the Other. His novel *Contact* tells of governments willing to spend half a trillion dollars to send a messenger to another world. That messenger, played in the movie by Jodie Foster, did indeed make contact and then returned to find her report discounted by scientists and welcomed by the masses. Sagan's novel revealed more than he may have intended.

Christians claim there are times, though perhaps less frequent than we would lead others to believe, when we do make personal contact with the Creator of the universe. "I have seen things that make all my writings seem like straw," wrote Thomas Aquinas about one such encounter.

In the movie *Contact,* Jodie Foster lounges against the Very Large Array radio dishes day after day, night after night, until one day a distinctive pattern of sound crackles through the headphones and she sits bolt upright. *Something is there!* For Christians too, contact can bring a kind of shock. Listen to C. S. Lewis:

> It is always shocking to meet life where we thought we were alone. "Look out!" we cry, "it's *alive.*" And therefore this is the very point at which so many draw back—I would have done so myself if I could—and proceed no further with Christianity. An "impersonal God"—well and good. A subjective God of beauty, truth and goodness, inside our own heads—better still. A formless life-force surging through us, a vast power which we can tap—best of all. But God Himself, alive, pulling at the other end of the cord, perhaps approaching at an infinite speed, the hunter, king, husband—that is quite another matter. There comes a moment when the children who have been playing at burglars hush suddenly: was that a *real* footstep in the hall? There comes a moment when people who have been dabbling in religion ("Man's search for God!") suddenly draw back. Supposing we really found Him? We never meant it to come to *that!* Worse still, supposing He had found us?

I too have felt the tug at times, a tug strong enough to jerk me out of cynicism and rebellion, strong enough to wrench my life in a new direction. Yet for long stretches, achingly long stretches, I have also sat with my headphones on, desperate for some message from the other world, yearning for reassuring contact, and heard only static.

How can something as fundamental as a God who created us to know and love him become so tenuous? If God, as Paul told a sophisticated crowd of skeptics in Athens, "did this," meaning all creation, in order that we might reach out and find him, why not make himself more obvious?

Writers of the Bible lived in the "Holy Land," where bushes burst into flame, where rocks and volcanoes gushed sacred metaphors and the stars bespoke God's grandeur. No longer. The supernatural world has seemingly gone into hiding, leaving us alone with the visible. The thirst for God, though, for *contact* with the unseen, the hunger for love from a cosmic Parent who can somehow fashion meaning from this scrambled world, defiantly persists.

Those of us who live in a material world, in bodies covered by skin, understandably want God to connect with us in our world. I once visited the imposing shrine to the Virgin of Guadeloupe outside Mexico City. In a museum room, placards explain that the image of the Virgin miraculously appeared to an Indian on the site in 1531 and left her image on his coat, a tattered thing that now hangs dramatically inside. The eye of the Virgin supposedly retains the image of the Indian, and tourists scrutinize grainy blowups of the Virgin's iris in search of the man's tiny image. Other blowups feature her earlobe, on which the Song of Solomon is said to be inscribed. Thousands of pilgrims joined me that day, and we gazed at a statue of the Virgin from a mechanized slide-walk which smoothly transported us through the shrine even as priests conducted mass on the other side of a glass wall.

I don't know if Carl Sagan ever visited the Shrine of Guadeloupe, but I can guess his reaction if he did: people imagine what they want, as a form of projection or wish-fulfillment. We yearn for visibility, hoping to bring the supernatural down to our level of materiality. In 1999 an image of Jesus appeared on a glass office building in Florida, perceptible at least to some from a certain angle, and the next day a mile-long procession of cars snarled traffic on the street outside. Creatures of flesh and blood, we lose patience with anything that does not manifest itself on our terms.

Alan Turing, one of the pioneers in computers and artificial intelligence, proposed a method to answer the question, "Can computers think?" Put a keyboard and monitor on one side of a wall and X (either a person or machine) on the other. Ask X a series of questions, and wait for the answers to appear on the monitor. *Please write me a sonnet on the following subject [provide a topic]. Add 34957 to 70764. Do you play chess? [then pose a series of chess problems].* Turing suggested that a machine could be said to think if the question-asker could not ultimately determine from the answers whether X was a person or a machine. When he wrote the paper, in 1950, the odds worked heavily against the machine. Now artificial intelligence has advanced to the point where computers can defeat the best chess players in the world and counseling software can carry on extended dialogues with its "clients." A well-programmed machine could conceivably confound an interrogator for some time.

Since God remains invisible, people tend to remake God in their own image. The *Conversations with God* phenomenon comprises three books, all best-sellers with millions of avid readers, which the author claims were dictated to him by God. I met one of the books' devotees recently and asked him to describe the God he believes in. "God doesn't exist apart from us," he said. "He is the composite of all good energy in the world. We create God, all of us." In other words, God would never pass the Turing test.

Christians, in contrast, believe that God possesses all the qualities of personhood: unpredictable, relational, free, intelligent, emotional, sometimes cooperative and sometimes resistant. The problem is how to get God on the other side of a wall to answer our questions. He won't type back. God is not, say the scientists, empirically verifiable. We must believe in something—the instinct is as strong as thirst or hunger—but we no longer know what to believe. Traditional theology seems, to some people, like reading recipes to the starving—like an unslaked thirst.

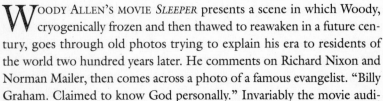

WOODY ALLEN'S MOVIE *SLEEPER* presents a scene in which Woody, cryogenically frozen and then thawed to reawaken in a future century, goes through old photos trying to explain his era to residents of the world two hundred years later. He comments on Richard Nixon and Norman Mailer, then comes across a photo of a famous evangelist. "Billy Graham. Claimed to know God personally." Invariably the movie audience laughs, and who can blame them? Such a notion does seem rather absurd—and yet nothing better expresses the promise dangled before us.

God is personal. Much of Christian theology, hammered out in the rarified atmosphere of Greek philosophy, obscures this plain fact by using impersonal phrases such as "Ground of all Being" or "Inevitable Inference" to describe God.* But the Bible, both Old Testament and New, portrays a God who affects us and is affected by us. "For the Lord

---

* Philosopher William James observed caustically, "Would martyrs have sung in the flames for a mere inference, however inevitable it might be?"

takes delight in his people," says the psalmist (149:4); at times God also takes great exception to his people, say the prophets. The personality of God leaps out of almost every page of the Bible. "God is love," says the apostle John. "Whoever lives in love lives in God, and God in him." It would be difficult to get more personal.

Why, then, do we find it so difficult to relate personally to this God? At various times people tended to pray to local saints, who seemed more accessible and less scary. Protestant Reformers and Catholic mystics, though, challenged us to relate to God directly, without intermediaries. And modern evangelicalism summons us to know God, to talk to God in conversational language, to love God as one might love a friend. Listen to the "praise songs" in modern churches, which sound exactly like love songs played on pop radio, with God or Jesus substituted as the lover.

The same evangelical tradition that spurs us on to greater intimacy also invites abuse. "I asked the Lord what to speak on and he said, Don't speak on pride, speak on stewardship." "The Lord told me he wanted a new medical center in this city." "God is whispering to me right now that someone in this audience is struggling with a broken marriage." I know for a fact that some statements exactly like these are deceitful, from speakers who say them sloppily or manipulatively. The wording implies a kind of voice-to-voice conversation that did not take place, and the fudged report has the effect of creating a spiritual caste that downgrades others' experiences.

Martin Marty, a Lutheran minister and popular writer, confesses he "can count on one hand the number of times in my life that 'immediacy' [with God] hit me enough to merit my talking about it to the person closest to me, and can count no times it was worth advertising to the public." He speaks instead of a season of abandonment by God, of dereliction, that descended on him during his wife's lengthy terminal illness.

Frederick Buechner is a writer I hold in the highest esteem both for his craft and his Christian commitment. He left a promising career as a novelist to attend seminary and seek ordination as a Presbyterian minister, only to return to writing as his primary "pulpit." In his memoir, Buechner records a scene of tense anticipation in which he lay in the warm sunlight pleading for a miracle, for some definite sign from the Lord.

> In just such a place on just such a day I lay down in the grass with just such wild expectations. Part of what it means to believe in God,

at least part of what it means for me, is to believe in the possibility of miracle, and because of a variety of circumstances I had a very strong feeling at that moment that the time was ripe for miracle, my life was ripe for miracle, and the very strength of the feeling itself seemed a kind of vanguard of miracle. Something was going to happen—something extraordinary that I could perhaps even see and hear—and I was so nearly sure of it that in retrospect I am surprised that by the power of autosuggestion I was unable to make it happen. But the sunshine was too bright, the air too clear, some residual skepticism in myself too sharp to make it possible to imagine ghosts among the apple trees or voices among the yellow jackets, and nothing like what I expected happened at all.

What he got was the soughing wind and the clack-clack of two apple branches scraping against each other. Had God spoken or not? Why wouldn't God use a vocabulary less susceptible to doubt and misinterpretation? For Buechner, at least, God did not.

While in his fifties Buechner spent a semester teaching at Wheaton College where he encountered the familiarity of evangelical language for the first time. "I was astonished to hear students shift casually from small talk about the weather and movies to a discussion of what God was doing in their lives. If anybody said anything like that in my part of the world, the ceiling would fall in, the house would catch fire, and people's eyes would roll up in their heads." Although he came to admire the students' fervency, it seemed to him at first that their God resembled a cosmic Good Buddy.

Do we, like billboards for Pepsi, fan a thirst we cannot quench? Just last week my church sang: "I want to know you more / I want to touch you / I want to see your face." Nowhere in the Bible do I find a promise that we will touch God, or see his face, not in this life at least.

> I die of thirst, here at the fountainside.
>
> RICHARD WILBUR

Modern American religion speaks in "friendly" terms with God even though, as C. S. Lewis points out in *The Four Loves,* friendship is the form of love that least accurately describes the truth of a creature's encounter with the Creator. How, then, can we have a "personal relationship" with a God who is invisible, when we're never quite sure he's there?

PART TWO

Faith

*When God Seems Absent,
Indifferent, or Even Hostile*

ROOM FOR DOUBT

We both believe, and disbelieve a hundred times an Hour,
which keeps Believing nimble.

EMILY DICKINSON

I MUST EXERCISE FAITH simply to believe that God exists, a basic require-
ment for any relationship. And yet when I wish to explore how faith
works, I usually sneak in by the back door of doubt, for I best learn about
my own need for faith during its absence. God's invisibility guarantees
I will experience times of doubt.

Everyone dangles on a pendulum that swings from belief to unbelief,
back to belief, and ends—where? Some never find faith. A woman asked
Bertrand Russell, the world's best-known atheist at the time, what he would
say if it turned out he had been wrong and found himself standing outside the Pearly Gates. His eyes lighting up, Russell replied in his high, thin
voice, "Why, I should say, 'God, you gave us insufficient evidence!'"

Others have faith, then lose it. Peter De Vries, product of a strict
Calvinist home and undergraduate studies at Calvin College, went on

to write savagely comic novels about the loss of faith. One of his characters "could not forgive God for not existing"—words that explain
much of De Vries's own God-obsessed work. His novel *The Blood of the
Lamb* tells of Don Wanderhope, father of an eleven-year-old girl who
contracts leukemia. Just as the bone marrow begins to respond to treatment and she approaches remission, an infection sweeps through the
ward and kills her. Wanderhope, who has brought in a cake with his
daughter's name on it, leaves the hospital, returns to the church where
he prayed for her healing, and hurls the cake at the crucifix hanging in
front of the church. The cake hits just beneath the crown of thorns, and
brightly colored icing drips down Jesus' dejected face of stone.

I feel kinship with those who, like Russell, find it impossible to believe
or, like De Vries, find it impossible to keep on believing in the face of
apparent betrayal. I have been in a similar place at times, and I marvel
that God bestowed on me an unexpected gift of faith. Examining my own
periods of faithlessness, I see in them all manner of unbelief. Sometimes
I shy away for lack of evidence, sometimes I slink away in hurt or disillusionment, and sometimes I turn aside in willful disobedience.
Something, though, keeps drawing me back to God. What? I ask myself.

"This is a hard teaching. Who can accept it?" said Jesus' disciples in
words that resonate in every doubter. Jesus' listeners found themselves
simultaneously attracted and repelled, like a compass needle brought
close to a magnet. As his words sank in, one by one the crowd of onlook-
ers and followers slouched away, leaving only the Twelve. "You do not
want to leave too, do you?" Jesus asked them in a tone somewhere
between plaintiveness and resignation. As usual, Simon Peter spoke up:
"Lord, to whom shall we go?"

That, for me, is the bottom-line answer to why I stick around. To my
shame, I admit that one of the strongest reasons I stay in the fold is the
lack of good alternatives, many of which I have tried. *Lord, to whom
shall I go?* The only thing more difficult than having a relationship with
an invisible God is having no such relationship.

GOD OFTEN DOES HIS work through "holy fools," dreamers who strike
out in ridiculous faith, whereas I approach my own decisions with

calculation and restraint. In fact, a curious law of reversal seems to apply in matters of faith. The modern world honors intelligence, good looks, confidence, and sophistication. God, apparently, does not. To accomplish his work God often relies on simple, uneducated people who don't know any better than to trust him, and through them wonders happen. The least gifted person can become a master in prayer, because prayer requires only an intense desire to spend time with God.

My church in Chicago, a delightful mixture of races and economic groups, once scheduled an all-night vigil of prayer during a major crisis. Several people voiced concern. Was it safe, given our inner-city neighborhood? Should we hire guards or escorts for the parking lot? What if no one showed up? At length we discussed the practicality of the event before finally putting the night of prayer on the calendar.

The poorest members of the congregation, a group of senior citizens from a housing project, responded the most enthusiastically to the prayer vigil. I could not help wondering how many of their prayers had gone unanswered over the years—they lived in the projects, after all, amid crime, poverty, and suffering—yet still they showed a childlike trust in the power of prayer. "How long do you want to stay—an hour or two?" we asked, thinking of the logistics of van shuttles. "Oh, we'll stay all night," they replied.

One African-American woman in her nineties, who walked with a cane and could barely see, explained to a staff member why she wanted to spend the night sitting on the hard pews of a church in an unsafe neighborhood. "You see, they's lots of things we can't do in this church. We ain't so educated, and we ain't got as much energy as some of you younger folks. But we can pray. We got time, and we got faith. Some of us don't sleep much anyway. We can pray all night if needs be."

And so they did. Meanwhile, a bunch of yuppies in a downtown church learned an important lesson: Faith appears where least expected and falters where it should be thriving.

Despite my innate skepticism, I yearn for the kind of faith that came so naturally to those senior citizens, childlike faith that asks God for the impossible. I do so for one reason: Jesus prized such faith, as the miracle stories in the Gospels make clear. "Your faith has healed you," Jesus would say, deflecting attention from himself to the healed person.

Miraculous power did not come from his side alone but somehow depended on the recipient.

Reading through all the miracle stories together, I see that faith comes in different degrees. A few people demonstrated bold, unshakable faith, such as a centurion who told Jesus he need not bother with a visit—just a word would heal his servant long-distance. "I tell you the truth, I have not found anyone in Israel with such great faith," Jesus remarked, astonished. Another time, a foreign woman pursued Jesus as he was seeking peace and quiet. At first Jesus answered her not a word. Then he replied sharply, telling her he was sent to the lost sheep of Israel, not to "dogs." Nothing could deter this stubborn Canaanite woman, and her perseverance won Jesus over. "Woman, you have great faith!" he said. These foreigners, the least likely people to demonstrate strong faith, impressed Jesus. Why should a centurion and a Canaanite, who both lacked Jewish roots, put their trust in a Messiah his own countrymen had trouble accepting?

In glaring contrast, the people who should have known better lagged in faith. Jesus' own neighbors doubted him. John the Baptist, his cousin and forerunner, later questioned him. Among the twelve disciples Thomas doubted, Peter cursed, and Judas betrayed, all after spending three years with Jesus.

The same law of reversal I observed in my church in Chicago seems to apply in the Gospels: Faith appears where least expected and falters where it should be thriving. What gives me hope, though, is that Jesus worked with whatever grain of faith a person might muster. He did, after all, honor the faith of everyone who asked, from the bold centurion to doubting Thomas to the distraught father who cried, "I do believe; help me overcome my unbelief!"

Noting the wide spectrum of faith represented in the Bible, I wonder whether people naturally divide into various "faith types" just as they divide into personality types. An introvert who approaches other people cautiously, I approach God the same way. And just as I tend to be calculated about my decisions, considering all sides, I also experience the curse of the "on the other hand" syndrome whenever I read a bright promise in the Bible. I used to feel constant guilt over my void of faith, and still I long for more, but increasingly I have come to terms with my level of faith. We are not all shy or melancholic or introverted; why should we expect to have the same measure or kind of faith?

DOUBT IS THE SKELETON in the closet of faith, and I know no better way to treat a skeleton than to bring it into the open and expose it for what it is: not something to hide or fear, but a hard structure on which living tissue may grow. If I asked every person to stop reading whose faith has wavered—as a result of a tragedy, or a confidence-shaking encounter with science or with another religion, or disillusionment with the church or individual Christians—I might as well end the book with this sentence. Why, then, does the church treat doubt as an enemy? I was once asked to sign *Christianity Today* magazine's statement of faith "without doubt or equivocation." I had to tell them I can barely sign my own name without doubt or equivocation.

"I don't know how the kind of faith required of a Christian living in the 20th century can be at all if it is not grounded on the experience of unbelief," wrote novelist Flannery O'Connor to a friend. "Peter said, 'Lord, I believe. Help my unbelief.' It is the most natural and most human and most agonizing prayer in the gospels, and I think it is the foundation prayer of faith." O'Connor got her characters wrong (the quote comes from the demoniac's father in Mark 9, not Peter) but her sentiments right. Doubt always coexists with faith, for in the presence of certainty who would need faith at all?

In my childhood I heard the old Scottish chorus, "Cheer up, ye saints of God, / there's nothing to worry about, / nothing to make ye feel afraid, / nothing to make ye doubt." I liked the rousing spirit of the song, especially if the singers rrrolled their "r's" in a Scottish brogue. Now, though, as I look at the words I wonder if the writer read the same Bible I read, a book whose heroes stagger from one daunting crisis to the next.

Job's friends reacted to his doubts with shock and dismay. "Stop feeling that way! Shame on you for having such scandalous thoughts!" they said in effect. God, who had his own differences with Job, nonetheless held up Job, not the friends, as the hero. Books such as Job, Ecclesiastes, Psalms, and Lamentations show beyond question that God understands the value of human doubt, amply portraying it in sacred scripture.

Modern psychology teaches that since you can't really eliminate your feelings you might as well go ahead and express them openly, and the Bible seems to agree. Those who honestly confront their doubts often find themselves growing into a faith that transcends the doubts.

I need only mention a few Christian stalwarts to establish the prevalence, perhaps inevitability, of doubt. Martin Luther battled constantly against doubt and depression. "For more than a week," Luther once wrote, "Christ was wholly lost. I was shaken by desperation and blasphemy against God." The Puritan Richard Baxter rested his faith on "probabilities instead of full undoubted certainties"; fellow-Puritan Increase Mather wrote entries in his diary such as "Greatly molested with temptations to atheism." A church in Boston delayed evangelist Dwight L. Moody's application to join, his beliefs seemed so uncertain. Missionary C. F. Andrews, a friend of Gandhi, found himself unable to lead his Indian congregation in the Athanasian Creed because of doubts. British mystic Evelyn Underhill admitted to times when "the whole spiritual scheme seems in question."

Reading the biographies of great people of faith, I must search to find one whose faith did *not* grow on a skeleton of doubt, and indeed grow so that the skeleton eventually became hidden. In his novel *The Flight of Peter Fromm,* Martin Gardner has a professor suggest that today's intellectually honest Christian must choose between being a truthful traitor or a loyal liar. Adam, Sarah, Jacob, Job, Jeremiah, Jonah, Thomas, Martha, Peter, and many other characters in the Bible demonstrate a third category: the loyal traitor, who questions, squirms, and rebels yet still remains loyal. God appears far less threatened by doubt than does his church.

The church owes a large debt to loyal traitors. At various times, church officials insisted on an earth 6000 years young, opposed medicines as obstructions against God's will, supported slavery, and ranked certain races (and also women) as inferior beings. Doubters questioned these and other dogmas, often bringing on themselves condemnation and persecution.

In *A Prayer for Owen Meany* novelist John Irving describes a teacher who made faith attractive because he valued doubt. Irving was probably alluding to his own boarding school teacher Frederick Buechner, whom he thanks at the front of the book. Buechner takes for granted that a relationship between an invisible God and visible humans will always involve an element of doubt: "Without somehow destroying me in the process, how could God reveal himself in a way that would leave no room for doubt? If there were no room for doubt, there would be no room for me."

HAVING SAID SO MANY laudatory things about doubt, I need also acknowledge that doubt may lead a person away from faith rather than toward it. In my case, doubt has prompted me to question many things that need questioning and also to investigate alternatives to faith, none of which measure up. I remain a Christian today due to my doubts. For many others, though, doubt has had the opposite effect, working like a nerve disease to cause a slow and painful spiritual paralysis. Nearly every week I answer a letter from someone tormented by doubts. Their suffering is as acute and debilitating as any suffering I know.

Although we cannot control doubt, which often creeps up on us uninvited, we can learn to channel it in ways that make doubt more likely to be nourishing than toxic. For starters, I try to approach my doubts with the humility appropriate to my creaturely status.

I have often wondered why the Bible does not give clear answers to certain questions. God had the perfect opportunity to address the problem of pain in his speech at the end of Job, the longest single speech by God in the Bible, yet avoided the topic entirely. The Bible treats other important issues with slight hints and clues, not direct pronouncements. I have a theory why, which I freely admit ventures into personal opinion.

I have a book on my desk titled *The Encyclopedia of Ignorance*. Its author explains that whereas most encyclopedias compile information that we know, he will attempt to outline the areas of science we cannot yet explain: questions of cosmology, curved space, the riddles of gravitation, the interior of the sun, human consciousness. I wonder if God has perhaps fenced off an area of knowledge, "The Encyclopedia of Theological Ignorance," for very good reasons. These answers remain in God's domain, and God has not seen fit to reveal them.

Consider infant salvation. Most theologians have found enough biblical clues to convince them that God welcomes all infants "under the age of accountability," though the biblical evidence is scant. What if God had made a clear pronouncement: "Thus saith the Lord, I will welcome every child under the age of ten into heaven." I can easily envision Crusaders of the eleventh century mounting a campaign to slaughter every child of nine or younger in order to guarantee their eternal salvation—which of course would mean that none of us would be around a millennium later to contemplate such questions. Similarly, the zealous conquistadors in Latin America might have finished off the native peoples for good if the Bible had clearly stated that God's overlooking "the times of ignorance" applied to all who had not heard the name of Jesus.

Reading church history, not to mention reflecting on my own life, is a humbling exercise indeed. In view of the mess we have made of crystal-clear commands—the unity of the church, love as a mark of Christians, racial and economic justice, the importance of personal purity, the dangers of wealth—I tremble to think what we would do if some of the ambiguous doctrines were less ambiguous.

Our approach to difficult issues should befit our status as finite creatures. Take the doctrine of God's sovereignty, taught in the Bible in such a way that it stands in unresolved tension with human freedom. God's perspective as an all-powerful being who sees all of history at once, rather than unfolding second by second, has baffled theologians and will always baffle theologians simply because that point of view is unattainable to us, even unimaginable by us. The best physicists in the world struggle to explain the multidirectional arrows of time. A humble approach accepts that difference in perspective and worships a God who transcends our limitations.

Hyper-Calvinists show what happens when we seize prerogatives that no human can bear. Thus Malthusians opposed vaccination for smallpox because, they said, it interfered with God's sovereign will. Calvinist churches discouraged early missionaries: "Young man . . . when God pleases to convert the heathen, He'll do it without your help or mine," they told William Carey, ignoring the obvious fact that *we* are the ones chosen by God to carry the good news worldwide. After Calvin drew a solid line between the elect and the reprobate, his followers then inferred that we humans can discern who falls on which side of that line. The Book of Life belongs in the category of "theological ignorance," something we cannot know and for which (thankfully) we must trust God.

Of course, we must and should investigate some of the issues occupying the margins of doctrine. I have found consolation, for example, in C. S. Lewis's depiction in *The Great Divorce* of hell as a place that people choose, and continue to choose even when they end up there. As Milton's Satan put it, "Better to reign in Hell than serve in Heaven." Still, I must insist that the most important questions about heaven and hell—who goes where, whether there are second chances, what form the judgments and rewards take, intermediate states after death—are opaque to us at best. More and more, I am grateful for that ignorance, and grateful that the God who revealed himself in Jesus is the one who determines the answers.

⟶ ❦ ⟵

OVER TIME, I HAVE grown more comfortable with mystery rather than certainty. God does not twist arms and never forces us into a corner with faith in himself as the only exit. We can never present the Final Proof, to ourselves or to anyone else. We will always, with Pascal, see "too much to deny and too little to be sure . . ."

I look to Jesus, God laid bare to human view, for proof of God's refusal to twist arms. Jesus often made it harder, not easier, for people to believe. He never violated an individual's freedom to decide, even to decide against him. I marvel at how gently Jesus handled the reports of John the Baptist's doubts in prison, and how tenderly he restored Peter after his brusque betrayal. And Jesus' story of the prodigal son reveals a divine attitude of forgiveness-in-advance that may seem indulgent and risky, but it did restore a dead son to life.

"You will know the truth, and the truth will set you free," said Jesus. I love that sweeping, magisterial statement, because I have concluded its converse is also true: "Truth" that does not set free is not truth. Those who heard Jesus make the statement took up stones to kill him. They were unprepared for that kind of freedom, and so the church has often been. Read Aldous Huxley's *The Devils of Loudon,* any biography of Joan of Arc, or an account of the Salem witch trials, and you will see the extremes of a church threatened by freedom.

The church environment I grew up in had no room for doubt. "Just believe!" they told us. Anyone who strayed from the defined truth risked punishment as a deviant. In Bible College my brother received an "F" on a speech that, in the 1960s, had the effrontery to suggest that rock music is not inherently immoral. Although my brother was a classical musician who in fact had no taste for rock music, he could find no biblical support for the arguments about rock music made at that school. I have heard my brother speak many times—he was a competitive debater—and saw the notes for his presentation, and have no doubt that he received an "F" for one reason: the teacher disagreed with his conclusion. More, the teacher concluded that *God* disagreed with his conclusion. A failing grade in an undergraduate class hardly ranks with the punishment meted out by the judges in Salem or Loudon. My brother did not lose his life; he left the school. He also left the faith, however, and has never returned—in large part, I believe, because he did not observe truth setting people free and never found a church that makes room for prodigals.

I had a very different experience from my brother's. In my pilgrimage I found a grace-filled church and a community of Christians who formed a safe place for my doubts. I note in the Gospels that Jesus' disciple Thomas kept company with the other disciples even though he could not believe their accounts of Jesus' resurrection—the *sine qua non* of any doctrinal statement—and it was amid that community that Jesus appeared in order to strengthen Thomas's faith. In a similar way, my friends and colleagues at *Campus Life* magazine, then *Christianity Today,* and LaSalle Street Church in Chicago created a haven of acceptance that carried me along when my faith wavered. I could say before a church class I taught, "I know I should believe this, but truthfully, I'm having trouble right now." I feel sad for lonely doubters; we all need trustworthy doubt-companions.

The church at its best prepares a safe and secure space that belief may one day fill; we need not bring fully formed belief to the door, as a ticket for admission. When I began to write openly about doubt, and questioned some of the dogmas of evangelicalism, I expected rejection and punishment, such as I had received in adolescence. Instead I found that the angry, condemnatory letters were vastly outnumbered by others from readers who affirmed my questions and my right to question. Gradually those doubts settled into a lesser place, or found resolution, and they did so, I think, because fear melted away. I learned that the opposite of faith is not doubt, but fear.

One of John Donne's Holy Sonnets contains the mysterious line, "Churches are best for prayer, that have least light." The phrase can be taken several ways, the most literal referring to cathedrals lit only by candles. Given Donne's own harrowing history with the church, though, most readers see a further meaning: Churches that leave room for mystery, that do not pretend to spell out what God himself has not spelled out, create an environment most conducive to worship. After all, we lean on God out of need, not out of surplus.

Why then, do so many churches strive to appear bright and well-lit?

———— ∞ ————

IN A FAMOUS ALLEGORICAL dilemma, a fourteenth-century French monk told of a donkey who confronts two equally attractive, equally distant bales of hay. The animal stares, hesitates, stares some more, and eventually perishes because he has no logical justification for moving toward one bale or the other.

Without an element of risk, there is no faith. Nathaniel Hawthorne wrote of Herman Melville, "He can neither believe nor be content in his disbelief." Like the donkey torn between two bales, this middle ground may represent the greatest danger, because it removes passion in a person's relationship with God. Faith becomes a kind of intellectual puzzle, which is never biblical faith.

Faith means striking out, with no clear end in sight and perhaps even no clear view of the next step. It means following, trusting, holding out a hand to an invisible Guide. As Thomas Graham, dean of a theological school, put it, faith is reason gone courageous—not the opposite of reason, to be sure, but something more than reason and never satisfied by reason alone. A step always remains beyond the range of light.

One year a friend came to visit me in late June for the specific purpose of climbing mountains. Late-season snow made all but a few mountains inaccessible, so we settled on one of the easiest, Mount Sherman. Normally, a hiker can follow a gentle trail that winds right to the obvious summit. As we started from the trail head, however, we realized that a summer snowstorm had changed everything. Occasionally the clouds would part enough to give us a view of what we thought might be the summit, but then the sky would close tight around us in a total whiteout.

False summits—and most mountains have them—present a trial for the climber. For three hours you glance every few seconds at the top. Your eyes are pulled by a force like gravitation; you cannot resist looking at the massive peak that is luring you up its side. Then, just when you reach the top, you realize it is not the top at all. Perspective from below has fooled you. You see the real summit a half-mile ahead. Or is that too a false summit?

In the climb up Mount Sherman, we began in snow and clouds and ended in snow and clouds, and saw little in between. When a true white-out settles in, you lose all orientation with the horizon and cannot tell if you are ascending, descending, or walking upside down. You strike out blind—which, on mountains as craggy as the Rockies, may well prove fatal.

My partner and I discussed turning back and decided against it. We sat and waited for the clouds to clear a little, picked a spot and marked a compass bearing, then struck out again. When the clouds closed in, we sat in the wet snow and waited for another break.

Aware of avalanche danger, we deliberately chose a longer route that circled the gentler slopes of the mountain. In the cloud cover, we would hear the ominous crackling sounds of avalanches breaking loose from the other peaks around us. The heavy air made each one sound as if it was bearing right down on us, though intellectually we knew differently— we thought. Sitting in snow in the middle of a cloud, with a sound like sonic booms ricocheting all around makes one question maps, compasses, sense organs, and reason itself.

We had judged correctly, though, and no avalanches hit nearby. Clouds parted long enough to give us a glimpse of a ledge leading directly to the true summit, and with care we managed to make it. The sign-in cylinder at the top, buried in snow, indicated that we were the first hikers that season to ascend Mount Sherman. Then came the fun part. Clouds broke up, we could choose our slopes, and what took four hours to ascend took less than an hour to descend—on our backs, sliding like tobogganers down slopes slick with new snow.

> When we get our spiritual house in order, we'll be dead. This goes on. You arrive at enough certainty to be able to make your way, but it is making it in darkness. Don't expect faith to clear things up for you. It is trust, not certainty.
>
> FLANNERY O'CONNOR

That climb, as I reflected on it later, recapitulated what I have learned about the pilgrimage of faith. It involves miscalculations, thrills and hardship, long periods of waiting and long periods of simply trudging. No matter how thoroughly I prepare, make precautions, and try to eliminate risk, I never succeed. Always there are times of whiteout, when I can see nothing and avalanches roar down around me.

When I reach the summit though, nothing in the world compares to that feeling of accomplishment and exaltation. Yet Mount Sherman is, after all, only one 14,000-foot mountain in Colorado. I have fifty-two to go.

FOUR

FAITH UNDER FIRE

*It is not as a child that I believe and confess Jesus Christ.
My hosanna is born of a furnace of doubt.*

FYODOR DOSTOEVSKI

I IDENTIFY WITH THE poet Anne Sexton, who said she loved faith but had little. My own skeptical traits I acquired largely in church: listening to "testimonies" I later learned were faked, seeing the hypocrisies of spiritual leaders, hearing people praise God for miraculous healing the week before they died. Virtually any "answer to prayer," I discovered, had other possible explanations, and I hastened to find them. Eventually I outgrew the stage of wanting to poke holes in other people's faith, but the habit of skepticism lingers, along with a strong aversion to faith abuse.

Because I have written about pain and suffering, I have a file drawer filled with letters from earnest Christians who pray—for their child with a birth defect, for an inoperable brain tumor, for reversal of paralysis—who seek anointing with oil and follow every biblical admonition, and yet who find no relief from suffering, no reward for their faith. I have also asked

51

numerous Christian physicians if they have ever witnessed an undeniable medical miracle. Most think for a minute and come up with one possibility, maybe two.

Strangely, spending my time writing about the Christian faith makes it no easier. A friend commented about Christians in general, "If you repeat anything to yourself often enough, you can believe it." Is that what I do? I go over and over the words, trying to get them just right. But how can I know whether I truly believe them or am just repeating them to myself, like a telephone solicitor rehearsing a sales pitch? When dealing with an invisible God, doubts inevitably steal in.

For reasons such as these I have always hesitated to write about faith, afraid of causing someone else to lose theirs. Although I do not want to discourage anyone's simple faith, neither do I want to raise unrealistic expectations of what faith might achieve. "Tempting God means trying to get more assurance than God has given," said the wise bishop Lesslie Newbigin. I have to face the honest fact that Christians live in poverty, get sick, lose their hair and teeth, and wear eyeglasses at approximately the same rate as everyone else. Christians die at exactly the same rate: 100 percent.

We live on a fallen planet full of suffering from which even the Son of God was not exempt. During their lifetimes, Jesus and the apostle Paul* both prayed for easier ways to cope on such a planet, and neither got relief. The sociologist Bronislav Malinowski drew this distinction between magic and religion: In magic, people try to get the gods to perform their will, while in religion people try to conform to the will of the gods. Christian faith means conforming to the will of God whatever it may mean. "My Father, if it is possible, may this cup be taken from me," Jesus prayed in Gethsemane. It was not possible, and he added submissively, "Yet not as I will, but as you will."

George Everett Ross makes the same point as Malinowski in different words:

> I have served in the ministry thirty years, almost thirty-one. I have
> come to understand that there are two kinds of faith. One says

---

* Paul describes his dire circumstances in 1 Corinthians: "To this very hour we go hungry and thirsty, we are in rags, we are brutally treated, we are homeless. . . . Up to this moment we have become the scum of the earth, the refuse of the world." In the next letter he tells of his unsuccessful prayers to have a "thorn in the flesh" removed.

if and the other says though. One says: "If everything goes well, if my life is prosperous, if I'm happy, if no one I love dies, if I'm successful, then I will believe in God and say my prayers and go to the church and give what I can afford." The other says though: though the cause of evil prosper, though I sweat in Gethsemane, though I must drink my cup at Calvary—nevertheless, precisely then, I will trust the Lord who made me. So Job cries: "Though he slay me, yet will I trust Him."

I have friends who see a demon behind every bush and an angel behind every vacant parking place, and I sometimes marvel at what their simple faith accomplishes. When there is no miracle, however, when they need something closer to long-term fidelity than short-term wonder, I note that they turn to people with a more cautious and longsuffering faith.

The Bible models both simple faith and hang-on-against-all-odds fidelity. Job, Abraham, Habakkuk and his fellow prophets, as well as many of the heroes of faith mentioned in Hebrews 11, endured long droughts when miracles did not happen, when urgent prayers dropped back to earth unanswered, when God seemed not just invisible but wholly absent. We who follow in their path today may sometimes experience times of unusual closeness when God seems responsive to our every need; we may also experience times when God stays silent and all the Bible's promises seem glaringly false.

O N MY TRAVELS OVERSEAS I have noticed a striking difference in the wording of prayers. Christians in affluent countries tend to pray, "Lord, take this trial away from us!" I have heard prisoners, persecuted Christians, and some who live in very poor countries pray instead, "Lord, give us the strength to bear this trial."

Paradoxically, difficult times may help nourish faith and strengthen bonds. I see this in human relationships, which tend to solidify in times of crisis. My wife and I both have grandmothers who have lived past 100 (in the year 2000 they entered their third century!). Talking with them and their friends, I detect a trend that seems almost universal in the reminiscences of older people: they recall difficult, tumultuous times with a touch of nostalgia. The elderly swap stories about World War II and the

Great Depression; they speak fondly of hardships such as blizzards, the childhood outhouse, and the time in college when they ate canned soup and stale bread three weeks in a row.

Ask a strong, stable family where they got such strength, and you may very well hear a story of crisis: huddling together in a hospital waiting room, waiting anxiously for some word of a runaway son, sorting through the rubble after a tornado, comforting a daughter after her broken engagement. Relationships gain strength when they are stretched to the breaking point and do not break.

Seeing this principle lived out among people, I can better understand one of the mysteries of relating to God. Faith boils down to a question of trust in a given relationship. Do I have confidence in my loved ones — or in God, as the case may be? If I do stand on a bedrock of trust, the worst of circumstances will not destroy the relationship.

Abraham climbing the hill with his son at Moriah, Job scratching his boils under the hot sun, David hiding in a cave, Elijah moping in a desert, Moses pleading for a new job description — all these heroes experienced crisis moments that sorely tempted them to judge God as uncaring, powerless, or even hostile. Confused and in the dark, they faced a turning point: whether to turn away embittered or step forward in faith. In the end, all chose the path of trust, and for this reason we remember them as giants of faith.

Unfortunately, not everyone passes these tests of faith with flying colors. The Bible is littered with tales of others — Cain, Samson, Solomon, Judas — who flunked. Their lives give off a scent of sadness and remorse: Oh, what might have been.

One Christian thinker, Søren Kierkegaard, spent a lifetime exploring the tests of faith that call into question God's trustworthiness. A strange man with a difficult personality, Kierkegaard lived with constant inner torment. Again and again he turned to biblical characters like Job and Abraham, who survived excruciating trials of faith. During their times of testing, it appeared to both Job and Abraham that God was contradicting himself. *God surely would not act in such a way — yet clearly he is.* Kierkegaard ultimately concluded that the purest faith emerges from just such an ordeal. Even though I do not understand, I will trust God regardless.

I have learned much from Kierkegaard and his unbalanced view of faith. I say unbalanced because Kierkegaard focuses so intently on the great ordeals of faith and has little to say about the day-to-day maintenance aspects of a relationship with God. He describes "knights of faith," those few individuals selected by God for some extraordinary feat. They were tested as today we might test a jet plane: not to destroy but rather to gauge the limits of usefulness. "Would it not have been better, after all, if he were not God's chosen?" Kierkegaard once asked about Abraham. No doubt Abraham himself asked that question during his ordeals, but I doubt he asked it at the end of his life.

For the believer, faith revolves around a crisis in personal relationship more than intellectual doubts. Does God deserve our trust, no matter how things appear at the time?

———— ✑ ————

A CHRISTIAN AUTHOR WHOM I love and respect writes, "The way God arranges things sometimes seems uniquely designed to frustrate us: a tire goes flat on the way to the hospital, the sink backs up an hour before overnight company arrives, a friend lets you down during a time when you most need support, you suddenly develop laryngitis the day of your presentation to important buyers." To Christians in places like Pakistan and Sudan, these trials must seem obscenely insignificant. Yet I know well that a series of annoyances exactly like these can introduce a seed of doubt in my relationship with God and undermine my basic trust.

I find myself stumbling over my friend's phrase "The way God arranges things," however. Does God indeed position a nail in the road so that I will run over it on the way to the hospital? Does he wind hairs around the sink trap so that it will clog just before company arrives? I too instinctively blame God when bad things happen, calling into question any relationship of trust. Should I? Does God arrange flat tires, computer crashes, and viral germs in my life as custom tests of faith, similar to the tests of faith that Abraham and Job endured? I doubt it.

If the Book of Job teaches one lesson, especially in God's speech at the end, it is that human beings have no business, let alone competence, in trying to figure out all the intricacies of why things happen. Instead, God challenged Job to do any better:

Do you have an arm like God's,
    and can your voice thunder like his?
Then adorn yourself with glory and splendor,
    and clothe yourself in honor and majesty.
Unleash the fury of your wrath,
    look at every proud man and bring him low,
look at every proud man and humble him,
    crush the wicked where they stand.

God restrains from continual interference with what takes place on earth, declining to humble every proud man and crush the wicked where they stand, for reasons that continue to perplex their victims. We, like Job, assume that God has somehow arranged all events, then draw conclusions that are patently false: *God doesn't love me. God is not fair.* Faith offers the option of continuing to trust God even while accepting the limits of our humanity, which means accepting that we cannot answer the "Why?" questions.

When Princess Diana died in an automobile crash I got a phone call from a television producer. "Can you appear on our show?" he asked. "We want you to explain how God could possibly allow such a terrible accident." Without thinking, I replied, "Could it have had something to do with a drunk driver going ninety miles an hour in a narrow tunnel? How, exactly, was God involved?"

I could not make the television appearance, but his question prompted me to dig out a file folder in which I have stashed notes of things for which God gets blamed. I found a quote from boxer Ray "Boom-Boom" Mancini, who had just killed a Korean opponent with a hard right. At a press conference after the Korean boxer's death, Mancini said, "Sometimes I wonder why God does the things he does." In a letter to Dr. James Dobson, a young woman asked this anguished question: "Four years ago, I was dating a man and became pregnant. I was devastated! I asked God, 'Why have You allowed this to happen to me?'" Susan Smith, the South Carolina mother who pushed her two sons into a lake to drown, then blamed a phantom car-jacker for the deed, wrote in her official confession: "I dropped to the lowest point when I allowed my children to go down that ramp into the water without me. I took off running and screaming, 'Oh God! Oh God, no! What have I done? Why did you let this happen?'"

Exactly what role did God play in a boxer pummeling his opponent, a teenage couple losing control in a backseat, or a mother drowning her children? I wonder. Did God arrange these incidents as tests of faith? To the contrary, I see them as spectacular demonstrations of human freedom exercised on a fallen planet. At such moments, exposed as frail and mortal, we lash out against someone who is not: God.

Having examined every instance of human suffering recorded in the Bible, I have come away convinced that many Christians who face a trial of faith attempt to answer a different question than God is asking. By instinct we flee to the questions that look backward in time: What caused this tragedy? Was God involved? What is God trying to tell me? We judge the relationship on such incomplete evidence.

The Bible gives many examples of suffering that, like Job's, have nothing to do with God's punishment. In all his miracles of healing, Jesus overturned the notion, widespread at the time, that suffering—blindness, lameness, leprosy—comes to people who deserve it. Jesus grieved over many things that happen on this planet, a sure sign that God regrets them far more than we do. Not once did Jesus counsel someone to accept suffering as God's will; rather he went about healing illness and disability.

The Bible supplies no systematic answers to the "Why?" questions and often avoids them entirely. A flat tire, a backed-up sink, a case of laryngitis—these tests, however minor, may well provoke a crisis of trust in our relationship with God. Yet we dare not tread into areas God has sealed off as his domain. Divine providence is a mystery that only God understands, and belongs in what I have called "The Encyclopedia of Theological Ignorance" for a simple reason: no time-bound human, living on a rebellious planet, blind to the realities of the unseen world, has the ability to comprehend such answers—God's reply to Job in a nutshell.

———— ❧ ————

CHRISTIANS OFTEN READ THE Bible in such a way that exaggerates God's promises, setting themselves up for later disillusionment. "Look at the birds of the air," Jesus once said; "they do not sow or reap or store away in barns, and yet your heavenly Father feeds them. . . . See how the lilies of the field grow. They do not labor or spin." From such verses, readers infer that God will always provide, which then brings about a major crisis of faith when drought and famine arrive.

But how does the heavenly Father feed the birds and make the lilies grow? He does not cause black-oiled sunflower seeds to appear magically on the ground like manna in the wilderness. He feeds the birds by furnishing the planet with forests, wildflowers, and worms—and we humans know well that our subdivisions and strip malls can have a disastrous impact on the bird population. The lilies of the field may grow without labor, but their growth also depends on the regular systems that produce weather. In years of severe drought, they neither labor nor spin nor survive.

"Are not two sparrows sold for a penny?" Jesus also said. "Yet not one of them will fall to the ground apart from the will of your Father. And even the very hairs of your head are all numbered. So don't be afraid; you are worth more than many sparrows." Some take that passage as a comfort: "His eye is on the sparrow," goes the song, "And I know he watches me." Ironically, Jesus said it in the midst of dire warnings to his followers that they would face floggings, arrest, and even execution—hardly much comfort.* Jacques Ellul points out a common mistranslation: the Greek text simply has, "apart from your Father," and says nothing about God's will:

> It is to make things plain that "will" has been added. But the addition changes the meaning completely. In the one case, God wills the death of the sparrow, in the other death does not take place without God being present. In other words, death comes according to natural laws, but God lets nothing in his creation die without being there, without being the comfort and strength and hope and support of that which dies. At issue is the presence of God, not his will.

We tend to view God's interactions with events on earth as coming "from above," like light rays or hailstones or Zeus's lightning bolts falling to the ground from the heavens. Thus God in heaven reaches down to

---

* One of Doris Betts's characters has a more realistic view: "God knows the sparrows fall, but they keep falling. Ain't creation just one dead bird after another?"

intervene on earth through events like the ten plagues. Perhaps we would do better to picture God's interaction as an underground aquifer or river that rises to the surface in springs and fountainheads. Father Robert Farrar Capon, in *The Parables of Judgment*, makes this shift in perspective from above to below, presenting God's acts as "outcroppings, as emergences into plain sight of the tips of the one, continuous iceberg under all of history. Thus, when we draw in our same previous series of mighty acts, they become not *forays into history* of an alien presence from above but *outcroppings within history* of an abiding presence from below."

In other words, God does not so much overrule as underrule. His presence sustains all creation at every moment: "in him [Christ] all things hold together," said Paul. His presence also flows into individuals who align themselves with him; God's Spirit, an invisible companion, works from within to wrest good from bad.

MANY CHRISTIANS QUOTE THE verse Romans 8:28, "And we know that in all things God works for the good of those who love him," with the implication that somehow everything will turn out for the best. The Greek original text is more properly translated, "In everything that happens, God works for good with those who love him." That promise, I have found to hold true in all the disasters and hardships I have known personally. Things happen, some of them good, some of them bad, many of them beyond our control. In all these things, I have felt the reliable constant of a God willing to work with me and through me to produce something good. Faith in such a process will, I'm convinced, always be rewarded, even though the "Why?" questions go unanswered.

A story from John 9 illustrates the difference in approach. The story starts where many sick people start, with the question of cause. Encountering a man blind from birth, the disciples look backward to find out why. Who sinned to bring on this punishment, the blind man or his parents? (Think about the implication: had the man sinned *in utero*?) Jesus answers unequivocally: "Neither this man nor his parents sinned, but this happened so that the work of God might be displayed in his life." Redirecting their attention forward, Jesus poses a different question, "To what end?"

Jesus' response, I believe, offers a concise summary of the Bible's approach to the problem of pain. Thornton Wilder wrote *The Bridge of San Luis Rey* to investigate why five particular people died in a bridge collapse. When asked about a similar tragedy—why did eighteen people die in a construction accident?—Jesus refused to answer. Instead, he turned the question back on the askers: Would you be ready for death if a tower fell on you? In Jesus' view, even tragedy could be used to push a person toward God. Rather than looking backward for explanations, he looked forward for redemptive results.

To backward-looking questions of cause, to the "Why?" questions, the Bible gives no definitive answer. But it does hold out hope for the future, that even suffering can be transformed so that it produces good results. Sometimes, as with the blind man, the work of God is manifest through a dramatic miracle. Sometimes, as with Joni Eareckson and so many others who pray for healing that never comes, it is not. In every case, suffering offers an opportunity for us to display the work of God, whether in weakness or in strength. The "miracle" of Joni Eareckson— a teenager devastated by paralysis who becomes a prophetess for the disabled to the rest of the church—demonstrates that abundantly. Knowing Joni since her teenage days, I firmly believe the transformation worked in her is even more impressive than if she had suddenly regained her ability to walk. "Storms are the triumph of his [God's] art," said the poet George Herbert.

I am writing these words just after the tragedy at Columbine High School in Littleton, Colorado, not far from my home. Every day, newspapers and television programs here dissect the event in excruciating detail. The funerals of twelve students and one teacher have been broadcast live. Ministers, parents, school administrators, and everyone touched by the tragedy ask "Why?" and no one has an answer. The element of evil—hate-filled, racist teenagers spraying their classmates with automatic weapons—looms so large in this particular tragedy that no one publicly links God to the event. Some ask why God does not intervene at such a time, but no one suggests God *caused* that outbreak of violence.

You would have to live in Colorado to appreciate fully the answer to the other question posed by the tragedy: Can any good come out of such horror? Can it be redeemed? A week after the killings I visited the hill in

Clement Park on which fifteen crosses stood, sifted through the pile of flower bouquets, athletic jackets, stuffed animals, and other mementos, and read some of the handwritten notes of love and support that poured in from all over the world. I also read the notes written to the two killers, personal notes from other misfits and outcasts lamenting that Eric Harris and Dylan Klebold had not found friends to confide in who could ease their pain. I attended churches that spontaneously filled with hundreds of grieving worshipers the days and weeks following the event. I watched the *Today Show* as Craig Scott, brother of one of the victims, put his hand on the shoulder of the father of the one African-American student killed and comforted him, even as Katie Couric broke down on the air. I heard friends of students describe their classmates' bravery as a gunman pointed his weapon at their heads and demanded, "Do you believe in God?" I heard of other results: of youth groups swelling all over the city, of teachers apologizing to their classes for not having identified themselves as Christians, and inviting students to meet them after school for grief counseling, of the father of one victim becoming an evangelist and the father of another leading a gun-control crusade. Out of evil, even terrible evil such as the Columbine massacre, good may come.

For many people, it takes the jolt of tragedy, illness, or death to create an existential crisis of faith. At such a moment, we want clarity; God wants our trust. A Scottish preacher in the last century lost his wife suddenly, and after her death he preached an unusually personal sermon. He admitted in the message that he did not understand this life of ours. But still less could he understand how people facing loss could abandon faith. "Abandon it for what!" he said. "You people in the sunshine may believe the faith, but we in the shadow *must* believe it. We have nothing else."

> If knowing answers to life's questions is absolutely necessary to you, then forget the journey. You will never make it, for this is a journey of unknowables — of unanswered questions, enigmas, incomprehensibles, and most of all, things unfair.
>
> MADAME JEANNE GUYON

TWO-HANDED FAITH

For all that has been, thanks. For all that shall be, yes.

DAG HAMMARSKJÖLD

Y EARS AFTER THE AMERICAN Civil War had ended, someone asked George Pickett, the Confederate general who led "Pickett's charge" at Gettysburg, to explain why his side lost. He pulled on his whiskers for a moment, then replied, "Well, I kinda think the Yankees had a little somethin' to do with it."

To draw a more complete picture, I must mention a further way of looking at reality. The invisible God is not alone out there. The Bible insists we live in the midst of other unseen "powers," some devoted to good and some to evil. If one day we, like Job, have the opportunity to question God in person about matters that troubled us during our time on planet earth, God may well reply, "I think the Rebels had something to do with it."

As a cub reporter at the height of the Jesus movement in the 1970s, I interviewed a rock band appearing at a Christian music festival. They presented to me a view of the world I had never encountered:

> Yeah, man, we were really under attack. The Lord was with us in Indianapolis. His Spirit filled the place. So then Satan reached down as we were driving along the road and undid the trailer hitch from our bus. There goes all our amplifiers and instruments. The trip would have ended right there. But God stepped in. He guided that thing so it hit nothing, just coasted to a stop beside the road. We're back in business, man. The Lord's business!

In their Jesus-people lingo, the musicians presented a world that involved God and Satan waging a tug-of-war over every incident on earth.

After interviewing the band, I began listening to language used by Christians. A family leaves on a trip to the Middle East during a time of rising tensions: "We're in God's hands," they say. A man goes through a contentious divorce: "God is teaching me to look to him."

I have heard seminarians joke about a man who steps from a curb and narrowly misses being hit by a speeding car. "Providence was looking out for him," says an observer. A day later the man steps from the same curb and this time gets hit. After long months he recovers from serious injuries. "Isn't it marvelous how God spared him?" the observer remarks. Later, he steps from the same curb, is hit again, and this time dies from the injuries. "Well, God saw fit to take him home."

At times all of us fall into such thinking. The great Leo Tolstoy struggled to make sense of God's involvement during Napoleon's invasion. In *War and Peace,* he examines each feint and thrust of the enemy as it marches across Russia. Surely it cannot be God's will for the Corsican upstart to conquer Holy Russia! Is God sleeping? Can forces of evil prevail over forces of good? As the French army drives toward Moscow, Tolstoy fervently searches for some understanding of providence that might account for such a catastrophe. He finds nothing except the "irresistible tide of destiny."

Everyone who believes in God carries around a basic assumption of how God acts in relation with us. The French novelist Flaubert said that a great writer should stand in his novel like God in his creation: nowhere to be seen, nowhere to be heard. God is everywhere and yet invisible, silent, seemingly absent and indifferent. A few intellectuals may enjoy worshiping such an absentee God, but most Christians prefer Jesus' image of God as a loving father. We need more than a watchmaker who winds up the universe and lets it tick. We need love and mercy and for-giveness and grace—qualities only a personal God can offer.

Yet the more personal conception of God we have, the more unnerv-ing are the questions about him. Shouldn't a loving God intervene more often on our behalf? And how can we trust a God we can never confi-dently count on to come to our aid?

I ONCE MET A bona fide paranoid, a young woman utterly convinced the world was against her. Whatever happened she somehow worked into her conspiracy theory of a hostile world. If I tried to comfort her by saying some-thing like, "I think you took that comment in the wrong way. Martha was just trying to be helpful. She doesn't hate you," my peacemaking would only fuel her paranoia. *Aha, he's one of* them. *Martha probably put him up to this. He's trying to soften me up, break down my resistance.* Nothing anyone said or did could pierce through her protective armor of paranoia.

A paranoid person orients life around fear. My wife worked for a super-visor who became convinced, wrongly, that Janet had eyes on his job. Every suggestion Janet made at work, her supervisor took as an attempt to undermine him. Every compliment, he took as a subversive attempt to win him over. Nothing Janet said could convince him otherwise, and eventually she had to leave the job to preserve her own sanity.

I am learning that mature faith, which encompasses both simple faith and fidelity, works the opposite of paranoia. It reassembles all the events of life around trust in a loving God. When good things happen, I accept them as gifts from God, worthy of thanksgiving. When bad things hap-pen, I do not take them as necessarily sent by God—I see evidence in the Bible to the contrary—and I find in them no reason to divorce God. Rather, I trust that God can use even those bad things for my benefit. That, at least, is the goal toward which I strive.

A faithful person sees life from the perspective of trust, not fear. Bedrock faith allows me to believe that, despite the chaos of the present moment, God does reign; that regardless of how worthless I may feel, I truly matter to a God of love; that no pain lasts forever and no evil triumphs in the end. Faith sees even the darkest deed of all history, the death of God's Son, as a necessary prelude to the brightest.

A skeptic will respond that I have just presented a classic rationalization: beginning with a premise, I proceed to manipulate all evidence in support of that premise. The skeptic is right. I begin with the premise of a good and loving God as the first principle of the universe; anything contradicting that premise must have another explanation. In politics, says William Safire, "The candidate who takes credit for the rain gets blamed for the drought." How, then, can I "let God off the hook" in view of the terrible things that happen to people every day?

First, as I have argued, we must not assume that everything happens with God's approval. When two alienated teenagers walk into a high school, set off bombs and shoot nine hundred rounds of ammunition at their classmates, is that God's plan? A friend excitedly told me about the many "miracles" that happened in Columbine High School. The killers planted ninety-five explosive devices in the school, very few of which detonated. One student took two bullets at point-blank range directly in the face; "miraculously," the bullets lodged in thick jawbone on each side of his face, and he lived. Another student went home sick that day, and his parents praised God for his providential care. I hear such stories and rejoice at the outcomes, yet I wonder how such assertions sound to the parents who lost children in the massacre.

Many things happen in this world that are clearly against God's will. Read the prophets, God's designated spokesmen, who thunder against idolatry, injustice, violence, and other symptoms of human sin and rebellion. Read the Gospel accounts, where Jesus upsets the religious establishment by freeing people from disabilities the divines had deemed "God's will." Providence may be a great mystery, nonetheless I find no justification for blaming God for what God so clearly opposes.

The skeptic's question does not melt away, though. How can I praise God for the good things in life without censuring him for the bad? I can do so only by establishing an attitude of trust—paranoia in reverse—based on what I have learned in relationship with God.

I find a parallel in my human relationships. If I am waiting for my friend Larry at a rendezvous point, and he has not shown up an hour past the agreed-upon time, I do not start cursing his irresponsibility and thoughtlessness. Years of friendship have taught me that Larry is prompt and reliable. I assume that something—a flat tire? an accident?—over which he has no control has thwarted his plans.* Those I love, I credit for good things and try not to blame for bad, assuming instead other forces are at work. Together, we have developed a pattern of trust and discerning love.

Over time, both through personal experience and my study of the Bible, I have come to know certain qualities of God as well. God's style often baffles me: he moves at a slow pace, prefers rebels and prodigals, restrains his power, and speaks in whispers and silence. Yet even in these qualities I see evidence of his longsuffering, mercy, and desire to woo rather than compel. When in doubt, I focus on Jesus, the most unfiltered revelation of God's own self. I have learned to trust God, and when some tragedy or evil occurs that I cannot synthesize with the God I have come to know and love, then I look to other explanations.

———cy———

CONSIDER THE PLIGHT OF a spy operating behind enemy lines, who suddenly loses all contact with friendly forces back in the home country. Have they abandoned him, cut him off? If he fully trusts his government, he presumes instead that the communication line has been compromised and contacts have ended for his own protection. If captured and held hostage in Beirut or Teheran, he will have no evidence that anyone back home cares for him. A loyal spy, though, will trust that his government is scouring the diplomatic channels, offering rewards to informers, and perhaps launching a clandestine rescue effort. He believes, against all apparent evidence, that his government values him and his welfare.

C. S. Lewis gives further illustrations of times when trust pays off, even in conditions that seem to argue against it:

---

* In a mysterious passage in Daniel 10, the Bible describes a scene with close parallels. Daniel cannot understand why one of his prayers has not been answered. Then an angel shows up to explain what has been occurring in the unseen world: for three weeks the angel has been trying to overcome resistance from the "prince of the Persian kingdom" in order to answer Daniel's prayer, and only recently has gotten reinforcements from a heavenly power named Michael. I doubt Daniel ever prayed casually again.

In getting a dog out of a trap, in extracting a thorn from a child's finger, in teaching a boy to swim or rescuing one who can't, in getting a frightened beginner over a nasty place on a mountain, the one fatal obstacle may be their distrust. We are asking them to trust us in the teeth of their senses, their imagination, and their intelligence. We are asking them to believe that what is painful will relieve their pain and that what looks dangerous is their only safety. We ask them to accept apparent impossibilities: that moving the paw farther back into the trap is the way to get out—that hurting the finger very much more will stop the finger hurting—that water which is obviously permeable will resist and support the body—that holding onto the only support within reach is not the way to avoid sinking—that to go higher and onto a more exposed ledge is the way not to fall. To support all these *incredibilia* we can rely only on the other party's confidence in us—a confidence certainly not based on demonstration, admittedly shot through with emotion, and perhaps, if we are strangers, resting on nothing but such assurance as the look of our face and the tone of our voice can supply, or even, for the dog, on our smell. Sometimes, because of their unbelief, we can do no mighty works. But if we succeed, we do so because they have maintained their faith in us against apparently contrary evidence. No one blames us for demanding such faith. No one blames them for giving it. No one says afterwards what an unintelligent dog or child or boy that must have been to trust us. . . .

Now to accept the Christian propositions is *ipso facto* to believe that we are to God, always, as that dog or child or bather or mountain climber was to us, only very much more so.

In an unusually revealing letter to his friend Father John Calabria, Lewis applied this principle quite personally. In his fiftieth year, he could sense his writing talent slipping away. He was spending his time caring for his infirm mother and also for a friend's, in a chaotic house devastated by quarrels. "How long, O Lord?" Lewis writes. He explains the distractions to Calabria, asks for prayer, says that disruptions are keeping him from work on many books. He adds, "If it shall please God that I write more books, blessed be He. If it shall not please Him, again, blessed be He. Perhaps it will be the most wholesome thing for my soul that I lose both fame and skill lest I were to fall into that evil disease, vainglory."

Lewis's letter strikes like an arrow into my heart because I make my living writing books, am in fact writing this book in my fiftieth year, and have some idea what it meant for Lewis to come to that place of trust and submission. What loomed as a great sacrifice and loss, he interpreted instead as a potential blessing, for the single reason that he trusted God. Lewis believed that whatever entered his life, even the opposite of his own desires, God could turn into benefit and profit.

Gregory of Nicea once called St. Basil's faith "ambidextrous" because he welcomed pleasures with the right hand and afflictions with the left, convinced that both would serve God's design for him. The eighteenth-century spiritual director Jean-Pierre de Caussade echoed Basil. "A living faith is nothing else than a steadfast pursuit of God through all that disguises, disfigures, demolishes and seeks, so to speak, to abolish him." De Caussade sought to accept each moment as a revelation of God, believing that regardless of how things appear at a given time, all of history will ultimately serve to accomplish God's purpose on earth. He advised, "Love and accept the present moment as the best, with perfect trust in God's universal goodness. . . . Everything without exception is an instrument and means of sanctification. . . . God's purpose for us is always what will contribute most to our good."

Here is what ambidextrous, or "two-handed" faith means to me, in theory if not always in practice. I take "everything without exception" as God's action in the sense of asking what I can learn from it and praying for God to redeem it by improving me. I take nothing as God's action in the sense of judging God's character, for I have learned to accept my puny status as a creature—which includes a limited point of view that obscures unseen forces in the present as well as a future known only to God. The skeptic may insist this unfairly lets God off the hook, but perhaps that's what faith is: trusting God's goodness despite any apparent evidence against it. As a soldier trusts his general's orders; better, as a child trusts her loving parent.

A friend who struggles with depression wrote me, "I cannot explain my depression to anyone. It is nonrational, and flies in the face of my comfortable life. It colors my outlook on the entire world, and I harbor it as a secret point of view that no one else shares or can enter into. Nothing seems more real to me, when I am depressed. The darkness defines my life." She went on to tell me that since her conversion—which, as a Jew, she still hides from her family—the depression dominates her less often. "In fact, I'm beginning to see faith as the flip side of depression. It too colors everything. I cannot always explain it to others, and yet gradually it is bringing light into my dark life."

PARANOIA IN REVERSE, THE mirror image of depression—I have wandered into images of faith that are best illustrated, not analyzed. I think of the prophet Daniel's three friends who defied a tyrant by declaring, "If we are thrown into the blazing furnace, the God we serve is able to save us from it, and he will rescue us from your hand, O king. But *even if he does not,* we want you to know, O king, that we will not serve your gods or worship the image of gold you have set up." I think of Jesus on the cross who cried on the one hand, "My God, why have you forsaken me?" and on the other, "Father, into your hands I commit my spirit." Daniel's friends found miraculous deliverance, Jesus did not; both trusted God regardless.

Or I think of the apostle Paul's exalted state as described in the book of Philippians. His values seem topsy-turvy. His stint in prison he views as desirable, for that "hardship" has brought about many good results. Wealth or poverty, comfort or pain, acceptance or rejection, even death or life—none of these circumstances matter much to Paul. "I have learned the secret of being content in any and every situation, whether well fed or hungry, whether living in plenty or in want."

I think also of John Donne, the seventeenth-century poet and dean of St. Paul's Cathedral in London. Much of what I believe about God and suffering I have learned from Donne, who stands to me as a model of two-handed faith.

John Donne was a man acquainted with grief. During his term at London's largest church, three waves of the bubonic plague swept through the city, the last epidemic alone killing 40,000 people. Londoners flocked to Dean Donne for an explanation, or at least a word of comfort. Meanwhile Donne himself came down with an illness the doctors initially diagnosed as plague (it turned out to be a spotted fever, like typhus). For six weeks he lay tremulous at the threshold of death, listening to the church bells toll each new fatality, wondering if he would be next ("Never send to know for whom the bell tolls; it tolls for thee"). During this dark time Donne, forbidden to read or study but permitted to write, composed the book *Devotions*, a meditation on suffering. He was tuning his instrument at the door, he said—the door of death.

In *Devotions*, John Donne calls God to task. Sometimes he taunts God, sometimes he grovels and pleads for forgiveness, sometimes he argues fiercely. But not once does Donne leave God out of the process. The presence of God shadows every thought, every sentence.

Donne asked the "Why me?" question over and over. Calvinism was relatively new, and Donne pondered the notion of plagues and wars as "God's angels." He soon recoiled from that idea: "Surely it is not thou, it is not thy hand. The devouring sword, the consuming fire, the winds from the wilderness, the diseases of the body, all that afflicted Job, were from the hands of Satan; it is not thou." Still, he never felt certain, and the not-knowing caused him inner torment. Donne's book never answers the "Why me?" questions, as none of us can answer those questions that lie beyond the reach of humanity.

But even though *Devotions* does not resolve the intellectual doubts, it does record Donne's emotional resolution. At first—confined to bed, churning out prayers without answers, contemplating death, regurgitating guilt—he can find no relief from ever-present fear. Obsessed, he reviews every biblical occurrence of the word *fear*. As he does so, it dawns on him that life will always include circumstances that incite fear: if not illness, financial hardship, if not poverty, rejection, if not loneliness, failure. In such a world, Donne has a clear choice: to fear God or to fear everything else, to trust God or to trust nothing.

In his wrestling with God, Donne changes questions. He began with the question of origin—"Who caused this illness? And why?"—for which he found no answer. His meditations shift ever so gradually toward the question of response. The crucial issue, the one that faces every person who endures a great trial, is that same question of response: Will I trust God with my pain, my weakness, even my fear? Or will I turn away from him in bitterness and anger? Donne determines that it does not really matter whether his sickness is a chastening from God or merely a natural occurrence. In either case he will trust God, for in the end trust represents the proper fear of the Lord.

Donne likens the process to his changing attitude toward physicians. Initially, as they probed his body for new symptoms and discussed their findings in hushed tones outside his room, he could not help feeling afraid. In time, seeing their compassionate concern, he became convinced that they deserved his trust, even when their treatments involved pain. The same pattern applies to God. Although we often do not understand his methods or the reasons behind them, the underlying issue is whether God is a trustworthy "physician." Donne decides yes.

In a passage reminiscent of Paul's litany in Romans 8 ("For I am convinced that neither death nor life, neither angels nor demons . . . will be able to separate us from the love of God"), Donne checks off his potential fears. Great enemies? They pose no threat, for God can vanquish any enemy. Famine? No, God can supply. Death? Even that, the worst human fear, raises no permanent barrier to those who fear God. Donne concludes that his best course is to cultivate a proper fear of the Lord, for that fear can supplant all others. He prays, "as thou hast given me a repentance, not to be repented of, so give me, O Lord, a fear, of which I may not be afraid."

> Whatever faith may be, and whatever answers it may give, and to whomsoever it gives them, every such answer gives to the finite existence of man an infinite meaning, a meaning not destroyed by sufferings, deprivations, or death.
>
> LEO TOLSTOY

LIVING IN FAITH

To live in the past and future is easy. To live in the present is like threading a needle.

WALKER PERCY

M Y PASTOR IN CHICAGO, Bill Leslie, said he often felt like an old hand-operated water pump, the kind still found in some campgrounds. Everyone who came to him for help would pump vigorously a few times, and each time he felt something drain out of him. Ultimately he reached a place of spiritual emptiness, with nothing more to give. He felt dry, desiccated.

In the midst of this period, Bill went on a weeklong retreat and bared his soul to his assigned spiritual director, a nun. He expected her to offer soothing words about what a sacrificial, unselfish person he was, or perhaps recommend a sabbatical. Instead she said, "Bill, there's only one thing to do if your reservoir runs dry. You've got to go deeper." He returned from that retreat convinced that his faith depended less on his outer journey of life and ministry than on his inner journey toward spiritual depth.

In the foothills of the Rocky Mountains where I live, well-diggers drilled down 640 feet before striking water for our house. Even then the water only trickled until they used a technique called "fracking," short for hydro-fracturing. Pumping water down the well shaft at very high pressure, technicians shattered the granite into gravel and opened new seams for water flow. As I watched, pressures that to me seemed likely to destroy the well actually tapped new sources of water. I'm sure Bill Leslie would appreciate the analogy: extreme pressures, seemingly destructive, forced him to seek new sources of strength—the very reason he had pursued spiritual direction in the first place.

In a similar metaphor, the prophet Jeremiah writes of a bush that sets its roots in parched desert soil. In times of rainfall and prosperity the plant flourishes, but during drought its shallow roots shrivel and die. Jeremiah draws a contrast to the one who lives in faith:

> ... blessed is the man who trusts in the Lord,
>   whose confidence is in him.
> He will be like a tree planted by the water
>   that sends out its roots by the stream.
> It does not fear when heat comes;
>   its leaves are always green.
> It has no worries in a year of drought
>   and never fails to bear fruit.

The Bible makes no rosy promises about living only in springtime. Instead, it points toward faith that helps us prepare for arid seasons. Harsh winters will come, followed by scorching summers. Yet if the roots of faith go deep enough, tapping into Living Water, we can survive the drought times and flourish in times of plenty.

ACCORDING TO STANLEY HAUERWAS, the life of faith consists of patience and hope. When something comes along to test our relationship with God, we rely on those two virtues: patience formed by a long memory, and hope that our faithfulness will prove worth the risk. Jews and Christians have always emphasized these virtues, Hauerwas notes, for we believe that a God who is both good and faithful controls the universe; patience and hope keep faith alive during times that cast doubt on that belief.

I would paraphrase Hauerwas by saying the life of faith consists of living in the past and in the future. I live in the past in order to ground myself in what God has already done, as a way of gaining confidence in what he might do again. Relating to an invisible God involves certain handicaps: with no sensory evidence in the present, we must look backward to remind ourselves of who it is we are relating to. Every time God introduced himself as "the God of Abraham, Isaac, and Jacob," he reminded his chosen people of his history with them — a history that for all three forebears included seasons of testing and doubt.

I too learn about faith by looking back at Abraham, Isaac, and Jacob, for God proceeded in a most puzzling manner with all three. After God had promised to bring about a people as numerous as the stars in the sky, what followed more resembled a case study in family infertility. Abraham and Sarah entered their nineties before they saw their first child; that son (appropriately named Isaac, or "laughter") married a barren woman; the grandson Jacob had to wait fourteen years for the wife of his dreams, only to discover her barren as well. This tortuous path toward populating a great nation shows that God operates on a different timetable than impatient human beings expect. From Abraham, Isaac, and Jacob — and also Joseph, Moses, David, and a host of others — I learn that God moves in ways I would neither predict nor desire. Yet each of those Old Testament characters lived and died in faith, vowing to the end that God had indeed kept his promises.

All through the Psalms, David and the other poets peer over their shoulders to former times when God appeared powerless yet somehow triumphed, when trust seemed foolhardy yet proved prudent. Psalms that review the history of God's deliverance often betray the writer's misgivings over whether God will intervene so spectacularly again. Strong memories soothe a restless present, as any number of psalms can attest.

New Testament letters advise the same: Study the Scriptures diligently, as necessary road maps for contests of faith. Beyond the Bible, the testimony of the entire church bears witness of God's faithfulness. Where would my own faith be, I wonder, without Augustine, Donne, Dostoevski, Jürgen Moltmann, Thomas Merton, C. S. Lewis? Many times I have leaned on their words as an exhausted traveler might lean against a roadside monument.

"I find that I crave light as a thirsting man craves water," wrote Commander Richard Byrd during a six-month sojourn in a metal hut at the South Pole. In the Antarctic winter, the sun made no appearance for four of those months. "A funereal gloom hangs in the twilight sky. This is the period between life and death. This is the way the world will look to the last man when it dies." Three weeks before the sun was due to return, he wrote in his journal about the sun's reappearance, "I tried to imagine what it would be like, but the conception was too vast for me to grasp." How strange those words must have seemed when Byrd later edited that journal for publication, living out his days in a latitude that saw the sun's rays every day.

Although I do not keep a formal journal, my writings accomplish something similar. I pick up an article I wrote twenty-five years ago and marvel at the passion I felt over an issue I have hardly thought about since. Such anger, doubt, barely controlled cynicism! I find cries of lament penciled long ago in the margins of my Bible and give thanks that I made it through that particular valley. When exuberant, I look at my past writings and am shocked at the sloughs of despond I wallowed in; when depressed, I am shocked at the bright faith I used to have. Mainly, from the past I gain perspective that what I feel and believe right now I will not always feel and believe—which drives me to sink roots deeper, into layers of subsoil unaffected by El Niño or other vagaries of climate.

Remembering my relationship with God takes effort and intentionality. I cannot pull out a home video and watch our history and growth together; there are no photo albums of living in faith. I must consciously work at reviewing both the progress of the ache and the progress of the healing.

Reflecting on his own life, the apostle Paul wrote, "Here is a trustworthy saying that deserves full acceptance: Christ Jesus came into the world to save sinners—of whom I am the worst. But for that very reason I was shown mercy so that in me, the worst of sinners, Christ Jesus might display his unlimited patience." I imagine many people would dispute Paul for that title "worst of sinners." Paul looks back just long enough to remember his former state and to stake his claim, then turns ahead to the future: "Now to the King eternal, immortal, invisible, the only God, be honor and glory for ever and ever. Amen."

The creek by my house freezes over every winter. If I bend down close, though, I can hear it flowing beneath the ice, the sound muffled but unmistakable. Never does it stop. Under the frigid layers of winter lies proof of an inevitable summer.

***

OF PATIENCE AND HOPE, past and future, the life of faith consists. Martin Marty, who rated half the psalms as "wintry" in tone, also noted that 149 of the 150 eventually get around to hope.

Jürgen Moltmann, one of the premier theologians of our century, recounts in the slim book *Experiences of God* his personal journey toward hope. Drafted as a teenager in World War II, he was sent to the German front, where the British soon captured him. The next three years he spent in detention, shuttled from prison camp to prison camp in Belgium, Scotland, and England. Meanwhile Hitler's empire collapsed, exposing the moral rot at the center of the Third Reich, and all around him Moltmann saw how other Germans "collapsed inwardly, how they gave up all hope, sickening for the lack of it, some of them dying. The same thing almost happened to me. What kept me from it was a rebirth to new life...."

Apart from the cultural trappings of Christmas and other holidays, Moltmann had no Christian background. He had brought just two books with him into battle: Goethe's poems and the complete works of Nietzsche, in editions that Hitler had distributed to his troops. Neither nourished hope, to put it mildly. But a chaplain gave him a New Testament, which included the Psalms in an appendix.

"If I make my bed in hell, behold thou art there," Moltmann the prisoner read. Could God be present in that dark night? "I was dumb with silence, I held my peace, even from good; and my sorrow was stirred.... I am a stranger with thee, and a sojourner, as all my fathers were." As he read, Moltmann found words that perfectly captured his own feelings of desolation. He became convinced that God "was present even behind the barbed wire—no, most of all behind the barbed wire."

As Moltmann kept reading, he also found something new in the Psalms: hope. Walking the perimeter of the barbed wire at night for exercise, he would circle a small hill in the center of the camp on which stood a hut that served as a chapel. For him the hut became a symbol of God's presence radiating in the midst of suffering, and out of that symbol grew hope.

Upon release, Moltmann abandoned his plan to study quantum physics and turned instead to theology, founding a movement called "a theology of hope." We on earth exist, he concluded, in a state of contradiction between the cross and the resurrection. Surrounded by decay, we nonetheless hope for perfection, for a restoration of the cosmos. We have no proof that it can ever be attained, only a sign in history, the "foreglow" of the raising of Christ from the dead. Yet if we can sustain faith in that glorious future, it can transform the present—just as Moltmann's own hope of eventual release from prison camp transformed his daily experience there.

A future faith can alter the present, at the very least by allowing us to suspend judgment of God. A person without future faith logically assumes that the suffering and chaos on this planet reflect something of God; therefore, God is neither all-good nor all-powerful. Future faith allows me to believe that God is not satisfied with this world either and plans to restore the universe to its original design. Just as Moltmann came to believe in the possibility of life outside a prison camp someday, I can believe in a future time when God will reign with perfect justice.

"Away distrust: My God hath promised, he is just," wrote George Herbert. I need that reminder daily. With future faith, I can trust in that as-yet-unverified justice despite all the apparent contradictions on this groaning planet.

IN HIS AUTOBIOGRAPHY, *A Long Walk to Freedom,* Nelson Mandela recalls the scene when he first laid eyes on his granddaughter. At the time, he was working at hard labor on Robben Island in almost unbearable conditions, cutting lime in a quarry under a sun so bright it nearly blinded him. Only one thing kept the prisoners from despair, he writes: they sang together as they worked. The songs reminded them of family and home and tribe and the world outside they might otherwise forget.

During the fourteenth year of his imprisonment, Mandela gained permission for a visit from his daughter (he was generally forbidden visitors).

She ran across the room and embraced him. Mandela had not held his daughter since she was a young girl, and it was both poignant and dizzying to hug this fully grown woman, his child. Then she handed over her own newborn baby, Nelson's granddaughter, into his callused, leathery hands. "To hold a newborn baby, so vulnerable and soft in my rough hands, hands that for too long had held only picks and shovels, was a profound joy. I don't think a man was ever happier to hold a baby than I was that day."

Mandela's tribal culture had a tradition of letting the grandfather choose a new baby's name, and Nelson toyed with various names as he held that tiny, helpless baby. He settled on Zaziwe, which means Hope. "The name had special meaning for me, for during all my years in prison hope never left me—and now it never would. I was convinced that this child would be a part of a new generation of South Africans for whom apartheid would be a distant memory—that was my dream."

As it turned out, Mandela had served barely half his sentence and would not gain freedom for thirteen more years. The vision of hope, however, of Zaziwe, sustained him. Despite little present evidence at the time, he believed that the reality of apartheid in South Africa would someday crumble. The time would come, whether in his lifetime or his granddaughter's, when a new kind of justice would descend. Future faith determined his present.

Even for those who, unlike Mandela, do not live to see hope realized in this life, future faith holds out hope in resurrection. Dallas Willard knew a woman who refused to talk about life beyond death because, she said, she did not want her children to be disappointed if it turned out no afterlife existed. As Willard points out, if no afterlife exists, no one will have any consciousness with which to feel disappointment! On the other hand, if there is an afterlife, shouldn't we prepare for it?

When I lived in Chicago, we watched the steady physical deterioration in a church member named Sabrina. Young, slender, beautiful, stylish, Sabrina caught the eye of every man and the envy of every woman, until an inoperable brain tumor began its cruel work on her. Every month our church had a time of prayer for healing, and Sabrina and her husband went forward each month. Soon she was wearing colorful scarves to hide the effects of the chemotherapy. All too quickly, she began walking with a limp, in need of assistance just to make it down the aisle. Then she lost the use of all her limbs and attended church in a wheelchair. Then she went blind and was confined to bed. Toward the end, she could not speak and communicated by blinking her eyes at her husband's promptings.

Those of us who knew Sabrina cried out to God on her behalf. The pastors anointed her with oil. We wished and prayed for a miracle. We felt helpless and angry as our prayers went unanswered and we watched the inexorable progress of the disease.

At Sabrina's funeral, held in the same church, about half of those in attendance came from the congregation and half from her workplace. Her colleagues at work stared at the hymn books and the liturgy on the program as if they were written in a foreign language. All of us, regardless of faith background or beliefs, shared the sense of grief and outrage at what had happened to Sabrina. Yet her husband, her pastors, and her fellow-parishioners also shared something incomprehensible to the others attending: hope that Sabrina's life had not truly ended, hope that we would one day see her again.

"Lord, to whom shall we go?" asked Simon Peter in a moment of confusion. I feel his words deeply at every funeral I attend. Without resurrection faith, belief in a future beyond what we now know, death has the last word and proclaims its mocking victory. A "foreglow" of resurrection surely does not dispel the shadows, but it does bathe them in the new light of hope.

LEO TOLSTOY, WHO DID not disdain adding a moral lesson to his stories, ended his short story "Three Questions" this way: "Remember then: there is only one time that is important — Now! It is the most important time because it is the only time when we have any power."

A record of God's faithfulness in the past combines with hope in a better future for one end: to equip us for the present. As Tolstoy said, we have control over no other time. The past is unchangeable, the future unpredictable. I can only live the life directly before me. Faithful Christians pray, "Thy will be done, on earth as it is in heaven," and then proceed to enact God's will — love, justice, peace, mercy, forgiveness — in the present, on earth.

I have learned the importance of the present, by analogy, in the writing process. If I focus on previous books and articles I have written, fretting over my failures and relishing my successes, or if I concentrate on the future, worrying about deadlines and carrying the whole book in my mind, I will undergo paralysis in the present. I must devote myself to the word and sentence before me, to the present moment.

My friends in recovery groups live by the indispensable slogan, "One day at a time." The historian of Alcoholics Anonymous titled his work *Not-God* because, he said, the most important hurdle an addicted person must surmount is to acknowledge deep in the soul that he or she is not God. No mastery of manipulation and control, at which alcoholics excel, can overcome the root problem; rather, the alcoholic must recognize his or her own helplessness and fall back in the arms of the Higher Power. "First of all we had to quit playing God," concluded the founders of AA. Next, we must in faith allow God himself to "play God" in our lives, which involves daily, even moment-by-moment surrender.

If I reflect on my entire spiritual pilgrimage at once, I usually end up nostalgic for those times when God seemed so much closer. Faith, I have found, is not something I settle into, a skill I learn to master. It comes as a gift from God, and I need to pray for it every day, as I pray for daily bread. A friend of mine, paralyzed in an accident, traces her turning point in faith to this very principle. She could not face a life of total paralysis; she could, however, face one day at a time, with God's help. The Bible contains 365 commands to "fear not"—the most reiterated command in the Bible—as if to remind us daily that we will face difficulties that might naturally provoke fear.

"There is no fear in love," writes the apostle John, "but perfect love drives out fear...." He goes on to point to the source of that perfect love: "We love because he first loved us." In other words, the cure to fear is not a change in circumstances, rather a deep grounding in the love of God. I ask God to reveal his love to me directly, or through my relationships with those who also know him—a prayer I think God takes great delight in answering. When I get depressed about my present failures, I ask God to remind me of my true identity: one who will be made perfect and has already been forgiven. "You've got to go deeper," said the nun to my burned-out pastor. Sink the well into a water table that never runs dry.

Thomas Merton conceded that everything in modern city life conspires against such a surrender. We worry about money, about what we need to have and to know, about whom to compete with, and what is slipping out of our control. Ultimately this agitation, which Merton termed a "neurosis," drove him into a monastery, where at last he found a place for quietness and meditation. In fact, Merton's autobiography recounts the day he decided to enter the monastery rather than the army. In either course he would find happiness, he believed, if that were the course God wanted for him. "There is only one happiness: to please Him. Only one sorrow, to be displeasing to Him. . . ."

Merton found the secret to true freedom: If we live to please God alone, we set ourselves free from the cares and worries that press in on us. So many of my own cares trace back to concern over other people: whether I measure up to their expectations, whether they find me desirable. Living for God alone involves a radical reorientation, a stripping away of anything that might lure me from the primary goal of pleasing God. Living in faith involves me pleasing God, far more than God pleasing me.

I know a hand surgeon who specializes in reattaching fingers that have been partially or completely severed in accidents. When he enters the operating room, he knows he will be squinting into a microscope for six to eight hours, sorting out and stitching together the snarl of nerves, tendons, and blood vessels finer than human hairs. A single mistake, and the patient may permanently lose movement or sensation. He cannot take a coffee break or even a bathroom break. Once my friend got an emergency call at three o'clock in the morning and could hardly face the prospect of beginning such an arduous procedure. In order to add incentive and focus, he decided to dedicate the surgery to his father who had recently died. For the next few hours, he imagined his father standing beside him, his hand on his shoulder, offering encouragement.

The technique worked so well that he began dedicating his surgeries to people he knew. He would call them, often awakening them, and say, "I have a very demanding procedure ahead of me, and I'd like to dedicate the surgery to you. If I think about you while I'm performing it, that will help me get through." And then it dawned on him: should not he offer his life to God in the same way? The details of what he did each day—answering phone calls, hiring staff, reading medical journals, meeting with patients, scheduling surgeries—changed little, yet somehow the awareness of living for God gradually colored each of those mundane tasks. He found himself treating nurses with more care and respect, spending more time with patients, worrying less about finances.

———— ❧ ————

I HAVE VISITED CALCUTTA, India, a place of poverty, death, and irremediable human problems. There, the nuns trained by Mother Teresa serve the poorest, most miserable people on the planet: half-dead bodies picked up from the streets of Calcutta. The world stands in awe at the sisters' dedication and the results of their ministry, but something about these nuns impresses me even more: their serenity. If I tackled such a daunting project, I would likely be scurrying about, faxing press releases to donors, begging for more resources, gulping tranquilizers, grasping at ways to cope with my mounting desperation. Not these nuns.

Their serenity traces back to what takes place before their day's work begins. At four o'clock in the morning, long before the sun, the sisters rise, awakened by a bell and the call, "Let us bless the Lord." "Thanks be to God," they reply. Dressed in spotless white saris, they file into the chapel, where they sit on the floor, Indian-style, and pray and sing together. On the wall of the plain chapel hangs a crucifix with the words, "I thirst." Before meeting their first "client," they immerse themselves in worship and in the love of God.

I sense no panic in the sisters who run the Home for the Dying and Destitute in Calcutta. I see concern and compassion, yes, but no obsession over what did not get done. In fact, early on in their work Mother Teresa instituted a rule that her sisters take Thursdays off for prayer and rest. "The work will always be here but if we do not rest and pray, we will not have the presence to do our work," she explained. These sisters are not working to complete a caseload sheet for a social service agency. They are working for God. They begin their day with him; they end their day with him, back in the chapel for night prayers; and everything in between they present as an offering to God. God alone determines their worth and measures their success.

When his life's work was threatened, St. Ignatius of Loyola was asked what he would do if Pope Paul IV dissolved the Society of Jesus, to which he had devoted his energy and gifts. He replied, "I would pray for fifteen minutes, then I would not think of it again."

I cannot pretend to anything like the magisterial attitude of Ignatius or Mother Teresa's nuns. I admire, even revere them, and pray that some day I will attain something like the holy simplicity they embody. For now, all I can muster is a daily (and erratic at that) process of "centering" my life on God. I want my life to be integrated in the one true reality of a God who knows everything about me and desires for me only the good. I want to view all the distractions of my day from the perspective of eternity. I want to abandon myself to a God who can elevate me beyond the tyranny of my self. I will never be free from evil, or from distractions, but I pray that I can be freed from the anxiety and unrest that crowd in with them.

In the morning I ask for the grace to live for God alone, and yet when the phone rings with a message that strokes my ego, or when I open a letter from an irate reader, I find myself slipping back—no, tumbling back—to a self-consciousness in which other people, or circumstances, determine my worth and my serenity. I sense my need for transformation and keep going only because that sense is the one sure basis for potential change.

"The motions of Grace; the hardness of heart; external circumstances," Pascal jotted down in one of his cryptic notes. These three things encompass our lives. External circumstances press in: family strife, job pressures, financial worries, global concerns. The motions of grace, God's gifts within, seek to ground us in a deeper reality. Hardness of heart? Of the three, this alone falls somewhat under my control. All I can do is pray daily for God to "batter my heart," in John Donne's phrase, or better yet, to melt it with his love.

Transformation comes, in the end, not from an act of will, but an act of grace. We can only ask for it and keep asking.

> There is a Moment in each Day that Satan cannot find.
>
> WILLIAM BLAKE

MASTERY OF THE ORDINARY

In order to arrive at what you are not
You must go through the way in which you are not.

T. S. ELIOT

A S A FORM OF truth in advertising, I feel obligated to explore how faith works in actual daily practice, not just in theory. My own life of faith has included many surprises that no one had prepared me for. Of course, if the journey did not include a few potholes, dark stretches, and unexpected detours, we would hardly need faith.

Some monastics describe an integrated life in which spiritual strength flows outward to bathe every activity. Then again, most of them live in spiritual communities with scheduled prayer and worship times and have no cell phones and televisions to interrupt their days. What about the rest of us, who face to-do lists that never get done and live in a culture that conspires to drown out silence and fill all pauses?

When I begin the morning by intentionally centering on God, from that still point I hope that serenity and peace will expand to affect the rest of my day. Yet I have found that even if I get *only* that half-hour of calmness in an otherwise jumbled day, the effort still proves worthwhile. I used to think that everything important in my life—marriage, work, close friends, relationship with God—needed to be in order. One defective area, like one malfunctioning program on my computer, would cause the entire system to crash. I have since learned to pursue God and lean heavily on his grace even when, especially when, one of the other areas is plummeting toward disaster.

As one who writes and speaks publicly about my faith, I have also learned to accept that I am a "clay vessel" whom God may use at a time when I feel unworthy or hypocritical. I can give a speech or preach a sermon that was authentic and alive to me when I composed it, even though as I deliver it my mind is replaying an argument I just had or nursing an injury I received from a friend. I can write what I believe to be true even while painfully aware of my own inability to attain what I urge others toward.

Exercising faith in the present means trusting God to work through the encounter before me despite the background clutter of the rest of my life. As the recovery movement has taught us, our very helplessness drives us to God.* An addicted person may discover his or her weakness to be a gift disguised, for that is what presses daily toward grace—whereas the rest of us vainly try to deny our need. Anne Lamott, who writes openly about her alcoholism, says she has two favorite prayers: "Thank you, thank you, thank you" and "Help me, help me, help me."

I have visited William Cowper's home in the tiny stone village of Olney, England. Cowper wrote some of the church's most popular hymns—"O for a Closer Walk with God," "God Moves in a Mysterious Way His Wonders to Perform," "There Is a Fountain Fill'd with Blood"—and for a time shared a house with John Newton, converted slave-trader and author of "Amazing Grace." As I toured the sites where Cowper lived, however, I realized how little grace he actually experi-

---

* Bill W., one of AA's founders, wrote the psychiatrist Carl Jung a note of appreciation and received a reply in which Jung said it may be no accident that we refer to alcoholic drinks as "spirits." Perhaps, suggested Jung, alcoholics have a greater thirst for the spirit than other people, a spiritual thirst which is all too often misdirected.

enced. Tormented by fears that he had committed the unpardonable sin and hounded by rumors of an illicit affair, Cowper suffered a nervous breakdown, attempted suicide several times, and was kept straightjacketed in an insane asylum for his own protection. The last quarter of his life, he avoided church entirely.

> Where is the blessedness I knew
> When first I sought the Lord?
> Where is the soul-refreshing dew
> Of Jesus and his word?
> What peaceful hours I once enjoyed!
> How sweet their memory still!
> But they have left an aching void
> The world can never fill.
> Return, O Holy Dove, return
> Sweet messenger of rest!
> I hate the sins that made Thee mourn
> And drove Thee from my breast.

In the idealism of youth I would have pounced upon Cowper as a typical Christian hypocrite, one who wrote about what he could not put into practice. Now, though, as I ponder the grand words the poet left behind, I see his hymns as perhaps the only marks of clarity in a sadly troubled life. "Redeeming love has been my theme, / And shall be till I die," wrote Cowper. I believe he meant those words with all his heart as he wrote them for others to sing. Though he felt little of it personally, he left lasting proof of redeeming love in his treasury of hymns.

An artist like Cowper does not create in order to gain future glory but rather to grapple, to attend closely, to express both pain and praise. We who follow bestow the glory, because out of the artist's struggle comes abiding truth that speaks to our souls. God's grace may work that transformation in any of us, using the failures of the present as the very tools to shape us in God's image. As Cowper expressed it:

> Sometimes a light surprises
> The Christian while he sings
> It is the Lord who rises
> With healing in His wings,

When comforts are declining,
He grants the soul again
A season of clear shining,
To cheer it after rain.

———⌒⌒———

M Y TEACHING IS NOT my own," Jesus said. "It comes from him who sent me. If anyone chooses to do God's will, he will find out whether my teaching comes from God or whether I speak on my own." Note the sequence: Choose to do God's will, and the confidence will later follow. Jesus presents the journey of faith as a personal pilgrimage begun in uncertainty and fragile trust.

Some psychologists practice a school of behavior therapy that encourages the client to "act as if" a certain state is true, no matter how unreasonable it seems. We change behavior, says this school, not by delving into the past or by trying to align motives with actions but rather by "acting as if" the change should happen.* It's much easier to act your way into feelings than to feel your way into actions.

If you want to preserve your marriage but are not sure you really love your wife, start acting as if you love her: surprise her, show affection, give gifts, be attentive. You may find that feelings of love materialize as you act out the behavior. If you want to forgive your father but find yourself unable, act as if he is forgiven. Say the words, "I forgive you," or "I love you," even though you are not entirely convinced you mean them. Often the change in behavior in the one party brings about a remarkable change in the other.

Something similar works in my relationship with God. I wish all obedience sprang from an instinctive desire to please God—alas, it does not. For me, the life of faith sometimes consists of *acting as if* the whole thing is true. I assume that God loves me infinitely, that good will conquer evil, that any adversity can be redeemed, though I have no sure confirmation and only rare epiphanies to spur me along the way. I act as if God

---

* The poet Mark Van Doren used to tell his students, when studying *Don Quixote:* "One of the lessons of this book is that the way to become a knight is to act like a knight." Later he told Thomas Merton, "The way to become a saint is to act like a saint."

is a loving Father; I treat my neighbors as if they truly bear God's image; I forgive those who wrong me as if God has forgiven me first.

I must rely on this technique because of the inherent difference between relating to another human and relating to God. I go to the grocery store and run into a neighbor I have not seen for months. *Judy just went through a divorce,* I say to myself, remembering we have not heard from her lately. Seeing Judy prods me to act. I ask about her life, check on her children, maybe invite her to church. "We must get together with Judy and the kids," I tell my wife later that day, recalling the grocery store encounter.

With God, the sequence reverses. I never "see" God. I seldom run into visual clues that remind me of God *unless I am looking.* The act of looking, the pursuit itself, makes possible the encounter. For this reason, Christianity has always insisted that trust and obedience come first, and knowledge follows.*

Because of that difference, I persevere at spiritual disciplines no matter how I feel. I do this for one main goal, the goal of all spiritual discipline: I want to know God. And in pursuing a relationship with God, we must come on God's terms, not our own. The famed spiritual director Fénelon advised his students that in difficult times, "Prayer may be less easy, the Presence of God less evident and less comforting, outward duties may be harder and less acceptable, but the faithfulness which accompanies them is greater, and that is enough for God." We obey first and then find the source of Jesus' teaching.

Old Testament prophets were quite blunt as they set out the preconditions for knowing God, as in this verse from Micah: "And what does the Lord require of you? To act justly and to love mercy and to walk humbly with your God." Along the same line, the New Testament epistles repeatedly tell us that love for God, which means acting in loving ways toward God, nurtures the relationship and leads toward growth. I do not get to know God, then do his will; I get to know him *by* doing his will. I enter into an active relationship, which means spending time

---

*In *A Severe Mercy,* Sheldon Vanauken described the process this way: "Choosing to believe *is* believing. It's all I can do: choose. . . . I do not affirm that I am without doubt, I do but ask for help, having chosen, to overcome it. I do but say: Lord, I believe — help Thou mine unbelief."

with God, caring about the people he cares about, and following his commands—whether I spontaneously feel like it or not.

"How shall we begin to know You Who are if we do not begin ourselves to be something of what You are?" asked Thomas Merton. God is holy, Other. I can no more get to know God apart from some common ground than I can get to know a Hungarian person apart from common language. Merton adds:

> We receive enlightenment only in proportion as we give ourselves more and more completely to God by humble submission and love. We do not first see, then act: we act, then see. . . . And that is why the man who waits to see clearly, before he will believe, never starts on the journey.

How can we obey without certainty, when plagued by doubts? I have concluded that faith *requires* obedience without full knowledge. Like Job, like Abraham, I accept that much lies beyond my finite grasp, and yet I choose to trust God anyhow, humbly accepting my position as a creature whose worth and very life depend upon God's mercy.

M OST OF US FACE a lesser trial than what Job and Abraham endured, but a trial nonetheless. Faith also gets tested when a sense of God's presence fades or when the very ordinariness of life makes us question whether our responses even matter. We wonder, "What can one person do? What difference will my small effort make?"

I once watched a public television series based on interviews with survivors from World War II. The soldiers recalled how they spent a particular day. One sat in a foxhole all day; once or twice, a German tank drove by, and he shot at it. Others played cards and frittered away the time. A few got involved in furious firefights. Mostly, the day passed like any other day for an infantryman on the front. Later, they learned they had just participated in one of the largest, most decisive engagements of the war, the Battle of the Bulge. It did not *feel* decisive to any of them at the time, because none had the big picture of what was happening elsewhere.

Great victories are won when ordinary people execute their assigned tasks—and a faithful person does not debate each day whether he or she is in the mood to follow the sergeant's orders or show up at a boring job. We exercise faith by responding to the task that lies before us, for we have control only over our actions in the present moment. I sometimes wish the Gospel writers had included details about Jesus' life before he turned to ministry. For most of his adult life he worked as a village carpenter. Did he ever question the value of the time he was spending on such repetitious tasks?

Ignatius Loyola, founder of the Jesuits, saw that nearly all of his followers went through periods of futility. Their faith began to waver, they questioned their worth, they felt useless. Ignatius set down a series of tests to help identify the cause of spiritual despair. In every case, regardless of cause, Ignatius prescribed the same cure: "In times of desolation we must never make a change, but stand firm and constant in the resolutions and determination in which we were the day before the desolation, or in the time of the preceding consolation." He advised fighting spiritual battles with the very weapons hardest to wield at that particular time: prayer and meditation, self-examination, repentance. Obedience, and only obedience, offers a way out.

A person reared in a Christian home, who has absorbed the faith along with other family values from trusted parents, will one day face a crisis that puts loyalty to the test. She may have had religious experiences, may have felt something of the closeness of God. Without warning, that sense vanishes. She feels nothing except doubts over all that has gone before. Faith loses all support of feeling, and she wonders if she has been living under illusion. At such a moment it may feel very foolish to hold on to faith regardless. Yet, as Ignatius counsels, now is the time to "stand firm." Faith can survive periods of darkness but only if we cling to it in the midst of the darkness.

More often than I would care to admit, doubts gnaw away at me. I wonder about apparent conflicts in the Bible, about suffering and injustice, about the huge gap between the ideals and reality of the Christian life. At such times I plod on, "acting as if" it is true, relying on the habit of belief, praying for the assurance that eventually comes yet never shields me against the doubts' return.

As a pianist, I find that my competency depends on one thing above all: consistent practice. I take little joy in practicing scales and arpeggios, and most of the time I skip them in favor of more melodic pieces. When I do so, however, I find that the grander pieces themselves seem more like work than joy. I do not play scales for their own sake, but in order to play the grander pieces I must build on the daily mastery of the ordinary.

———— ✧ ————

As Andrew Greeley said, "If one wishes to eliminate uncertainty, tension, confusion and disorder from one's life, there is no point in getting mixed up either with Yahweh or with Jesus of Nazareth." I grew up expecting that a relationship with God would bring order, certainty, and a calm rationality to life. Instead, I have discovered that living in faith involves much dynamic tension.

Throughout church history, Christian leaders have shown an impulse to pin everything down, to reduce behavior and doctrine to absolutes that could be answered on a true-false test. Significantly, I do not find this tendency in the Bible. Far from it, I find instead the mystery and uncertainty that characterize any relationship, especially a relationship between a perfect God and fallible human beings.

In a memorable phrase that became the virtual cornerstone of his theology, G. K. Chesterton said, "Christianity got over the difficulty of combining furious opposites, by keeping them both, and keeping them both furious." Most heresies come from espousing one opposite at the expense of the other.

A church uncomfortable with paradox tends to tilt in one direction or the other, usually with disastrous consequences. Read the theologians of the first few centuries as they try to fathom Jesus, the center of our faith, who was somehow fully God and fully man. Read the theologians of the Reformation as they discover the majestic implications of God's sovereignty, then strive to keep their followers from settling into a resigned fatalism. Read the theologians of today as they debate the intricacies of written revelation: a Bible that expresses God's words to us that is nonetheless authored by individuals of widely varying intelligence, personality, and writing style.

The first shall be last; find your life by losing it; no achievement matters apart from love; work out your salvation with fear and trembling for it is God who works in you; God's kingdom has come but not fully; enter the kingdom of heaven like a child; he who serves is greatest; measure self-worth not by what others think of you but by what you think of them; he who stoops lowest climbs highest; where sin abounds grace abounds more; we are saved by faith alone but faith without works is dead—all these profound principles of life appear in the New Testament, and none easily reduces to logical consistency. "Truth is not in the middle, and not in one extreme, but in both extremes," the British pastor Charles Simeon remarked. With some reluctance, I have come to agree.

Consider the basic makeup of human beings. Inside every person on earth, we believe, the image of God can be found. Yet inside each person there lives also a beast. Any religious or political system that does not account for both extremes—furious opposites, in Chesterton's phrase—will sorely fail. As a Jewish rabbi put it, "A man should carry two stones in his pocket. On one should be inscribed, 'I am but dust and ashes.' On the other, 'For my sake was the world created.' And he should use each stone as he needs it."

The dynamic tension inside each one of us works itself out in daily life, revealing what truly lies inside our hearts. Scott Peck's book *The Road Less Traveled* spent more time on *The New York Times* best-seller list than any book in history, and I believe the secret of its success unfolds from the very first sentence: "Life is difficult." Peck raised a thoughtful protest against the how-to, problem-solving books that normally occupy such lists—and especially occupy the Christian best-seller lists.

When a woman gives birth to a profoundly retarded child, no "how-to" book will remove the pain. Poverty and injustice do not go away despite our best programs. Kids in the most affluent suburbs shoot their classmates at school. Marriage problems don't get solved. Death snares us all eventually. And any faith that does not account for complexities such as these cannot last. Quite simply, being human is hazardous to health. Unlike angels, human beings get cancer, lose their jobs, and go hungry. We need a faith that somehow allows the possibility of joy in the midst of suffering as well as realism in the midst of praise.

I used to believe that Christianity solved problems and made life easier. Increasingly, I believe that my faith complicates life, in ways it should be complicated. As a Christian, I cannot *not* care about the environment, about homelessness and poverty, about racism and religious persecution, about injustice and violence. God does not give me that option.

The Quaker philosopher Elton Trueblood agrees: "In many areas the gospel, instead of taking away people's burdens, actually adds to them." He cites John Woolman, a successful Quaker merchant who lived a comfortable life until God convicted him of the offense of slavery. Woolman gave up his prosperous business, used his money to purchase slaves' freedom, wore undyed suits to avoid using dye produced by slave labor, traveled on foot in solidarity with slaves who were not permitted to ride in carriages, and refused to eat sugar, rum, molasses, and other products tainted by slave labor. Largely because of this "quiet revolutionary," by 1787 not a single American Quaker owned a slave. Trueblood writes:

> Occasionally we talk of our Christianity as something that solves problems, and there is a sense in which it does. Long before it does so, however, it increases both the number and the intensity of the problems. Even our intellectual questions are increased by the acceptance of a strong religious faith. . . . If a man wishes to avoid the disturbing effect of paradoxes, the best advice is for him to leave the Christian faith alone.

At the heart of the gospel lies the paradox of the yoke. Jesus offers us comfort—"Come to me, all you who are weary and burdened, and I will give you rest"—but the comfort consists in taking on a new burden, his own burden. "Take my yoke upon you and learn from me, for I am gentle and humble in heart, and you will find rest for your souls. For my yoke is easy and my burden is light."

Jesus offers a peace that involves new turmoil, a rest that involves new tasks. The "peace of God, which transcends all understanding" promised in the New Testament is a peace in the midst of warfare, a calmness in the midst of fear, a confidence in the midst of doubt. Living as resident aliens in a strange land, citizens of a secret kingdom, what other kind of peace should we expect? In this world restlessness, and not contentment, is a sign of health. The Bible uses the word "pondering" to describe how a person sorts through this kind of tension. When Jesus' mother Mary encountered things she could not rationally resolve, she held them inside her soul, "pondering" them, carrying the tension rather than trying to eliminate it.

My father-in-law, a lifelong Bible teacher with strong Calvinist roots, found his faith troubled in his final years. A degenerative nerve disease confined him to bed, impeding him from most of the activities that gave him pleasure. His thirty-nine-year-old daughter battled a severe form of diabetes. Financial pressures mounted. During the most severe crisis, he composed a Christmas letter and mailed it to others in the family. Many things that he had once taught, he now felt uneasy about. What could he believe with certainty? He came up with these three things: "Life is difficult. God is merciful. Heaven is sure." These things he could count on. When his daughter died of diabetic complications the very next week, he clung to those truths ever more fiercely.

PAUL MENTIONS THREE CHRISTIAN virtues — faith, hope, love — at the end of 1 Corinthians 13, his great chapter on love, and each one enfolds a paradox.

Love involves caring about people most of us would prefer not to care about. In Paul's words, love is patient, does not envy, is not self-seeking, is not easily angered, keeps no record of wrongs; it always protects, always trusts, always hopes, always perseveres. Such a program may seem reasonable on another planet run by different rules, but not on our planet where people act with injustice, meanness, and vengeance. By nature we keep records, right wrongs, and demand our rights; love does not.

Hope gives us the power to look beyond circumstances that otherwise appear hopeless. Hope keeps hostages alive when they have no rational proof that anyone cares about their plight; it entices farmers to plant seeds in spring after three straight years of drought. "Hope that is seen is no hope at all," Paul told the Romans. He mentions some of the good things that might come out of difficulties: "Suffering produces perseverance; perseverance, character; and character, hope." He lists hope at the end, instead of where I would normally expect it, at the beginning, as the fuel that keeps a person going. No, hope emerges *from* the struggle, a byproduct of faithfulness.

As for faith, it will always mean believing in what cannot be proven, committing to that of which we can never be sure. A person who lives in faith must proceed on incomplete evidence, trusting in advance what will only make sense in reverse. As Dennis Covington has written,

"Mystery is not the absence of meaning, but the presence of more meaning than we can comprehend."

For several centuries *Pilgrim's Progress* sold more copies annually than any book except the Bible. Rereading it recently, I was struck by how John Bunyan's version of the Christian life differs from what I read in most Christian books today. Every few pages the pilgrim makes some stupid mistake and nearly loses his life. He takes wrong turns and detours. His only companion sinks in the Slough of Despond. The pilgrim yields to worldly temptations. He flirts with suicide and decides again and again to abandon the quest. At one such moment, Mr. Hopeful assures him, "Be of good cheer, my brother, for I feel the bottom, and it is sound."

> Nothing that is worth doing can be achieved in our lifetime; therefore we must be saved by hope. Nothing which is true or beautiful or good makes complete sense in any immediate context of history; therefore we must be saved by faith. Nothing we do, however virtuous, can be accomplished alone; therefore we must be saved by love.
>
> REINHOLD NIEBUHR

Acting in courageous faith, the pilgrim continues his journey and in the end arrives at his destination, the Celestial City. *Pilgrim's Progress* proved a reliable guidebook for millions of Christians over the years. Cheery, problem-solving books offer a much more attractive road map today, but I cannot help wondering what we have lost along the way.

PART THREE

God

Contact with the Invisible

EIGHT

KNOWING GOD,
OR ANYONE ELSE

*It is incomprehensible that God should exist, and it is
incomprehensible that He should not exist; that the soul
should be joined to the body, and that we should have no
soul; that the world should be created, and that it should
not be created ...*

BLAISE PASCAL

ONE NIGHT I SAT up until 2:00 A.M. listening to two friends recount
their difficulties in relating to God. Stanley told of a lifelong struggle to believe that he mattered, and that God cared about him. Judy
interrupted, with a tone of impatience stretched to the breaking point.
"I can't tell you how many times I've tried to make contact with God!
All I get for my efforts is a sense of cold, disapproving silence."

Because I knew these friends well, I could not help surmising they might
be projecting their own family dysfunctions onto God. Judy had lost her
mother at an early age, and though her father had worked valiantly to raise
three daughters in a stable home, he had never conveyed much warmth. She
viewed him as a kind of schoolteacher, or athletic coach, who would judge
her performance and then raise the bar a notch higher. As for God, Judy said
that a single phrase used at her mother's funeral, "God took her because

he needed her more than we did," formed a block in her relationship with God that she has yet to overcome.

Stanley came from a large, lively family of seven that had no lack of warmth. Still, as the fourth child, and a twin at that, he had the persistent, nagging sense of being overlooked. Teachers in school invariably compared him to his older siblings. His father never quite mastered the skill of telling him apart from his twin, even though the two were not identical. "If I suddenly disappeared from my family, it might take a week or two for anyone to notice," he said with a wry smile.

That evening reminded me that everyone has an image of God distorted in some way—we must, of course, since God transcends our ability to imagine him. Our experiences of family and church combine with stray hints from literature and movies (Hawthorne's *The Scarlet Letter,* Jonathan Edwards's "Sinners in the Hand of an Angry God") to determine what image of God we carry around. How then, do we know the true God?

If Judy and Stanley had been describing one of my friends whom they had misjudged, I could introduce them to my friend to help them form a different, truer picture. How can I do that with God? I tried that evening, saying to them, "The God you are describing to me—that God does not exist." We had a stimulating discussion, despite the late hour, but in the end they went away with the same image of God imprinted from childhood.

———— ക്ക ————

KNOWING AN INVISIBLE GOD, we assume, has little in common with knowing a living, breathing person. Or does it? Actually, the more we understand how the mind works, the more it becomes clear that all knowledge—of God, people, or anything else—involves uncertainty and demands an act of faith.

The process of knowing takes place in the brain, the most isolated part of the human body. The brain never sees: even if a surgeon exposed it to light, brain matter would see nothing. The brain never hears: so cushioned is it against shock that brain cells can detect only the loudest sounds, like a jet airplane, which cause them to vibrate. The brain has no touch or pain cells: a neurosurgeon must anesthetize to cut through skin and skull, but once inside he can move or cut brain tissue without hurting a conscious patient. Its temperature varies no more than a few degrees, so it never feels heat or cold.

Because of the brain's isolation, everything that forms my knowledge of the world reduces down to a sequence of electrical signals, like dots and dashes of the Morse code, reporting in from millions of nerve sensors. Think of the voice that comes to you over the telephone. Someone on the other end speaks, and electronic equipment converts those sound waves into electrical signals that pass through relay stations to be reassembled on your end as vibrations that produce audible sounds. If the caller uses a cell phone, the sound is translated into packets of digital code and broadcast through the air, like a radio transmission, before entering your telephone receiver. Yet you "hear" your mother's voice in a way that seems like reality. In much the same way, the isolated brain must rely on messages in digital code from its sensory organs.

The doorbell rings and I run upstairs to answer it. Tom, the UPS driver, has a package for me. I greet him, sign for the package, and return to my desk to resume work. It would take a computer programmer to appreciate fully the marvel involved in that simple act. Sound receptor cells in my ear first detected the frequency of my doorbell, approximately an octave above the piano's "middle C," and then interpreted the much more variable pitch of Tom's baritone voice. Computer software now has the ability to recognize individual voice prints, and even words spoken clearly. No computer, however, has yet mastered the much more difficult task of recognizing a human face.

The human eye's 130,000,000 receptor cells reported instantly on the shape, texture, and color of Tom's lips, eyes, eyebrows, nose, and hair. I did not have to consciously assemble the data; my brain did it effortlessly, running the reports from eye cells through a memory bank of all the faces I know and identifying Tom in a fraction of a second.

A color-blind person would not notice Tom's blue eyes, and a deaf person would miss the pitch of his voice. For all of us, in fact, exceptions or illusions creep in, misinforming the isolated brain and giving every person who has ever lived a different perception of the world. Yet so resourceful is the brain that it fills in the gaps and creates a sense of reality regardless. A great composer like Beethoven can "hear" an entire symphony in his head even when totally deaf.

I mention this anatomical background to illustrate that my knowledge of other people, like Tom the UPS driver, necessarily depends on an act of faith. Although my closeted brain has stored away an image of my friends and acquaintances, I realize that the image involves a large measure of trust. I trust that Tom is not wearing a mask or a fake mustache, and that he indeed works for UPS and is not a burglar scouting my house. I think I know him, but how can I be sure? Perhaps Tom is an identical twin who job-shares with his brother.

So many times people have surprised and misled me. I have learned that one of my best friends had a secret life of sexual addiction, that another was abused by her father for fifteen years. I thought I knew these friends, only to discover I was missing vital information about them. All human relationships rest on a platform of uncertainty that preserves the mysterious quality of otherness. In knowing one another, we always fall short.

Nevertheless, at the most basic level I trust that these friends actually exist as individual persons much like me. Can I know that for sure? The problem of "other minds" poses a major puzzle that has exercised philosophers for many years.* I know that I exist, and I think I know my own mind. But how do I know your mind? I believe, for example, that when you shut a car door on your finger, something happens inside you that closely resembles what I experience when I slam a car door on my own finger. Yet I cannot know for certain, because I cannot get inside your mind; I must take your word for it when you tell me how much it hurts.

How do you know that I exist? You are reading my words on a page, yes, but perhaps "Philip Yancey" is actually a pseudonym. Perhaps this book is being written by a ghost writer or by a programmer at Fuller Seminary who cleverly devised software to crank out books of popular theology. If you try to contact me over the Internet, you will never know whether it is "I" responding or simply a concocted screen name. (A friend of mine spent two years corresponding with a young woman in a chat room, only to find it was actually a young man pulling a practical joke on

---

* Here is how George Berkeley, the eighteenth-century philosopher, stated the problem: "It is plain that we cannot know the existence of other spirits [persons], otherwise than by their operations, or the ideas by them excited in us. I perceive certain motions, changes and combinations of ideas, that inform me that there are certain particular agents like myself which accompany them and concur in their production."

her.) To me, I am an "I"; to everyone else I am a "you," and that distinction introduces a powerful strain of uncertainty.

Admittedly, most people do not go around questioning whether other minds and persons exist. We take it for granted without giving it much thought. Yet individual minds will always mosaic a different version of the same person. Think of the authors of the four Gospels — Matthew, Mark, Luke, and John — each struck by different aspects of Jesus' personality and life. As they reflected on what they knew about him, different words and scenes came to mind. Or consider the twelve disciples: all of them followed Jesus around for three years, but what different conclusions Judas and John drew about him! Later, a Pharisee named Saul of Tarsus thought he had Jesus figured out, until a personal encounter radically changed his opinion and altered the direction of his life. "Knowing" another person is a tricky matter involving much approximation and mystery.

THE PROCESS OF KNOWING other people may shed light on how we know God. In the first place, I recognize that knowing "other minds," whether other persons or God, always requires an act of faith. Alvin Plantinga, a contemporary philosopher, applies this fact to the question of God's existence. I cannot be certain of God's existence, he acknowledges; I cannot *prove* it rationally. Yet neither can I be certain of anyone else's existence; they may all be products of my imagination. I do believe I am not alone in the universe, but because I cannot get inside of any other person's mental state I must accept this belief by analogy—or by faith. Plantinga goes so far as to say, after much philosophical argument, that we have as much evidence for believing in God as we do for believing in other people.

In addition, I must assume that my senses never furnish a complete representation of another person. I can learn a lot about you through watching you, listening to you, touching you. Yet there always remains a part of you inaccessible to me, the person inside your body, the real "you." I discern this most clearly in disabled people who have lost the close, dependable connection between mind and body.

I had a wonderful friend with cerebral palsy who for years was mistakenly confined to a home for the mentally retarded. Her arms flailed about spastically, she could not walk, and she made grunting sounds instead of words. Most who met her—tragically, even her own family—assumed she was retarded. In time, though, professionals recognized that Carolyn had a fine mind locked inside that uncooperative body. She moved to a more appropriate home, attended high school, and then college. Eventually she became a writer. Once, at her college, a friend read a chapel address Carolyn had written. Students sat in total silence and listened to Carolyn's eloquent words as she slumped in a wheelchair onstage beside her friend at the microphone. (She had chosen a text from 2 Corinthians, "We have this treasure in jars of clay.") All had seen her wheelchair on campus, and some had even cracked cruel jokes at her expense; few had made the effort to get to know the remarkable mind at work inside Carolyn's twisted body.

Another friend, Don, is currently fighting the degenerative nerve disease ALS, or Lou Gehrig's disease. I knew Don as a rugged outdoorsman who ran a horse ranch and led white-water canoeing expeditions. When I last visited him, though, he sat in a wheelchair. Though he could still talk, the nerves controlling voice and language could not keep up with his mental instructions. He stumbled over words and the simplest phrases stumped him. He preferred to type his thoughts into a laptop computer, which would then speak for him in a weird Darth Vader-type voice. Anyone walking into the room would see a man sitting very still, saying nothing, with a gentle smile at times crossing his face. But the disembodied words that came out of the computer, and the lucid e-mail messages I get from Don to this day, prove that inside that placid exterior, a lively and witty mind endures.

I am thankful that modern technology allows people like Don and Carolyn to communicate even when they lose the bodily functions that produce speech. Stephen Hawking, one of the world's most brilliant scientists, can only move one finger of one hand, and yet through the same software Don uses, Hawking can address scientific gatherings. (An Englishman, he says he resents the program's American accent.) I read a book "written" by a Frenchman who could only blink his left eyelid; a nurse would run her finger across the alphabet on a poster board until he blinked at the letter he wanted, then begin all over again until he signaled the next letter of the word. Even if these people lost *all* ability to communicate, through total paralysis or a stroke-induced *aphasia,* I would assume that somewhere inside them the mind would live on. Inevitably, however, we must rely on other people's bodies to convey to us their minds.

The adaptations I've had to make in communicating with disabled friends brings up an interesting theological question. Since God has no body, how can we perceive him? How can we communicate with God? Could it be that we possess the capacity for direct knowledge of God, meaning without reliance on the body and its senses? If so, our knowledge of God would operate differently than our knowledge of other persons. Conceivably, a spirit-God could use a kind of direct intuition to communicate to people, in a process governed by different rules, for God doesn't need our bodies in order to access our minds. As Tennyson wrote in a poem, "Closer is he than breathing, and nearer than hands and feet."

Jesus clearly hinted that after his death a new way of knowing would open up: not the normal process of an isolated brain forming pictures of reality but an internal and direct path of knowledge. "When the Counselor comes, whom I will send to you from the Father, the Spirit of truth who goes out from the Father, he will testify about me," Jesus said. "But when he, the Spirit of truth, comes, he will guide you into all truth."

Every creature on earth has a way to connect to the environment around it, a means to pick up and process what is out there. I will call this mechanism *correspondence.* In some cases, an animal's correspondence can far exceed our human abilities. Bats detect insects by sonar; eels stun their prey with electricity; pigeons navigate by magnetic fields; bloodhounds drink in a world of smell unavailable to us.*

Perhaps the unseen world requires an inbuilt set of correspondences activated through some sort of spiritual quickening. God is not "out there" in the material world, and we can only perceive him by gaining a new ability to correspond. "The man without the Spirit does not accept the things that come from the Spirit of God, for they are foolishness to him, and he cannot understand them, because they are spiritually discerned,"

---

* Voltaire's story "Micromages" imagines alien visitors who live 15,000 years and have seventy-two senses with which to perceive the world. Human beings, far more "handicapped," detect a tiny sliver of the electromagnetic spectrum: infrared and ultraviolet rays pass through us without our noticing, as do the frequencies that carry radio, television, and cellular telephone messages.

said Paul. "Now this is *eternal* life," said Jesus: "that they may know you, the only true God, and Jesus Christ, whom you have sent." At the heart of the Christian story lies the promise of direct correspondence with the unseen world, a link so profound as to be likened to a new birth, and the key to life beyond organic death.

As the pathway into the unseen world, the Bible presents faith, which Hebrews defines as "being sure of what we hope for and certain of what we do not see." Moses "saw him who is invisible," that chapter goes on to say, indicating an unusual correspondence at work. From the first page to the last, the Bible renders an account of another reality operating simultaneously to, but usually hidden from, the material reality of earth.

The invisible world may sometimes "borrow" the visible world in an attempt to communicate, as with the burning bush that Moses saw with his physical eyes. Except in these unusual instances, we humans rely primarily on "means of grace," such as the church, spiritual disciplines, and the sacraments, to correspond with the unseen world. Prayer, for example, operates somewhat like breathing: it keeps us alive spiritually. As Evelyn Underhill observed, "We are creatures of sense and spirit, and we must live an amphibious life."

According to the Bible, the greatest distinction between human beings is not based on race, intelligence, income, or talent. It is a distinction based on correspondence with the unseen world. The "children of light" have that correspondence; the "children of darkness" do not. One day we will achieve a complete, rather than partial correspondence with that world. As the apostle John said, "Dear friends, now we are children of God, and what we will be has not yet been made known. But we know that when he appears, we shall be like him, for we shall see him as he is."

IN DISCUSSING THE PROBLEM of "other minds," I have not told the whole story. The reason philosophers obsess over such questions and most people do not is that philosophers sit in book-lined rooms and allow abstractions to float around in their minds while the rest of us are picking up clothes at the cleaners, getting the kids ready for school, fighting battles at the PTA or city council, or taking care of an elderly relative.

We believe in other minds because we encounter them all day long. We *relate* to them.

In truth, we become who we are in large part because of those relationships. We do not enter the world as discrete minds dropped magically into waiting bodies. Our experiences, mainly our relationships, form us as persons. Feral children, those rare but documented cases of children raised by wild animals, never truly develop the ability to relate to others and can hardly be classified as persons in any meaningful sense. Similarly, children who have been locked in closets for years in appalling instances of child abuse never develop language skills and seem permanently stunted.

The human being takes longer to mature than any other animal. An antelope can drop out of its mother's womb, stand, and master the basics of running and eating in a matter of hours. Human babies, in contrast, must depend helplessly on other people for many months. A baby cannot truly become a person apart from human relationships.

Likewise, I conceive of the spiritual life as a capacity built into the human person, but one that can only develop in relationship with God. "I call you into my soul," said Augustine, "which you prepare to accept you by the longing that you breathe into it." Although we all have the capacity, our spiritual longing will remain unfulfilled until we make contact, and then develop the skills of spiritual "correspondence." Considered in this way, Jesus' striking image of being born again makes perfect sense. Conversion, the process of connecting to spiritual reality, awakens the potential of brand new life. And as God's children we become who we are through relationship with God and God's people.

I think of the person who has influenced my Christian life more than any other: the missionary surgeon Paul Brand. Over a fifteen-year period of time, I wrote three books with Dr. Brand. I accompanied him on trips to India and England where together we retraced the main events in his life. I spent hundreds of hours asking him every question I could think of about his experiences with medicine, life, and God. I interviewed his former patients, his colleagues, his family, his operating-room scrub nurses (the very best source, I found, to learn the truth about a surgeon's character!). Dr. Brand is both a good and a great man, and I have everlasting gratitude for the time we spent together. At a stage in my spiritual development when

I had little confidence to write about my own faith, I had absolute confidence writing about his.

I changed because of my relationship with Dr. Brand, who became a channel of spiritual growth for me. My faith strengthened as I had a living model of a person enhanced in every way by his own relationship with God. I now view justice, lifestyle, and money issues largely through his eyes; I see the natural environment differently; I look at the human body, and especially pain, in a very different light. My relationship with Dr. Brand affected me deeply, in my core, on the inside. Yet as I look back, I can think of no instance in which he imposed himself on me or manipulatively sought to change me. I changed willingly, gladly, as my world and my self encountered his.

A similar process works, I believe, with God. I become who I am as a Christian by relating to God. In ways mysterious and often hard to describe—yet never coercive or manipulative—I have changed over time because of my contact with God.

If I could interview the biblical characters Jeremiah, Jacob, Job, James, and Jude, each would give me a different answer to the question, "Tell me about your relationship with God—what is it like?" If I asked that question of David or the other psalmists, I would get starkly different answers from the same person! The relationship varies from one psalm to the next, and even varies within the same psalm. Psalm 143, for example, reflects on "the days of long ago," when God seemed close and intimate, then cries out, "Do not hide your face from me." David, especially, understood perhaps better than anyone who has ever lived, the dynamic, living relationship that takes place between a person and God.

Indeed, I see many parallels between getting to know God and getting to know a human person. I first learn a person's name. Something in his personality attracts me to him. I spend time with my new friend, learning what activities we have in common. I give gifts and make small sacrifices for that friend. I do things to please my friend that I wouldn't do otherwise. I share happy times and sad times; we laugh together and weep together. I reveal my deepest secrets. I take risks of relationship. I make commitments. I fight and argue, then reconcile. All these stages of relationship apply to God as well.

Ah yes, someone objects, *you make these parallels sound so smooth. I have many successful relationships with other people. I can see them, touch them, hear them. But when I try to relate to an invisible God, nothing happens. I never have the sense that God is even there.* I do not discount such an objection, because at times in my life I have wondered the same thing. Even now, my relationship with God rests or falls on faith (though, as I have pointed out, all relationships do).

You can see the problem by watching scenes of religious experience in movies. They are, in a word, boring. A saint kneels and prays, and the action comes to a halt. Something is happening, we presume, but not such that the camera can record. The process is invisible — which, for most people, holds far less interest than something engaging our bodies, like sex.

I know that my relationship with God will not exactly parallel my relationship with human beings, and in some ways will radically differ. God is infinite, intangible, and invisible. If I may use such language, we humans have little sympathy for the problems that must confront a Being who desires to relate to us. Baron von Hugel drew the analogy of a man's relations with a dog.* The parallel was generous to us. An infinite God relating to human beings presents far more of a challenge than a man relating to his dog — perhaps a man communicating with a wood tick is a closer analogy.

Communication between such unequal creatures will inevitably cause confusion and disappointment on both sides. What we humans want out of a relationship may well run at cross-purposes with what God wants. We want God to be like us: tangible, material, perceptible (hence the long history of idolatry). We want God to speak in audible words that we can clearly understand (Ezra Stiles of Yale studied Hebrew in order to converse with God in his native language!).

---

* "Our dogs know us, and love us thus most really, yet they doubtless know us only vividly, not clearly; we evidently strain their minds after a while — they then like to get away amongst servants and children; and, indeed, they love altogether to escape from human company. . . . And yet, how wonderful! Dogs thus require their fellow-dogs, the shallow and clear, but they also require us, the deep and dim; they require indeed what they can grasp. . . . The source and object of religion, if religion be true and its object be real, cannot, indeed, by any possibility, be as clear to me even as I am to my dog."

Apart from the Incarnation and rare epiphanies, however, God shows little interest in corresponding on our level. God has, in the common phrase "been there, done that," and has no reason to confine himself to time and space any longer than necessary. Rather, God seeks from us correspondence in a spiritual realm and seems more interested in other kinds of growth: justice, mercy, peace, grace, and love—spiritual qualities that can work themselves out in a material world. In short, God wants us to be more like him.

An ancient Orthodox writer wrote, "God cannot be grasped by the mind. If he could be grasped, he would not be God." We are profoundly different, God and I, which explains why friendship is not the primary model used in the Bible to describe our relationship. Worship is.

AFTER SURVIVING INTERNMENT IN a Nazi concentration camp, Viktor Frankl went on to become a famous therapist. He recalls a time when, fearing death at any moment, he and another prisoner were forced by Nazi guards to march toward an unknown destination.

> ... as we stumbled on for miles, slipping on icy spots, supporting each other time and again, dragging one another up and onward, nothing was said, but we both knew; each of us was thinking of his wife. Occasionally I looked at the sky, where the stars were fading and the pink light of the morning was beginning to spread behind a dark bank of clouds. But my mind clung to my wife's image, imagining it with an uncanny acuteness. I heard her answering me, saw her smile, her frank and encouraging look. Real or not, her look was then more luminous than the sun which was beginning to rise.
>
> A thought transfixed me: For the first time in my life I saw the truth as it is set into song by so many poets, proclaimed as the final wisdom by so many thinkers. The truth—that love is the ultimate and the highest goal to which men can aspire. Then I grasped the meaning of the greatest secret that human poetry and human thought and belief have to impart: *The salvation of man is through love and in love....*

For the first time in my life I was able to understand the meaning of the words, "The angels are lost in perpetual contemplation of an infinite glory."

As I read Frankl's memoir, I know beyond doubt who I would be thinking of if I were ever put in a place of terror and suffering and imminent death. Like Frankl, I would fix all my remaining powers of concentration on the face of my wife, who has shared my life and has taught me the meaning of love. I wonder if I could ever have learned to love God had I not learned first, through her, to love. If we become persons through relationship, the person I am today is due in large measure to her. Painfully shy, socially inept, emotionally damaged though I was when I met her, she nevertheless looked past those handicaps and graced me with her love and attention.

She is visiting her family two thousand miles away as I write these words, and yet she "lives" inside me. The history we have shared fills my mind and shapes my very personality. All day today I have felt her absence as a kind of presence. I think of what she might be doing just now. I pray for her. I miss her.

As I think of the ways Janet affects me, I understand why the Bible so often turns to love and marriage for pictures of the relationship God wants with us. Viktor Frankl, thinking of his wife, understood for the first time the meaning of a worship that had always eluded him. We are not angels lost in perpetual contemplation, however, but flawed human beings who prove inconstant in our love contract with God as well as with our human partners.* My own marriage, which has endured for three decades, is based on an underlying covenant that we both renegotiate daily. Fidelity, not romance, has kept us together.

Early in our marriage an older and wiser couple counseled, "Don't depend on romantic love. It won't last. Love is a decision, not a feeling." Honeymoon-blinded, I dismissed their advice as symptomatic of an older

---

* Thomas Green, a priest who has spent his life exploring spirituality and has written seven books on prayer, makes an interesting observation. He estimates that about the same proportion of people have a very successful prayer life as have a very successful marriage. Tangibility is not the issue, he says, for tangibility does not ensure the success of human relationships either.

generation out of touch with its feelings; now, years later, I would agree. Yes, marriage lives on love, but it is the kind of love that parenthood demands, or Christian discipleship: a gritty decision to go forward, step by step, one foot in front of the other.

For me, much has remained the same since my decision to follow Christ. Some things have grown harder and more complex. Yet, as with marriage, I have found life with God to be far more satisfying. Following Christ was a starting point, a choice of a path to walk down. I am still plodding that same path—for more years even than I have been married. God too lives inside me, his absence a kind of presence, changing me, orienting me, reminding me of my true identity.

Differences will always exist between a covenant of marriage and a covenant with God. Both covenants require fidelity; only one requires faith in the sense of being "certain of what we do not see." I never doubt my wife's existence because each morning, except when one of us is traveling, I can reach over and touch her to get tangible proof.

By nature God is a self-revealer; he must make himself known. Yet God is a self-concealer as well. "The secret things belong to the Lord our God," Moses told the Israelites. We live dangling between the secret things, withheld perhaps for our own protection, and the revealed things. The God who satisfies our thirst is also the great Unknown, the one no one can look upon and live. Perhaps it takes God's absence and presence both for us to remain ourselves, or even to survive.

> One so often hears people say, "I just can't handle it," when they reject a biblical image of God as Father, as Mother, as Lord or Judge; God as lover, as angry or jealous, God on a cross. I find this choice of words revealing, however real the pain they reflect: if we seek a God we can "handle," that will be exactly what we get. A God we can manipulate, suspiciously like ourselves, the wideness of whose mercy we've cut down to size.
>
> KATHLEEN NORRIS

PERSONALITY PROFILE

*God gives us just enough to seek him, and never enough
to fully find him. To do more would inhibit our freedom,
and our freedom is very dear to God.*

RON HANSEN

CERTAIN "PERSONALITY TRAITS" OF God make any relationship with him a daunting challenge. Books of theology tend to use inert words—omniscient, impassible, imperturbable—to describe God's personality, but the Bible tells of a God who is anything but inert. This God enters history, sides with the underdog, argues with people (sometimes letting them win), and may either exert or consciously curb his power. In the Bible life with God reads more like a mystery story, or a romance, than a theology text. What I find in its pages differs markedly from what I expect, and what most people expect, in getting to know God. The following aspects of God's personality may surprise and perplex someone seeking a personal relationship.

GOD IS SHY. By that, I do not mean bashful or timid, like a junior high boy at a party. God may speak in a voice like thunder, and when he shows up in person, humans fall terrified to the ground. Rather, God is shy to intervene. Considering the many things that must displease him on this planet, God exercises incredible — at times maddening — self-restraint.

The Bible presents the goal of creation as a time of Sabbath rest when God and all his creatures can enjoy peace and harmony. History keeps disturbing that rest, however, with loud and jangling interruptions. In the Old Testament, especially, God overcomes his shyness when evil or suffering escalates to a point of crisis. Sometimes God intervenes with a direct personal appearance, sometimes through natural phenomena, most often by tapping an individual to convey words on God's behalf.

Compared to the sacred writings of other religions, though, the Bible offers few scenes of linkage between the seen and unseen worlds. We tend to focus on the miracles and the dramatic appearances such as to Moses in a burning bush and to the prophets in dreams and visions. Yet these are tucked in between periods from which we have no record of the unseen world making an appearance. Usually the intervention comes only after many cries and prayers, delayed by decades or even centuries. God is not impetuous, but shy to act.

Why this quality? I cannot speak for God, of course, but the answer must in part reflect the "problem" of an invisible Being relating to people in a material world. If indeed an unseen world exists parallel to this one, as the Bible insists, we lack the sensors to detect it. I have never met a Christian with Elisha's ability to see chariots of fire. Even when we develop a correspondence with the unseen world, we do so by faith that the book of Hebrews defines as being "certain of what we do not see."

God faces almost the opposite situation. Unlike us, God has an all-encompassing point of view that takes in the world we see as well as other realms hidden to us. Moreover, God sees all our history at once, as a ball of yarn compared to the short, consecutive scraps of thread we experience. Unconstrained by a body, God exists in every place at once. (We should count it fortunate that God is spirit, for an infinite *material* being would fill all spaces, leaving no room for anything else.)

The same barrier that keeps us from God keeps God from us, though in an entirely different way. Every time God chooses to manifest himself in our world, he must accept limitations. He "con-descends" (literally, descends to be with) to our point of view.

Moses saw a burning bush that bedazzled him, changing the course of his life and of history. Out of flames of fire he heard the voice of God speaking. Yet God experienced that same burning bush as an accommodation, a limitation. The bush appeared before Moses in the Sinai wilderness, but not in China and not in Latin America. Thus began what critics call the "scandal of particularity." Why would God choose Israel out of all the available tribes? Why would God incarnate himself in the person of Jesus and settle in a backwater province of Palestine? God had little choice, to put it crudely, if he wished to communicate in a way humans could understand. To impinge on our world, God must subject himself to the rules of time and space. Any correspondence between the invisible and visible worlds, between God and human beings, works two ways, affecting both parties.

An analogy: conceivably we humans may one day master whale language, so that we can lower an underwater transmitter and communicate through squeaks and clicks in a way that whales understand. In doing so, we will interpret ourselves downwards, in a self-limiting way comprehensible to whales. They will not receive the full essence of what it means to be a human being; we can only "talk" about fish and plankton and oceans, not about laptop computers and skyscrapers and major league baseball. That analogy gives a small picture of what it must be like for an all-powerful, all-knowing God to communicate with human beings.

In short, God must set the pace of communication, so that we can only know God as he chooses to make himself known. The unequal partnership between the invisible God and material human beings guarantees that much will remain shrouded in mystery. God can know all of us; we can never know all of God. As God himself told Jeremiah, "Am I only a God nearby and not a God far away?"

The Bible does contain clear hints about one reason God restrains himself from interfering more directly, more often: God holds back out of mercy, for our benefit. The apostle Peter answers scoffers who doubt God's control over history with these words, "With the Lord a day is like a thousand years, and a thousand years are like a day. The Lord is not slow in keeping his promise, as some understand slowness. He is patient with you, not wanting anyone to perish, but everyone to come to repentance."

As I look back on God's spectacular interventions in the Old Testament—Noah's flood, the tower of Babel, the ten plagues of Egypt, the Assyrian and Babylonian invasions—I feel mostly gratitude for this quality of divine shyness. In the words of John Updike, "The sensation of silence cannot be helped: a loud and evident God would be a bully, an insecure tyrant, an all-crushing datum instead of, as He is, a bottomless encouragement to our faltering and frightened being."

GOD HIDES. ACCORDING TO the Jewish philosopher Martin Buber, "The Bible knows of God's hiding His face, of times when the contact between Heaven and earth seems to be interrupted. God seems to withdraw Himself utterly from the earth and no longer to participate in its existence. The space of history is then full of noise, but as it were, empty of divine breath." Do we live in such a time now, I sometimes wonder: full of noise but empty of God? And why would God flash his presence brightly one moment and not the next, like a firefly too quick to catch?

Isaiah said it bluntly: "Truly you are a God who hides himself." In a meditation on this verse, Belden C. Lane remarks that he used to fret about how his children played hide-and-seek. His son would bellow out "Ready!" when he had found a good hiding place, which of course instantly gave him away. Lane, the father, kept reviewing the point of the game—"You're supposed to hide, not give your position away!"—until one day it dawned on him that from his son's perspective *he* had missed the point of the game. The fun comes in being found, after all. Who wants to be left alone, undiscovered?

"God is like a person who clears his throat while hiding and so gives himself away," said Meister Eckhart. Perhaps God also feels pleasure in being found?

Lane's daughter used another, more subtle technique. She would pretend to run and hide, then sneak back to her father's side while he was still counting with his eyes shut tight. Though he could hear her excited breathing as she stood inches away from him, he never gave her away. Instead he would feign delight as he opened his eyes to announce, "Ready or not, here I come!" only to see his daughter touch home base before he even began the search. Lane reflects,

She was cheating, of course; and, though I don't know why, I always let her get away with it. Was it because I longed so much for those few moments when we stood close together, pretending not to hear nor to be heard—caught up in a game that for an instant dissolved the distance between parent and child, that set us free to touch and seek and find each other? It was a simple, almost negligible act of grace, my not letting on that I knew she was there. Yet I suspect that in that one act I may have mirrored God for my child better than in any other way I could. Still to this day, it seems, God is for me a seven-year-old daughter, slipping back across the grass, holding her breath in check, wanting once again to surprise me with a presence closer than I could ever have expected. "Truly thou art a God who hidest thyself," the prophet once declared. A playfulness as well as a dark mystery lies richly intertwined in that grand and complex truth.

Does God play hard to get for the sake of discovery? Again, I cannot speak for God. The Bible sometimes portrays God as the initiator, the Hound of Heaven in pursuit. Yet just when we think we have God, we suddenly feel like Isaiah searching for the One who absconds, *Deus absconditus*. Now you see God, now you don't.

We do know that in his relationships with people God places a premium on faith, which can only be exercised in circumstances that allow for doubt—circumstances such as God's hiddenness. Jesus answered those who questioned God's shyness and reticence with these words: "And will not God bring about justice for his chosen ones, who cry out to him day and night? Will he keep putting them off? I tell you, he will see that they get justice, and quickly." He added this somber warning, "However, when the Son of Man comes, will he find faith on the earth?" And later the apostle John wrote, "This is the victory that has overcome the world, even our faith."

If God merely wanted to make his existence known to every person on earth, God would not hide. However, the direct presence of God would inevitably overwhelm our freedom, with sight replacing faith. God wants instead a different kind of knowledge, a personal knowledge that requires a commitment from the one who seeks to know him.

My own understanding of God's hiddenness traces back not to the childhood game of hide-and-seek but rather to my first visit to a natural history museum. I gawked at the huge stuffed grizzly bears and the woolly mammoths and the yellowed skeletons of whales and dinosaurs hanging from the ceiling. One exhibit, however, kept beckoning me: a display of animal camouflage. When I first walked past it, I saw side-by-side scenes of winter and summer foliage. Only when I returned and stared intently did I notice the animals hiding in the diorama: a ferret chasing a snowshoe hare in the winter scene, praying mantises, birds, and moths in the summer. A placard detailed how many animals were hidden, and I spent half the day lingering there, trying to locate them all.

Elsewhere I have told of what finally brought me to God: not the Bible or Christian literature or anyone's sermons. I turned to God primarily because of my discovery of goodness and grace in the world: through nature, through classical music, through romantic love. Enjoying the gifts, I began to seek the giver; full of gratitude, I needed Someone to thank. Like the animals in the diorama, God had been there all the while, waiting to be noticed. Though I still had no proof, only clues, the clues led me to exercise faith.

One year I left a New Year's Eve party shortly before midnight to get a jump on traffic. We had driven for two hours to attend the party in Colorado Springs and hoped to make it a few miles out from town before tipsy revelers joined the traffic stream. Unknown to me at the time, some hardy mountaineers have a tradition every New Year's Eve. They stuff backpacks full of fireworks and hike through the snow and dark to the summit of Pike's Peak. As I was driving along, suddenly, at the stroke of midnight, red, blue, and yellow fireworks came shooting off the mountain. There was no sound because of the distance. The bits of light made up huge, gorgeous flowers that floated slowly and silently in the sky, illuminating behind them Pike's Peak itself, a snowy monument that filled our line of vision and dwarfed everything else in sight. It had been there all along, the mountain, but we had no eyes to see it.

"Surely the Lord was in this place, and I was not aware of it," Jacob declared. If we miss God's presence in the world, could it be that we have looked in the wrong places, or perhaps looked without seeing at the grace before our eyes?

------ ∾ ------

GOD IS GENTLE. I know no better way to convey this truth than by contrast. Mark 9 gives a vivid description of possession by an evil spirit, in the words of a distraught father who describes to Jesus his son's affliction:

> Whenever it seizes him, it throws him to the ground. He foams at the mouth, gnashes his teeth and becomes rigid. I asked your disciples to drive out the spirit, but they could not.... It has often thrown him into fire or water to kill him. But if you can do anything, take pity on us and help us.

Recognizing Jesus, the spirit immediately flung the boy into one of his fits. I can easily picture this scene, for I have seen someone in the throes of a *grand mal* epileptic seizure — brain cells misfiring, muscles locked in premature rigor mortis, jaw violently clenched.

Contrast that scene with possession by the Holy Spirit. "Quench not the Spirit," Paul warns in one place; "grieve not the holy Spirit of God," he says in another. God humbles himself so deeply that he puts himself somehow at our mercy. Whereas an evil spirit throws a person into fire or water, creating a grotesque caricature of a human being, a sovereign God takes up residence in that same person and says, "Don't hurt me." You can only grieve, or hurt, someone who has emotions, who cares deeply.

I see the same gentleness and refusal to coerce in the life of God's Son. In dealing with people, he states the consequences of a choice, then hands the decision back to the other party. Jesus showed a fathomless respect for human freedom: even as people killed him he prayed, "Father, forgive them, for they do not know what they are doing."

Parents know the precarious balance between guiding and manipulating their children. It may be true that "Father knows best" and Mother knows even better. But the goal of parenthood is not to produce clones who replicate the lives of their parents, rather to produce mature adults who make their own choices. Some parents achieve that goal better than others. Our heavenly Father, it seems, "errs" on the side of human freedom, subjecting himself to our choices and working from within his creation rather than acting on it from outside.

This pattern may shed light on God's other personality traits. Why is God shy? Why does God hide? Why so gentle? God recognizes that *we* are the ones on the journey, not himself. The journey does not transpire like a treasure hunt, such that if we follow the instructions and look hard enough we will find the treasure. No, the journey itself is the goal. The very quest for God, our determined pursuit, changes us in the ways that matter most. The silence and darkness we encounter, the temptations, and even the sufferings can all contribute to God's stated goal of shaping us into persons more like he intended — more like his Son.

Coercion has never succeeded very well in remaking people, which is why few doctrinaire Marxists and fewer still doctrinaire Nazis remain in the world. Even Utopians have had to agree that human change occurs best from the inside out. That may explain why, as John V. Taylor says,

> ... [God's] ceaselessly repeated word to every detail of his creation is: "Choose! I have set before you life and death, the blessing and the curse; therefore choose life. Stay as you are and drop out; change, however painfully, and move towards life." Whenever I learn a little more of the processes of creation I am amazed afresh at the unbelievable daring of the Creator Spirit who seems to gamble all the past gains on a new initiative, inciting his creatures to such crazy adventure and risk.

GOD'S PRESENCE VARIES. "How faint the whisper we hear of him," said Job during the long period of God's silence. By the end of the book, he could have amended that to "How loud the roar we hear of him!" Within the pages of one book the same person experiences an overwhelming sense of God's presence and also God's absence.

I have mentioned believers such as Martin Marty and Frederick Buechner who report no unmistakable signs of God's presence. I could as easily have recounted the opposite pattern: Augustine's vision, or George Fox's or Julian of Norwich's, or any number of the visitations recorded in William James's *The Varieties of Religious Experience*. The

Bible reveals the same fluid pattern: Rather than hold up a model of God's presence for all to strive for, it presents a God who sometimes withdraws and sometimes comes close. In Solomon's day God descended spectacularly on the temple; in Hezekiah's day he quietly withdrew; in Jonah's day he pursued the prophet like a bloodhound.

Julian of Norwich experienced both the presence and absence of God in quick succession. Her seventh revelation tells of times of being "fulfilled with the everlasting sureness," which lasted but a little while, when she found herself "in heaviness, and weariness of my life, and irksomeness of myself, that scarcely I could have patience to live." Her spiritual moods rose and fell in seesaw fashion about twenty times, she said.

I have learned one absolute principle in calculating God's presence or absence, and that is that I cannot. God, invisible, sovereign, who according to the psalmist "does whatever pleases him," sets the terms of the relationship. As the theologian Karl Barth insisted so fiercely, God is *free:* free to reveal himself or conceal himself, to intervene or not intervene, to work within nature or outside it, to rule over the world or even to be despised and rejected by the world, to display himself or limit himself. Our own human freedom derives from a God who cherishes freedom.

I cannot control such a God. At best I can put myself in the proper frame to meet him. I can confess sin, remove hindrances, purify my life, wait expectantly and — perhaps hardest of all — seek solitude and silence. I offer no guaranteed method to obtain God's presence, for God alone governs that. Solitude and silence merely supply the state most conducive to attending to the still small voice of God. There is, however, a sure way to promote God's absence. C. S. Lewis sets it out clearly:

> Avoid silence, avoid solitude, avoid any train of thought that leads off the beaten track. Concentrate on money, sex, status, health and (above all) on your own grievances. Keep

---

Were God to disclose but a little of that which is seen by saints and angels in heaven, our frail natures would sink under it. . . . Such a bubble is too weak to bear a weight so vast. Alas! No wonder therefore it is said, No Man can see God and live.

JONATHAN EDWARDS

---

the radio on. Live in a crowd. Use plenty of sedation. If you must read books, select them very carefully. But you'd be safer to stick to the papers. You'll find the advertisements helpful; especially those with a sexy or a snobbish appeal.

Lewis adds that he cannot give advice on pursuing God, having never had that experience. "It was the other way round; He was the hunter (or so it seemed to me) and I was the deer. . . . But it is significant that this long-evaded encounter happened at a time when I was making a serious effort to obey my conscience."

TEN

IN THE NAME OF THE FATHER

The whole law of human existence lies in this: that man be able to bow down before the infinitely great.

FYODOR DOSTOEVSKI

DOROTHY SAYERS COMBINED TWO careers that have more in common than first meets the eye. Thanks to the BBC and PBS, most people know her as the author of detective stories based on the character Lord Peter Wimsey. Others know her as a lay theologian in the tradition of G. K. Chesterton and C. S. Lewis. In both endeavors she tracked down mysteries with wit and ingenuity.

Sayers' seminal book *The Mind of the Maker* follows the trail of perhaps the greatest mystery of all, the Trinity. The average Christian has little comprehension of this doctrine, but we cannot know God, or fathom the nature of God's contacts with us, without some basic grasp of the Trinity.

We understand God best, Dorothy Sayers suggests, by thinking of God as a creative artist. Imagine God as an engineer or watchmaker or immovable force, and you will go astray. God's image shines through us most clearly in the act of creation—comprising the three stages of Idea, Expression, and Recognition—and by reproducing this act we may begin to grasp, by analogy, the Trinity.

I apply Sayers' notion to the creative form I know best: writing. Every writer begins with an Idea. Consider this book, for instance. For several years I read other books, talked to people, and scribbled notes on scraps of paper relating to a vague Idea. I had no title in mind, no clear concept of what shape the book might take, only a strong desire to explore my own questions about how we visible humans can relate to an invisible God. Sometimes friends would ask, "What are you working on, Philip?" and I would try to explain, but their blank looks told me that my original Idea was impenetrable.*

Finally the time came to begin writing, to choose the best Expression for my Idea. I write in the medium of nonfiction prose although theology can, as Dante and Milton proved, be expressed in other forms such as epic poetry. John Wesley wrote sermons, his brother hymns. Every artist chooses a medium—poem, pottery, opera, painting, novel, choral mass, movie, photograph, quilt, sculpture, song—to express the Idea with which he or she begins.

My Expression changes shape daily. Just yesterday I moved a huge block of text from one chapter to another, then deleted several pages entirely. On average I end up cutting a hundred pages from the first draft of each of my books. As I edit, I realize that some pages, over which I labored many days, disrupt the original Idea by causing the book to bog down or go in conflicting directions. The Idea has a life of its own, and over time I have learned to follow instincts alerting me when my Expression misrepresents the Idea. Similarly, my friends who write fiction tell me that story itself leads them in ways they neither planned nor anticipated. Regardless of the medium, every human creator seeks to express the Idea perfectly, and falls short. When Michelangelo visited the Sistine Chapel after its completion, I'm sure he noticed every flaw and imperfection.

The act of creation does not end, though, when I finish the work: another person must receive it. That final step, in fact, is being fulfilled

---

* Most writers I know have a mild panic attack when asked the question, "What are you working on?" I want to reply, "I don't know yet. Let me finish writing it, and then I can tell you." The Idea exists only as the first stage in the creative process.

at this very instant as you read this sentence. An artist creates for one purpose, to communicate, and the creative process will remain unfinished until at least one other person receives it. Dorothy Sayers calls this last step Recognition.

A successful work of art summons up a response in the receiver. In fact, when we encounter great art something akin to a chemical bonding takes place and our very bodies respond: muscles, heart rate, breathing, perspiration. Playwright Arthur Miller said he never relaxed until he sat in the audience and looked in people's eyes. If he saw the spark of recognition — "My God, that's me!" — he knew he had succeeded with his play. Recognition completes the cycle of creativity.

Dorothy Sayers's book deftly draws the analogy to the Trinity. Although God is one, within that unity we can distinguish the work of three distinct persons. God the Father is the Idea, or Essence, of all reality. "I am that I am," he introduced himself to Moses, in a Hebrew word perhaps more accurately translated, "I will be whatever I will be." Everything that exists — *everything* — flows from that Essence.

We learn something about God from all of creation — quasars and pulsars, aardvarks and anteaters, and especially human beings — but God the Son represents the perfect Expression of the Essence. "The Son is the radiance of God's glory and the exact representation of his being," wrote the author of Hebrews; "He is the image of the invisible God," said Paul. To see what God is like, simply look at Jesus.

The final step in God's creative revelation came to fruition at Pentecost, when God took up residence inside human persons. Something of God's Essence, the same Spirit who hovered over the waters at Creation, now lives inside flawed human beings, giving us the Recognition of a new identity: "And by him we cry, 'Abba, Father.' The Spirit himself testifies with our spirit that we are God's children." God's act of creation reached a climax.

⌘

GOD MADE MAN BECAUSE he loves stories," Elie Wiesel says. And a central part of that story involves God's interaction with his creatures. In the terms of Dorothy Sayers's analogy of the artist, God wrote a play into motion on planet earth and set the characters free. Every artist, not to mention every parent, knows what it is like to create something, then fling it out on the world for others to do with what they will. Creation means letting go, setting free, and in God's case this meant allowing his human creation to foul all the rest.

Not content to let the unruly characters spoil the plot, however, God devised ways to enter their history. John wrote that the Word "who was with God in the beginning ... became flesh and made his dwelling among us"—an event from which most of the world still dates its calendars. In three short years of ministry Jesus did more to convey God's Essence than all the prophets combined. "Lord, show us the Father and that will be enough for us," asked one of his disciples in a moment of uncertainty. Jesus replied, "Anyone who has seen me has seen the Father.... The words I say to you are not just my own. Rather, it is the Father, living in me, who is doing his work."

Later, when Jesus was preparing to depart planet Earth, he gave his disciples a Trinitarian formula, urging them to "make disciples of all nations, baptizing them in the name of the Father and of the Son and of the Holy Spirit." The Incarnation and Pentecost each divulged something new about God and caused an upheaval in the way people thought about God.

It took the brightest minds of the early church almost five centuries to come up with lasting formulations to express the concept of the Trinity.* In the unseen world, no confusion exists about how three persons can be one God. On our side of the curtain, however, we learn about the three persons the only way time-bound creatures can learn anything: in sequence. We learn first of God the Father from the Old Testament. We then learn of Jesus from the Gospels and of the Spirit primarily from the book of Acts and the Epistles.

I was discussing the Trinity with friends in a small group, seeking to connect abstract theology to practical life, when Elisa made this reflection. "You know, that's how I got to know God, through the three persons of the Trinity. I first got acquainted with God the Father in church, where I learned that God is holy, scary, deserving of our worship. Later, as a teenager, I became acquainted with Jesus, a man I wanted to follow for the rest of my life. And then—it was almost like

---

* The very word "person" comes out of that long debate. Theologians borrowed a word—*persona* in Latin, *porsopon* in Greek—used for the mask which actors wore on stage in order to express how one Being could be expressed in three persons.

a second conversion — I became aware of the power of the Spirit, of God living inside me."

In a simple and personal way, Elisa neatly captured the progression of God's revelation as perceived by us time-bound humans. God first revealed himself as holy and transcendent to a tribe he nudged, as a parent nudges a child, through early stages of development. "The fear of the Lord is the beginning of wisdom" could stand as the enduring lesson of the Old Testament. Jesus introduced a new stage of intimacy. "I no longer call you servants," he told his disciples; "Instead, I have called you friends, for everything that I learned from my Father I have made known to you." As he then prepared to leave he promised the Spirit, a Comforter who would achieve an intimacy so close that we somehow participate in the very actions of God on earth: God does his work through us.

IN MY ROLE AS journalist, I have met some famous people: Billy Graham, sitting presidents, Olympic athletes, writers of national reputation. I relate to them in a very different way, however, than I relate to my neighbors or my family. Just to contact them I have to go through layers of agents and appointment secretaries, and I take for granted that my time with them will be brief and tightly focused. We never sit around and shoot the breeze, and they learn almost nothing about me.

I relate to my neighbors much more casually. Rarely do I make an appointment to see them. I run into them at the mailbox or as they walk their dogs along our road. We talk about the weather, about sports or plans for the holidays or the danger of forest fires or anything else we have in common. I call on them for help if my car gets stuck in snow or if I need someone to sign for a package in my absence. On some lonely weekend night, we may decide spontaneously to go out to dinner together.

With my family, I relate in an entirely different way. I communicate more regularly and on a more intimate level. If I get alarming news from a doctor after a medical test, I tell them first. I do not have to play a role within my family; our kinship defines the relationship.

Knowing a God who is three persons has certain parallels with knowing people. A relationship with God depends on what God wants us to know about him, and is circumscribed by changing roles. If I asked an Israelite in the Old Testament, "Describe a personal relationship with God," I would get a very different answer than if I asked the same question of one of Jesus' disciples or of the apostle Paul. For that reason, in the remainder of this chapter and in the next two, I will consider each person of the Trinity individually.

My choice of words may seem irreverent, but I intend to look at the Trinity in light of the "advantages" and "disadvantages" each person brings to the process of knowing God. No human being could possibly grasp the full Essence of God. We know the invisible God only as God reveals himself to us, in various Expressions. And whenever the invisible God con-descends in a way that we can perceive in our material world, we benefit in certain ways and suffer in others.

As the author Tim Stafford has pointed out, although theologians tend to emphasize God's qualities—omnipotence, holiness, sovereignty, omniscience—that is not the normal way we know personal beings. We identify physical objects by their qualities, but we get to know people mainly through their stories. "Tell me about yourself," I say early in a relationship, expecting to hear about where my new acquaintances grew up, what kind of family they have, where they went to school. Over time, as the friendship deepens, we share experiences and create our mutual stories. (As it happens, Tim Stafford is a close friend and former colleague of mine, and just mentioning his name brings to mind sharp memories of shared stories: sitting by a tennis court early in the morning waiting for the sun to rise, being frightened awake by a screech owl on a camping trip, running together along a deserted beach in Africa.)

In a similar way, we know God the Father primarily through stories from the Old Testament. God has the capacity to relate to all creation at once, upholding its existence, as the Hebrews celebrated in their psalms of nature and thanksgiving. Yet God also chose to relate on a closer level with a tribe of people descended from Abraham, Isaac, and Jacob. So closely did God get involved, in fact, that he "moved in" with them, first in a tent in the wilderness, later in a temple built by Solomon.

God shared a camping experience with the Hebrews not because he needed a place to live, but because they needed his actual presence in order to get to know him. Most important, God established a "covenant" with

Israel, a contract that set the terms for both parties. As the scholar Perry Miller has said, when you have a covenant with God you no longer have a remote, unapproachable Deity; you have a God you can count on. You know what to expect.

In addition, God made rare but dramatic appearances to individuals. God spoke to Cain, and to Abraham and Samuel, and gave Noah detailed instructions about the ark. Moses both saw and heard a burning bush; later God addressed him "face to face." Jacob wrestled with a night visitor, got a new name, and limped away grateful, marveling, "I saw God face to face, and yet my life was spared."

In each of these stories God, who relates to the physical world at all points, decided to impinge upon it in one particular point, to choose a body or bush or dream as a vehicle of his presence. God could be seen and heard by humans through their physical sensors of eyes and ears. In the cloud and pillar of fire in the Sinai wilderness, the display continued for some time.

The poet George Herbert reflected nostalgically on this time:

Sweet were the dayes, when thou didst lodge with Lot,
Struggle with Jacob, sit with Gideon,
Advise with Abraham . . .

WHO HAS NOT YEARNED for the kind of sure, almost palpable relationship with God that Abraham or Moses enjoyed? My book *Disappointment with God* explored three questions many Christians ask: Is God hidden? Is God silent? Is God unfair? It struck me with great force as I wrote the book that those questions did not trouble the Hebrews in the Sinai wilderness. They saw evidence of God every day, heard him speak, and consorted under terms of a fair contract signed in God's own hand.

Out of this relationship emerged the Jews' great gift to the world: monotheism, the belief in one sovereign, holy God. The prophets scorned idols made of sticks and rocks and worshiped instead the real God, the Maker of that wood and stone.

Modern Americans, who tend to treat God more like a cosmic Good Buddy, could use a refresher course from the Old Testament on God's majesty. Pastor and author Gordon MacDonald has said that his own love for God has moved away from a sentimental model, which never satisfied, to something closer to a father/son model. He is learning to reverence, obey, and thank God; to express appropriate sorrow for blunders and sin; to pursue a quietness in which he might hear God whisper. In other words, he is seeking a relationship with God appropriate to the profound difference between the two parties. MacDonald adds this warning: "The most costly sins I have committed came at a time when I briefly suspended my reverence for God. In such a moment I quietly (and insanely) concluded that God didn't care and most likely wouldn't intervene were I to risk the violation of one of His commandments."

I have found that I must turn to other cultures in order to counterbalance the American evangelicals' familiar approach to God. For example, a friend in Japan wrote that he has understood the proper spirit of prayer more by listening to Japanese Christians than from the teaching of American missionaries. "We know how to come to God as humble servants with boldness," he says. "You don't have to tell Japanese people about hierarchy. When they learn that God is the Lord they immediately know all the implications of that. They know who's boss and that is never questioned. When they pray they use language that combines the highest forms of speech and the most intimate phrases of love and devotion. When they ask for something they ask with true humility, knowing they have no right to what they're asking except that God gives them the very right to ask and promises to answer."

The Old Testament stresses the wonder that this sovereign, holy God desires contact with his flawed creatures. God *wants* to relate to people, which explains why he kept pursuing the rebellious Israelites. A God mighty enough to extract his people from the most powerful empire on earth was nonetheless eager to con-descend and dwell among them in a tent. At every point, no matter how far his people fell away, God proved himself as Immanuel, the God with us. He made clothes for Adam and Eve after their rebellion, gave Abraham and Moses one chance after another, endured the indignities of Israel's unfaithfulness, and still came back with more love to offer.

In fact it was God's compassion, not power, that first impressed the Hebrews. The nation of Israel took a major leap the moment they realized God cared about their plight in Egypt: "When they heard that the Lord was concerned about them and had seen their misery, they bowed down and worshiped." How different was their God from the remote, often cruel gods of the Egyptians.

The Old Testament spells out one clear "advantage": this majestic God has an infinite capacity for contact with individual human beings. Unlike famous people, God need not employ appointment secretaries and limit his time with each person. "God loves each one of us as if there was only one of us to love," said Augustine.

God the Father can treat all of creation with unrelieved attention, as Jesus indicated with his comment about every hair on a person's head being numbered. Earlier, I referred to my friend Stanley, who said, "I can't believe that, in a world of six billion people, God knows my name." Precisely because God is infinite he can invest in six billion people, one at a time, without feeling any sense of drain or diminution. That is what it means to be God. The Old Testament reveals a Father with a limitless appetite for love.

WHAT "DISADVANTAGES" TO KNOWING God might the Old Testament present? Perhaps the best way to answer that impertinent question is to quote a modern Jew, for whom the Old Testament represents God's complete written revelation. Judaism, says Gershom Scholem, still addresses itself to the "vast abyss" between God and Man. A modern Jew, he confesses he "mainly perceives the remoteness." Scholem has missed the message of a God who desires intimacy.

Love tends to decrease as power increases, and vice versa. The same power that repeatedly overwhelmed the Israelites made it difficult for them to perceive God's love. A parent stands tall to instill respect in his child and stoops down low for hugs and affection. In the Old Testament, God stood tall. If you want to know what kind of "personal relationship with God" the Israelites enjoyed, listen to their words: "We will die! We are lost, we are all lost! Anyone who even comes near the tabernacle of the Lord will die." And again, "Let us not hear the voice of the Lord our God nor see this great fire anymore, or we will die."

"The voice of God / To mortal ear is dreadful," wrote Milton. New Testament writers, trained in Hebrew schools and mostly reared in faithful Jewish homes, showed little sense of nostalgia for the Old Testament era. They honored it as a time of preparation for a further revelation in Jesus. According to Paul, a Jew who acknowledged many benefits of the Old Covenant (see Romans 9–11), that arrangement failed in its most important goal: It did not nourish spiritual growth.

The brighter the light, the darker the contrasting shadow. God's shadow loomed so large that it inhibited growth. Like dependent children, the Israelites complained and rebelled so often that an easy two-week journey ended up lasting forty years. When God the parent ushered them into the Promised Land and drew back from such close involvement—the manna ceased when they crossed the Jordan River—they took the first halting steps and fell flat on their faces. A portent of things to come.

I have concluded that most Christians today avoid the Old Testament for the simple reason that they find the God depicted there scary and remote. In Doris Lessing's wry phrase, "Jehovah does not think or behave like a social worker." Jehovah behaves, instead, like a holy God trying desperately to communicate to cantankerous human beings. In my own reading of the Old Testament, I used to look for ways to make God more acceptable, less fierce. Now I concentrate on making myself more acceptable to God, which was the point of the Old Testament, after all. God sought intimacy with his people, surely, albeit only on his terms.

Listen to God's own verdict on Old Testament times: "But my people would not listen to me; Israel would not submit to me. So I gave them over to their stubborn hearts to follow their own devices."

"Inquire among the nations," God moaned to Jeremiah, as if in a state of shock: "Who has ever heard anything like this? A most horrible thing has been done by Virgin Israel. . . . My people have forgotten me. They have forsaken me."

After citing these and dozens of similar passages, Abraham Heschel remarks, "The heart of melancholy beats in God's words. . . . God is mourning Himself." Heschel continues,

> With Israel's distress came the affliction of God, His displacement,
> His homelessness in the land, in the world. . . . For Israel's deser-

tion was not merely an injury to man; it was an insult to God. This was the voice of God Who felt shunned, pained, and offended.

Israel's experience shows that God can be driven away or forced into hiding as a result of what people do. Sometimes God allows *us* to determine the intensity of his presence.

------ ᴄᴠᴢ ------

ONE SCENE FROM THE Old Testament captures both sides of a relationship with God the Father. It occurs in 1 Kings 18, at a time when Israel has sunk to one of its lowest points. King Ahab and Queen Jezebel are hunting down and slaughtering God's prophets, replacing them with their own court prophets who serve pagan gods. In a classic confrontation, Elijah challenges 850 of these prophets to a duel. As he mocks and taunts them, they slash themselves with spears and swords until the blood flows, crying to their gods all day long with no response. Finally, as the red sun drops toward the Mediterranean, Elijah builds an altar, douses it three times with four large jugs of water—this after a three-year drought—and calls on God to make himself known. "Then the fire of the Lord fell and burned up the sacrifice, the wood, the stones and the soil, and also licked up the water in the trench. When all the people saw this, they fell prostrate and cried, 'The Lord—he is God! The Lord—he is God!'"

If the story had ended there, we might look back with more nostalgia on Old Testament times. It did not. No revival broke out among the Hebrews. King Ahab, watching from the front row at Mount Carmel, left a legacy as one of Israel's wickedest kings. He and his wife quickly reestablished their dominance over government and religion. And Elijah himself, who had just called down fire from heaven and defeated 850 prophets in a single day, fled for his life in fear of Jezebel. "I have had enough, Lord," he moaned. "Take my life."

In an act of great tenderness, God visited Elijah in his time of despair. What happened next speaks volumes about what style works best when an omnipotent God decides to communicate with tiny human beings:

Then a great and powerful wind tore the mountains apart and shattered the rocks before the Lord, but the Lord was not in

For this is what the high and lofty One says—
> he who lives forever, whose name is holy:
"I live in a high and holy place,
> but also with him who is contrite and lowly in spirit,
to revive the spirit of the lowly
> and to revive the heart of the contrite."

ISAIAH 57:15

the wind. After the wind there was an earthquake, but the Lord was not in the earthquake. After the earthquake came a fire, but the Lord was not in the fire. And after the fire came a gentle whisper.

The gentle whisper, Elijah heard. God had accommodated himself to his prophet in a soft voice almost like silence.

ELEVEN

ROSETTA STONE

*We crave nothing less than perfect story; and while we chat-
ter or listen all our lives in a din of craving—jokes, anec-
dotes, novels, dreams, films, plays, songs, half the words of
our days—we are satisfied only by the one short tale we
feel to be true: History is the will of a just god who knows us.*

REYNOLDS PRICE

STEP BACK FOR A moment and contemplate God's point of view. A
spirit unbound by time and space, God had borrowed material
objects now and then—a burning bush, a pillar of fire—to make himself obvious on planet earth. Each time, God adopted the object in order
to convey a message, as an actor might don a mask, and then moved on.
In Jesus, something new happened: God *became* one of the planet's creatures, an event unparalleled, unheard-of, unique in the fullest sense of
the word.

The God who fills the universe imploded to become a peasant baby
who, like every infant who has ever lived, had to learn to walk and
talk and dress himself. In the Incarnation, God's Son deliberately
"handicapped" himself, exchanging omniscience for a brain that
learned Aramaic phoneme by phoneme, omnipresence for two legs and

an occasional donkey, omnipotence for arms strong enough to saw wood but too weak for self-defense.* Instead of overseeing a hundred billion galaxies at once, he looked out on a narrow alley in Nazareth, a pile of rocks in the Judean desert, or a crowded street of Jerusalem.

The disciple John, who knew Jesus well, could have been making a personal confession when he penned these words: "He was in the world, and though the world was made through him, the world did not recognize him." Little wonder. His disciples kept expecting him to throw his weight around, like a real God. He tidied up a temple once, but what about Herod's palace, the Roman Senate, or the Colosseum? God's perfect Expression was, scandalously, not what anyone could have come up with on their own.

Oh, the Gospels record that Jesus retained access to certain unusual powers. He sensed events preternaturally at times and had a sharp premonition of how his life would end. He could heal broken bodies, even off site if pressed. Once he modified the weather. Yet no one could mistake the carpenter from Nazareth for the dazzling figure described in the book of Revelation, the second person of the Trinity who would, in Milton's words, "ascend / The throne hereditary, and bound his reign / With Earth's wide bounds, his glory with the Heavens." And no one could mistake Jesus' voice, which toward the end weakened to a cry and a gasp, for the withering roar of Jehovah.

In 1996 a pop song by Joan Osborne made the charts, asking what difference it would make if God were one of us, "just a slob like one of us," a stranger on a bus commuting home. Some found the words sacrilegious—exactly the reaction of Jesus' family, neighbors, and countrymen, who had equal difficulty envisioning God as "one of us." By any measure Jesus led a tragic life: rumors of illegitimacy, taunts of insanity from his family, rejection by most who heard him, betrayal by friends, the savage turn of a mob against him, a series of justice-mocking trials, execu-

---

* Here is how Augustine expressed the paradox:
  Man's maker was made man that He, Ruler of the stars, might nurse at His mother's breast; that the Bread might hunger, the Fountain thirst, the Light sleep, the Way be tired on its journey; that Truth might be accused of false witnesses, the Teacher be beaten with whips, the Foundation be suspended on wood; that Strength might grow weak; that the Healer might be wounded; that Life might die.

tion in a form reserved for slaves and violent criminals. A pitiful story, to be sure, and that is the heart of the scandal: we do not expect to pity God.

How do you know God personally? In Jesus' day the answer was shockingly simple: you know him the same way you know anybody. You introduce yourself, shake hands, strike up a conversation, inquire about his family. Because of Jesus we need never question God's desire for intimacy. Does God really want close contact with us? Jesus gave up Heaven for it. In person he reestablished the original link between God and human beings, between seen and unseen worlds.

Swiss physician and author Paul Tournier mentions one obvious "advantage" in relating to the second person of the Trinity. Before the current regime took over in Iran, he addressed a mosque in Teheran at the invitation of an ayatollah. Tournier told the attentive Moslems that he, a Protestant from Geneva, felt close to them because John Calvin had given his followers a keen sense of God's immeasurable greatness, akin to the profile of Allah. That poses a danger, though, because a person who lives in constant awareness of the vast distance between God and his creation can drift toward fatalism. Tournier went on to say that, unlike Islam, Christianity offers the balance of intimacy with Jesus.

Jesus revealed a newly intimate side to God, a relationship so personal that he used the word "Abba," or "Daddy" to address him.* A spiritual sung in slave days in the American South captures this most practical advantage of Incarnation. Slaves had trouble approaching the exalted God; words like Master and Lord did not go down easily. They needed not an awesome, distant God, but an up-close, personal God whom they could visualize and love.

> My God is so high, you can't get over Him,
> He's so low, you can't get under Him,
> He's so wide, you can't get around Him,
> You must come in, by and through the Lamb.

Jesus "came down from heaven," descending so far that in the process he made us more comprehensible to God. Not only do we understand

---

* To show the change in emphasis: the Old Testament refers to God as Father 11 times, the New Testament 170 times.

God better because of Jesus; God understands *us* better. As another spiritual expresses it,

> Nobody knows the trouble I've seen,
> Nobody knows but Jesus. . . . Glory, Hallelujah!

Because of Jesus, God senses our human condition in a different way. Hebrews goes so far as to say that Jesus "learned obedience" and "was made perfect" through suffering. These words, full of mystery, imply that the Incarnation had meaning for God as well as for us. As a spirit being, God had never felt physical pain—how could he, lacking nerve cells? He "learned" about pain, just as we humans learn about it, through personal experience. Among the many limitations God accepted in coming to earth was physical suffering, which Jesus came to know in the worst way. He was, quite literally, dying to be with us.

The author of Hebrews drew an important lesson from this fact. "For we do not have a high priest who is unable to sympathize with our weaknesses, but we have one who has been tempted in every way, just as we are—yet was without sin"; therefore he "is able to deal gently with those who are ignorant and are going astray. . . ." Because of Jesus, God fully understands what it means to be human. Truly, nobody knows the trouble we've seen—nobody but Jesus.

I keep returning to this fact about Jesus because both as a Christian and as a writer I have spent a disproportionate share of my time exploring the mysteries of pain and suffering. I come away with as many questions as answers. Nonetheless, I have learned one important principle: not to judge God by some misfortune that befalls me or someone I love. My questions about providence and suffering are *primarily* answered in the person of Jesus, not in day-to-day events I may encounter now. When the Son of God visited earth he brought healing and not pain, and when he left earth he promised to return one day to restore it to God's original intent. His own resurrected body he offered as proof.

I cannot learn from Jesus why bad things occur—why an avalanche or flood decimates one town and not its neighbor, why leukemia strikes one child and not another—but I can surely learn how God feels about such tragedies. I simply look at how Jesus responds to the sisters of his good friend Lazarus, to a widow who has just lost her son, or a leprosy victim banned outside the town gates. Jesus gives God a face, and that face is streaked with tears.

In a fine analogy, H. Richard Niebuhr likened the revelation of God in Christ to the Rosetta stone. Before its discovery Egyptologists could only guess at the meaning of hieroglyphics. One unforgettable day they uncovered a dark stone that rendered the same text in Greek, ordinary Egyptian script, and previously undecipherable hieroglyphics. By comparing the translations side by side, they mastered hieroglyphics and could now see clearly into a world they had known only in a fog. Niebuhr goes on to say that Jesus allows us to "reconstruct our faith." We can trust God because we trust Jesus. If we doubt God, or find him incomprehensible, unknowable, the very best cure is to gaze steadily at Jesus, the Rosetta stone of faith.

USING A DIFFERENT IMAGE than Niebuhr, I envision Jesus as the "magnifying glass" of my faith, a phrase that needs some explanation. I am the proud owner of *The Oxford English Dictionary* which contains every word in the English language. The dictionary comes in two versions. Libraries and bibliophiles purchase a twenty-volume version that retails for $3,000. By joining a certain book club, however, I obtained a special one-volume edition for only $39.95. It contains the full text of the dictionary, with the one drawback of typesetting shrunken so small that no one on earth can read it unaided. Next, I purchased a splendid magnifying glass — the kind jewelers use, the size of a dinner plate, mounted on a swivel arm, with a buzzing fluorescent light built in. With that, and the occasional assistance of another, hand-held magnifying glass, I can pore over the shades of meaning of any word in English.

I have learned about magnifying glasses, using my dictionary. When I train the glass on a word, the tiny print shows up crisp and clear in the center, or focal point, while around the edges it grows progressively distorted. In an exact parallel, Jesus has become the focal point of my faith, and increasingly I am learning to keep the magnifying glass of my faith focused on Jesus. In my spiritual journey as well as in my writing career I have long lingered in the margins, pondering unanswerable questions about the problem of pain, the conundrums of prayer, providence versus free will, and other such matters. When I do so, everything becomes fuzzy. Looking at Jesus, however, restores clarity.

For instance, the Bible leaves unanswered many questions regarding the problem of pain, but in Jesus I see unmistakable evidence that God is not the author of particular sufferings. One of Jesus' main contributions, for me, has been the decisive revelation of God as "the God of all comfort."

To consider another example, Why doesn't God answer my prayers? I do not know, but it helps me to realize that Jesus himself knew something of that frustration. In Gethsemane he threw himself on the ground, crying out for some other way—and there was no other way. He prayed that the church would demonstrate the same unity as the godhead, a prayer that has not come close to being answered. He prayed "Thy will be done, on earth as it is in heaven," whereas any day's newspaper makes clear that prayer has not yet been answered.

Equally, I can worry myself into a state of spiritual indigestion over questions like "What good does it do to pray if God already knows everything?" Jesus silences such questions: If Jesus saw the need to pray, sometimes so urgently that he spent all night at it, so should I.

I admit that many standard Christian doctrines bother me. What about hell—will it really involve an eternity of torment? What of those who live and die without ever hearing about Jesus? I fall back on the response of Bishop Ambrose, mentor of Augustine, who was asked on his deathbed whether he feared facing God at judgment. "We have a good Master," Ambrose replied with a smile. I learn to trust God with my doubts and struggles by getting to know Jesus. If that sounds evasive, I suggest it accurately reflects the centrality of Jesus in the New Testament. We start with him as the focal point and let our eyes wander with care into the margins.

As a major advantage in knowing God, then, Jesus offers a close-up portrait of God's own vantage point. What bothers me about this planet—injustice, poverty, racism, sexism, abuse of power, violence, disease—bothered him as well. By looking at Jesus, I gain insight into how God feels about what goes on down here. Jesus expresses the Essence of God in a way that we cannot misconstrue.

"Better a little faith dearly won ... than perish on the splendid plenty of the richest creeds," wrote Henry Drummond. For me, that core of faith "dearly won" rests squarely in the center, in Jesus.

———— ❧ ————

THE APOSTLE PAUL MADE a sweeping claim about Jesus in the book of Colossians: "And having disarmed the powers and authorities, he made a public spectacle of them, triumphing over them by the cross." To Paul, Jesus' death offers the further unforeseen advantage of triumph. My skepticism rears up on reading that claim: *Sure, Paul. Look around you. Does this world really resemble one in which God has triumphed over "the powers"?* Then I recall that Paul wrote these words while under arrest in Rome, a hostage of the greatest power of his day. Soon, probably under Nero, he would join Jesus in the gallery of martyrs.

We know from other passages that the apostle staked his life on his belief that what God accomplished in his Son's resurrection, defeating the ultimate destructive power of death, he would accomplish for the entire groaning planet. In this particular passage in Colossians, however, Paul says nothing about the resurrection and keeps his gaze fixed on the cross. To what triumph could he be referring?

In recent years a French philosopher and anthropologist named René Girard has explored that very question, explored it so deeply, in fact, that to the consternation of his secular colleagues he converted to Christianity. It struck Girard that Jesus' story cuts against the grain of every heroic story from its time. The myths from Babylon, Greece, and elsewhere celebrated strong heroes, not weak victims. In contrast, from the very beginning Jesus took the side of the underdog: the poor, the oppressed, the sick, the "marginalized." Indeed, Jesus chose to be born in poverty and disgrace, spent his infancy as a refugee, lived in a minority race under a harsh regime, and died as a prisoner, unjustly accused.

Jesus admired people like a Roman soldier who cared for his dying slave; a tax collector who gave away his fortune to the poor; a member of a minority race who stopped to help a man accosted by thieves; a sinner who prayed a simple "Help!" prayer; a shamed woman who reached out in desperation to touch his clothing; a beggar who ate crumbs from a rich man's table. He disapproved of religious professionals who refused to help the wounded for fear of soiling themselves; a proud clergyman who looked down on sinners; the rich who offered only crumbs to the hungry; a responsible son who shunned his prodigal brother; the powerful who lived on the backs of the poor.

When Jesus himself died ignominiously as an innocent victim, it introduced what one of Girard's disciples has called "the most sweeping historical revolution in the world, namely, the emergence of an empathy for victims." Nowhere but in the Bible can you find an ancient story of an innocent yet heroic victim dragged to his death. To the ancients, heroes were heroic and victims were pitiable.

According to Girard, societies have traditionally reinforced their power through "sacred violence." The larger group (say, German Nazis or Serbian nationalists) picks a scapegoat minority to direct its self-righteous violence against, which in turn bonds and emboldens the majority. The Jewish and Roman powers tried that technique against Jesus and it backfired.* Instead, the cross shattered the longstanding categories of weak victims and strong heroes, for the victim emerged as the hero.

The apostle Paul touched on a deep truth about Jesus' paradoxical contribution in his claim to the Colossians. A public spectacle it was when Jesus exposed as false gods the very powers and authorities that men and women take such pride in. The most refined religion of the day accused an innocent man, and the most renowned justice system carried out the sentence.

As one of Flannery O'Connor's Southern characters commented, "Jesus thrown everything off balance." The gospel centered on that cross ushered in a stunning reversal of values that went on to affect the entire world. Today the victim occupies the moral high ground: witness recent Nobel Peace Prizes awarded to a black South African clergyman, a Polish union leader, a Holocaust survivor, a Guatemalan peasant woman, a bishop in persecuted East Timor. That the world honors and cares for the marginalized and disenfranchised, concluded Girard, is a direct result of the cross of Jesus Christ.

---

* The high priest Caiaphas expressed the scapegoat formula perfectly when he said of Jesus, "It is better for you that one man die for the people than that the whole nation perish."

Women, the poor, minorities, the disabled, environmental and human rights advocates—all these draw their moral force from the power of the gospel unleashed at the cross, when God took the side of the victim. In a great irony, the "politically correct" movement defending these rights often positions itself as an enemy of Christianity, when in fact the gospel has contributed the very underpinnings that make possible such a movement.

God's Expression in Jesus took the world by surprise, and two millennia later the reverberations have not stopped. In a culture that glorifies success and grows deaf to suffering, we need a constant reminder that at the center of the Christian faith hangs an unsuccessful, suffering Christ, dying in shame.

ROBERTA BONDI, A PROFESSOR of church history, tells a very personal story of how Jesus' compassion for the underdog melted her resistance against God and helped correct a distorted image. She had long struggled with the phrase "God the Father," mainly because her human father had been for her a harsh and distant figure. He tolerated no imperfections or weakness, no disobedience from his children or his wife, no questioning or asking why. He had a clear picture of a woman's place: sweet and pliant, quiet and submissive.

Try as she might, Roberta never managed to be pliant or quiet, and so went through childhood bearing the heavy burden that she had failed her father. He left the family before Roberta turned twelve and she saw him only once a year after that. Anger spread like an infection inside her, and whenever she heard someone say "God the Father," the anger flared up.

Bondi's scholarly career led her to Oxford where, ironically, she studied the "early church fathers." In the writings of Christian monks of the Egyptian desert, she discovered a different image of a heavenly Father: a gentle God who especially loves the ones the world despises and who understands our weaknesses, temptations, and sufferings. She tried using the word "Father" in prayer, with limited success until one day she came across Jesus' last, long conversation with his disciples before his arrest and death.

In that scene, as Jesus talks about going away to the Father, the disciples stare at him without comprehending until at last Philip blurts out, "Lord show us the Father, and that will be enough for us." Jesus answers:

"Don't you know me, Philip, even after I have been among you such a long time? Anyone who has seen me has seen the Father. How can you say, 'Show us the Father'?"

"Anyone who has seen me has seen the Father!" It struck Bondi, the church historian and theologian, as a startling new concept. If Jesus shows special concern for the poor, widows, and social rejects, then so does the Father. If Jesus has women friends and values them, so does the Father. Bondi had wrongly projected her own fractured image of fatherhood onto God; instead, she realized, God's ideal should offer a strong corrective to human fathers who fall short. Through the lens of Jesus, God made visible, she saw God anew.

As Bondi read the Gospels with open eyes, individual stories took on an entirely new coloring. For example, in the account of Lazarus in John 11 she noticed Jesus' interactions with the two sisters. The same Jesus who can access the Father's power to raise Lazarus from the dead also melts in sympathy, weeping along with his friends Mary and Martha. More, he allows the two sisters to scold him for being late. Still stinging from her own childhood, Bondi noted in contrast that the sisters seem not at all intimidated by Jesus. They do not submissively accept what has happened as the will of God but rather pour out their hurt and anger to Jesus.

Gradually Bondi gained some picture of what a relationship with God might look like.

> I had been assuming that when Jesus told us to call God "Father" he had meant that as God's children we were to relate to that Father as *very little* children relate to the kind of benevolent, dominant parent who prefers toddlers to adolescents because toddlers are so sweet and adolescents are so complicated. . . . I could not afford to relate to a Father God who demanded that I live as a helpless child.

To her delight, she found that God far prefers a relationship with mature adults, such as Jesus had with his disciples.

"I no longer call you servants. . . . Instead, I have called you friends," Jesus announced to his disciples with an evident sense of relief, relishing the advantages of Incarnation.

Oᴺᴇ ꜱɪᴍᴘʟᴇ ꜰᴀᴄᴛ ꜱʜᴏᴡꜱ the "disadvantage" of Incarnation: few people acquainted with Jesus recognized his origin from God. Paul's fine summary in Philippians says it well, "Who, being in very nature God, did not consider equality with God something to be grasped, but made himself nothing. . . ." For the duration of his time on earth, Jesus forfeited the privileges of God and thus risked going unrecognized. People expect power from their God, not powerlessness, strength not weakness, largeness not smallness.

To appreciate the change, recall one of the many times when God spoke audibly in the Old Testament. After thirty-eight chapters of theorizing by Job and his friends, God roared out of a storm, flattening them all with his first words. Though God sidestepped the questions Job had so passionately raised, the very fact that God crossed the gap between two worlds, impinging on the material world enough to rattle human eardrums, silenced Job. He repented in dust and ashes.

In comparison, the Gospels record only three occasions when God spoke audibly. Twice (at Jesus' baptism and the Transfiguration) God said virtually the same thing: "This is my Son, whom I love; with him I am well pleased." The last occasion, when God spoke for the benefit of doubting Greeks (John 12), some of them heard growls of thunder rather than words. God's voice flattened no one during Jesus' time on earth. During the traumatic trials before Herod and Pilate, Jesus himself kept mostly silent and God the Father said not a word.

Jesus orchestrated no lightning displays, and no cloud of smoke surrounded him when he addressed a crowd. By overcoming the disadvantages of the Old Testament revelations of God,

> Gᴏᴅ wears himself out through the infinite thickness of time and space in order to reach the soul and to captivate it. If it allows a pure and utter consent (though brief as a lightning flash) to be torn from it, then God conquers that soul. . . . The soul, starting from the opposite end, makes the same journey that God made towards it. And that is the cross.
>
> Sɪᴍᴏɴᴇ Wᴇɪʟ

Jesus lost the advantages. He looked not at all like God; he looked, well, human. *Isn't that Mary's boy? The carpenter's kid from Nazareth?* they taunted him.

"Lord, show us the Father and that will be enough for us," Philip pled. Yet when Jesus replied by pointing to himself, it clearly was not enough: later that same evening Philip and all the others deserted him. There may be a touch of Philip in each of us, a longing to see God just once, the undeniable smoke-and-fire version, to settle our doubts. What God offers in response does not satisfy.

The world cannot get over the huge gap between what we expect of God and what he offered in Jesus. Other religions respect Jesus as a wise teacher and admirable leader but not God. New Agers search for something more mystical, more personally satisfying. The best Expression of God's Essence draws forth as much rejection in our day as it did in his own.

TWELVE

THE GO-BETWEEN

Truth strikes us from behind, and in the dark.

HENRY DAVID THOREAU

THE ITALIAN WRITER UMBERTO ECO (*The Name of the Rose, Foucault's Pendulum*) wrote a fascinating account of a trip across America titled *Travels in Hyper Reality* in which he remarked on our thoroughly material outlook on life. Even American mythology takes on tangible form, he observed: the Santa Clauses enthroned in every shopping mall at Christmastime and the huge animated characters strolling through Disneyland anytime. Ancient Greeks celebrated their heroes in epic poetry recited around a campfire; modern Americans shake hands with them in fuzzy suits.

Religious television intrigued Eco. "If you follow the Sunday morning religious programs on TV you come to understand that God can be experienced only as nature, flesh, energy, tangible image. And since no preacher dares show us God in the form of a bearded dummy, or as a Disneyland robot, God can only be found in the form of natural force, joy, healing, youth, health, economic increment." Eco concluded that Americans perceive their God in an almost tactile way. Where is the *mysterium tremendum*, Eco asked—the holy, numinous, ineffable God?

I wonder what Eco might have thought of a scene I saw in the Philippines, in a church that houses an ebony statue of Jesus. Pilgrims, some of whom crawl on their knees for miles to approach the statue, line up to touch its toes. They used to kiss the toes, but wear and tear on the statue prompted the church to cover it in Plexiglas, with only a cutout for the toes. Unfortunately for the undersized Filipino pilgrims, authorities also elevated the statue, so the faithful must jump high to touch the sacred toes. Now long lines of short people shuffle up to a certain point, then leap like basketball dunkers to reach the statue's toes, which are again showing signs of wear. Once a year the church allows the Black Nazarene to come outside in a public procession, and most years people get trampled to death in the frenzy.

According to Eco, we humans search for clear-cut signs of God's presence, as if still yearning for the burning bush or audible voice. As material beings, we devalue spirit as less real and want God to appear in the realm of matter, where we live. Jesus answered that wish for a time, an event we celebrate in sacred art, but the plain fact is that Jesus returned to the realm of the unseen.

"God is spirit," insisted Jesus—something every faithful Jew believed. But how to imagine a Spirit or visualize God apart from some visible form? Furthermore, how can a spirit relate to our world of matter? Can a spirit "see" without retinal cells to receive and focus light waves or "hear" without an eardrum to record molecular vibrations? And can we ever determine whether a spirit-God is interacting with life on this planet? In short, how can we believe in a God we cannot see? The Old Testament Israelites miserably failed such a challenge; despite many evidences of God, they repeatedly turned toward idols they could touch and see.

Some Christians, like those Umberto Eco encountered in America, want to reproduce those times when God made himself more obvious. They regard the Spirit as a pet version of the Israelites' God in the wilderness: He speaks to them directly, provides food and clothing, guarantees health, offers crystal-clear guidance. In other words, the Spirit changes the rules of life so that we need never experience cause for disappointment. I know too many sick and needy Christians to believe that.

I envision the Spirit not so much as touching our mundane lives with a supernatural wand as bringing the Recognition (Dorothy Sayers' word) of God's presence into places we may have overlooked. The Spirit may bring that jolt of Recognition to the most ordinary things: a baby's grin, snow falling on a frozen lake, a field of lavender in morning dew, a worship ritual that unexpectedly becomes more than ritual. Suddenly we see these momentary pleasures as gifts from a God who is worthy of praise.

To search for the Spirit is like hunting for your eyeglasses while wearing them. In John V. Taylor's words, "We can never be directly aware of the Spirit, since in any experience of meeting and recognition he is always the go-between who creates awareness." The Spirit is what we perceive with rather than what we perceive, the one who opens our eyes to underlying *spirit*-ual realities.

The Spirit's Recognition of other people may well defy convention, for it has little to do with body shape, annual income, and the trappings of power. Rather, the Spirit may lead us to the same groups Jesus ministered to—aliens, widows, prisoners, the homeless, the hungry, the sick—so that we gradually come to view "the least of these" as God views them.

A COLLEGE STUDENT TOLD me his way of picturing the Holy Spirit. "I first learned about the Spirit from childhood flannelgraph lessons. They portrayed him as a miniature human being, a kind of homunculus, living deep inside our bodies. I still carry that image with me. The Spirit lives somewhere inside me, in my brain perhaps, or my heart. Like a janitor trapped inside a building, he gets my attention by banging on the pipes of my conscience or my subconscious. If I ignore him, he shrinks. If I attend to him, he grows larger until he fills me."

Mention of the Holy Spirit summons up much confusion. If a person or group claims, "The Bible says," you can look for yourself. If they claim, "The Spirit told me," where can you look? There lies the problem: by definition the Spirit is invisible. Jesus drew a parallel for Nicodemus: "The wind blows wherever it pleases. You hear its sound, but you cannot tell where it comes from or where it is going." How can we detect a presence that has no shape, no identifiable form?

Nevertheless, no one who wants to know God can ignore the Spirit, who made a dramatic appearance on earth at a hinge moment. As Jesus said goodbye to his followers, he asked them first to do something very important: Wait, Jesus said. Return to Jerusalem and wait for the Holy Spirit.*

What has happened since Jesus' departure challenges faith and, in all honesty, drives many people away from God. In Jesus, God had deliberately joined a world infected with evil and fallen victim to it. With the Spirit, a holy God risked his reputation on the evil-infected persons themselves, by expanding the Incarnation to encompass all of Jesus' followers. The God who took on human flesh so that we could experience him in our material world still takes on human flesh—our flesh.

Yet read the sad, speckled history of the church. To put it mildly, mortal human beings do not embody God's Expression as well as Jesus did. Indeed, we are as likely to turn people away from God as toward him. "It is for your good that I am going away," Jesus told his dubious disciples as he promised them the Comforter. How so? What "advantages" are there to this final revelation of God?

Certainly, if a person desires a "personal relationship with God," the Spirit takes the word *personal* to a new level. No other religion makes such an extravagant claim: that the God of the universe exists not just as an external power whom we must obey, but as One who lives inside us, transforming from the inside out and opening a channel of direct correspondence to God. As Thomas Merton put it, "since our souls are spiritual substances and since God is pure Spirit, there is nothing to prevent a union between ourselves and Him that is ecstatic in the literal sense of the word."

Our relations with other people, as I have said, always involve a degree of uncertainty and doubt. Neighbors of a mass murderer often express surprise when the criminal is led away in handcuffs: "He was such a nice man."

---

* The Spirit was active all along, of course, hovering over the waters at creation and inspiring God's messengers throughout Old Testament history—378 passages in the Hebrew Bible mention the Spirit. Henri Nouwen observes that neglect of the Spirit is seen in the fact that for most people Pentecost is a nonevent. Calendars mark Christmas and Easter, but "Pentecost is spectacularly absent." Yet Pentecost, not the Resurrection, was the event that transformed the disciples into exuberant messengers of Good News.

All of us keep a part of ourselves, the inner self, hidden, and show the world only an outer self. In the Spirit, God overcomes that barrier. God now lives inside, in the inner self, and seeks ways to bring harmony to those two selves so that we are not split but have a unified identity.

We receive "gifts of the Spirit" from One who, by living inside us, knows precisely how each person's unique combination of personality, upbringing, and natural skills can be used in God's service. As Jürgen Moltmann points out, "the Spirit of life" is only encountered as the Spirit of this and that particular life — as specific and as varied as the people indwelled. The Spirit enhances and shapes but never overwhelms our individual personalities and talents.

According to one account, Queen Victoria had very different impressions of her two most famous prime ministers. When she was with William Gladstone, she said, "I feel I am with one of the most important leaders of the world." Benjamin Disraeli, on the other hand, "makes me feel as if I am one of the most important people in the world." Reading that description, I thought of the difference between reactions to Jehovah of the Old Testament and the indwelling Spirit: one provokes awe, while one provides nurture.

My friend Ken, a committed Christian who struggles with his faith, told me, "Frankly, I see more evidence for the Spirit than for the other two members of the Trinity. The hunger for God that I feel — that is a sign of the Spirit's presence in me. My fitful battles with lust, my conviction of pride, the strong sense of when I need to apologize, and when to forgive — these signs of God are to me every bit as impressive as a burning bush. They let me know God is still at work inside me."

I have a hunch that small victories like the ones Ken describes give God as much, and maybe more, pleasure than any miracle from biblical times. I also know many "ordinary" people who visit prisons, care for the dying, build houses with Habitat for Humanity, adopt unwanted babies, welcome refugee families. They do these things under the prompting of God's Spirit.

"Are you filled with the Spirit?" If you asked the apostle Paul such a question, he would likely respond by listing qualities that the Spirit produces: love, joy, peace, goodness, etc. Do you have those qualities? And do you express God's love for others? Each of Paul's letters ends with a call to practical acts of love and service: prayer, sharing with the needy, comforting the sick, hospitality, humility. We dare not devalue the "ordinary"—actually, most extraordinary—work of God making himself at home in our lives. These are the marks of the Spirit-filled life, signs of the invisible made manifest in our visible world.*

The Spirit cannot be kept like a personal pet, living in a small compartment somewhere inside us to be brought out at will. The living presence of God inside us should permeate everything we see and do. To adapt the college student's analogy, the Spirit is not a homunculus banging on pipes for our attention but rather an indwelling part of the entire building. The Spirit does not act *on* us so much as *with* us, as a part of us—a God of the process, not a God of the gaps.

∞

JESUS JOINED THE HUMAN race for a time so that he can now serve as our sympathetic advocate. In a tender passage, Paul shows that the Spirit adds a further contribution to our struggles here.

Romans 8 sums up the entire human condition—more, the entire planet: "We know that the whole creation has been groaning as in the pains of childbirth right up to the present time." And we humans "groan inwardly" as well, he adds. The planet and all its inhabitants are emitting a constant stream of low-frequency distress signals. Paul loved a good play on words, and the first two appearances of *groan* serve as stage props to set up his climactic conclusion: ". . . the Spirit helps us in our weakness. We do not know what we ought to pray, but the Spirit himself intercedes for us with *groans* that words cannot express."

I know well the helpless feeling of not knowing what I ought to pray: how to pray for a person in a dead-end marriage that seems to represent only stuntedness, not growth; for a victim of child abuse who as

---

* J. I. Packer chides the church:

"With a perversity as pathetic as it is impoverishing, we have become preoccupied today with the extraordinary, sporadic, non-universal ministries of the Spirit to the neglect of the ordinary, general ones. Thus, we show a great deal more interest in the gifts of healing and tongues—gifts which, as Paul pointed out, not all Christians are meant to partake anyway—than in the Spirit's oridinary work of giving peace, joy, hope, and love, through the shedding abroad in our hearts of knowledge of the love of God."

an adult finds it impossible to enjoy sex; for a parent of a child diagnosed with terminal cancer; for a Christian in Pakistan imprisoned for her faith; for a city council or court that does not share my core beliefs. What can I ask for? How can I pray?

The Spirit announces the good news that we need not figure out exactly how to pray. We need only groan. As I read Paul's words, an image comes to mind of a mother tuning in to her child's wordless cry. I know mothers who can distinguish a cry for food from a cry for attention, an earache cry from a stomachache cry. To me, the sounds are identical, but the mother instinctively perceives the meaning of the child's nonverbal groan. It is the inarticulateness, the very helplessness, of the child that gives her compassion such intensity.

God's Spirit has resources of sensitivity beyond even the wisest mother, and evidently it is our helplessness that God too delights in, our weakness allowing opportunity for his strength. Linking the *groans* of Romans 8, Paul tells of a Spirit who lives inside us, who detects needs we cannot articulate and expresses them in a language we cannot comprehend. When we don't know what to pray, the Spirit fills in the blanks.

The Greek word applied to the Holy Spirit, Paraclete or *paracletos,* meant "one who stands by the side," such as an advocate or defense attorney, an image that must have provided strong comfort to the persecuted early Christians. Those of us who face different trials — cancer in the family, a besetting addiction, a teenager adrift, a job failure — also need the inner presence of a Spirit who intercedes for us "with groans that words cannot express," or as one translation has it "with sighs too deep for words." The same Greek word described a kind of cheerleader called upon when an army prepared for a decisive battle. For fearful and intimidated troops, the *paracletos* made audible a voice of confidence and morale building. We have access to that kind of inner voice, the voice of God himself.

The Bible presents, if you will, a "trinity of groans," a progression of intimacy in God's involvement with his creation. The Old Testament tells us of a God above, a Father who attends to our dwarfish human needs. The Gospels tell of a further step, the God alongside, who became one of us, taking on ears, vocal cords, and pain cells. And the Epistles tell of the God within, an invisible Spirit who gives expression to our wordless needs. The "groaning" chapter of Romans 8 concludes with the bold promise that one day there will be no need for groans at all.

ONE OF MY WRITING colleagues very nearly abandoned his faith after a horrific series of health and emotional problems. During his darkest hour, he said, God stayed silent. Prayer did nothing for him. At the end, when finally he emerged from the valley of shadow, he told me, "You know what kept me from chucking the whole thing, from apostatizing? Just this. It would mean having to go to three or four people I respect more than anyone else in the world and tell them, 'You're deceived.' I could not bring myself to deny the reality of God's Spirit in their lives."

A mutual friend, listening in, had another opinion. "That's exactly why I'm tempted to apostatize! Frankly, I don't see the reality of God's Spirit in people's lives. I want some *direct* evidence of God."

The "disadvantage" of knowing God through the Holy Spirit is that, when God turned over the mission to his church, he truly turned it over. As a result, many people who reject God are rejecting not God but a caricature of him presented by the church. Yes, the church has led the way in issues of justice, literacy, medicine, education, and civil rights. But to our everlasting shame, the watching world judges God by a church whose history also includes the Crusades, the Inquisition, anti-Semitism, suppression of women, and support of the slave trade.

I often wish we could set aside church history, scrub away the many layers of sediment, and encounter the words of the Gospels for the first time. Not everyone would accept Jesus—they did not in his own day—but at least people would not reject him for the wrong reasons. What I long for, however, is not only impossible but unbiblical. I must remind myself of Jesus' words that it is *for our good* that he went away. The subsequent failures of the church are at once a sign of God's readiness to con-descend, and also a backhanded compliment to human beings: God entrusts us with his mission.

I find it much easier to accept the fact of God dwelling in Jesus of Nazareth than in the people who attend my local church and in me. Yet the New Testament insists this pattern fulfills God's plan from the beginning: not a continuing series of spectacular interventions but a gradual delegation of his mission to flawed human beings. All along, Jesus planned to die so that we, his church, could take his place. What Jesus brought to a few — healing, grace, hope, the good-news message of God's love — his followers could now bring to all. "Unless a kernel of wheat falls to the ground and dies," he explained, "it remains only a single seed. But if it dies, it produces many seeds."

Eugene Peterson has written of his labors as a pastor, trying to shepherd a congregation who seemed to him gossipy and immature, who reduced the Bible to trivia and grew frustrated when God didn't solve all their problems. The contrast between the actual congregation and the ideals of the church set forth in the New Testament bothered him greatly until he noticed an important detail in the book of Revelation. The early chapters describe immature churches like his as "lampstands." "They are places, locations, where the light of Christ is shown," notes Peterson. "They are not themselves the light. There is nothing particularly glamorous about churches, nor, on the other hand, is there anything particularly shameful about them. They simply are."

In an elegant analogy, John V. Taylor likens the Incarnation to a scene in Shakespeare's *Henry V*. On the eve of battle against an overwhelming enemy, King Henry dons a disguise and moves incognito among the common soldiers in the field. He overhears one swear that the king will have to pay on judgment day when the hacked and broken bodies rise up and accuse him of having bought victory with their lives. Henry knows all too well the burden that lies on his shoulders, a burden that he now transfers to his army.

> Yet he still believes it will prove worthwhile and, as morning breaks, he rallies his small force to believe in it with him. So he instills into them his own hope, his faith in the value of the enterprise....
>
> God does know more intimately than any the price his creatures have been paying for his huge adventure of making this universe of accident and freedom and pain as the only environment in which love could one day emerge to receive and delight in and respond to his joyous love. He still believes the outcome will outweigh the immense waste and agony, not least the agony of his seeming

indifference and inaction. So, knowing we cannot understand, cannot forgive what he is doing, God has come among us as a fellow-being and fellow-sufferer to make amends and to win back trust.

King Henry could not fight the battle on his own. He could join his soldiers, move among them, inspire them, and lead the charge. But the outcome at Agincourt, one of the greatest military victories of all time, depended on the efforts of common foot soldiers.

God's withdrawal behind human skin, his condescension to live inside common foot soldiers, guarantees that all will sometimes doubt and many will reject God altogether. The plan also guarantees that the kingdom will advance at a slow, tedious pace, which God, showing remarkable restraint, does not overrule. It took eighteen centuries for the church to rally against slavery, and even then many resisted. Poverty still abounds, as does war and discrimination, and in some places the church does little to help.

Etty Hillesum wrote this in a journal discovered after her death in a Nazi concentration camp:

> One thing is becoming increasingly clear to me: that You cannot help us, so we must help You to help ourselves. And that is all we can manage these days and also all that really matters: that we safeguard that little piece of You, God, in ourselves. And perhaps in others as well. . . . You cannot help us but we must help You and defend Your dwelling place inside us to the last.

It will sometimes appear that God cannot help us, or at least does not. It will appear that he has set us loose down here, alone amid the evil powers. In truth, we all want a divine problem-solver. Christians may feel the same impatience over the slow, unspectacular work of the Holy Spirit as Jews felt over Jesus the Messiah, who did not provide the kind of triumphant rescue they wanted.

The questions we ask of God, he often turns back on us. We plead for God to "come down"

> Christ was himself but one and lived and died but once; but the Holy Ghost makes of every Christian another Christ, an AfterChrist; lives a million lives in every age . . .
>
> GERARD MANLEY HOPKINS

and only reluctantly acknowledge that God is already here, within us, and that what God does on earth closely resembles what the church does. In short, the chief "disadvantage" to knowing God as Spirit is the history of the church—and the spiritual biography of you and me.

PART FOUR

Union

A Partnership of Unequals

MAKEOVER

Now, with God's help, I shall become myself.

SØREN KIERKEGAARD

D URING HIGH SCHOOL YEARS I sought to deconstruct and then reconstruct my identity. In the first place, I hated being Southern.
Television programs like "The Beverly Hillbillies" and "HeeHaw" embarrassed me, and I cringed every time I heard President Lyndon Johnson
open his mouth: "Mah fella Amuricuns . . ." Since the rest of the nation
in the 1960s seemed to judge Southerners as backward, ignorant, and
racist, I wanted to disassociate myself from my home region.

Vowel by vowel I worked to change my accent, succeeding so well
that people ever since have reacted with surprise when they hear I grew
up in the Deep South. I began a campaign to read great books in order
to remove provincial blinders. I shunned any "Yes ma'am, no sir" man-
nerisms that conformed to proper Southern tradition. One at a time I
faced my fears and tried to conquer them. I fought to gain control of my

emotions so that they became my servants, not my master. I even recon-figured my handwriting, training myself to form each letter in a new, more streamlined way than before.

By and large the makeover worked, giving me a personality that has fit comfortably in the decades since. I became less vulnerable and more open-minded and flexible — traits not cultivated in my upbringing but useful in my profession as a journalist. Childhood ghosts vanished. I thought I had escaped my past.

The problems showed up years later when I began to realize the lim-its to a self-constructed personality. In most ways important to God, I had failed miserably. I was selfish, joyless, loveless, and lacked compassion. With the notable exception of *self-control*, I lacked all nine of the fruits of the Spirit listed in Galatians 5. These qualities, I saw, cannot be constructed but must be grown, cultivated by God's indwelling presence. I agree with J. Heinrich Arnold that Christian discipleship "is not a question of our own doing; it is a matter of making room for God so that he can live in us."

I have since made it a regular practice to pray through the list in Galatians: love, joy, peace, patience, kindness, goodness, faithfulness, gen-tleness, and self-control. Do I dispense love, experience joy and peace, exhibit patience? I keep hitting against a glass ceiling, for though I excel at doubt and honest self-appraisal I see a frustrating lack of progress in qualities like joy and love. And just when I think I'm becoming more patient and gentle, I get cut off after waiting on hold for twenty min-utes on the telephone and start pounding the desk with my fist. As I am humbly aware, any progress in these areas comes as a result of God's work.

Ultimately I came to see that my entire project of reconstructing per-sonality had been misguided. God did not want to work with a wholly dif-ferent personality. God chose *me*. I saw this most clearly during a guided meditation at a spiritual retreat. The director asked me to focus on the story of Lazarus's resurrection in John 11. "Put yourself in the place of Lazarus as you read," he said. "He's alive again but wrapped in binding cloths. He needs help getting free of them. I want you to identify what binding cloths are wrapped around you, keeping you from being the fully alive person God intended."

I made a long list. It included such things as a lingering guilt that taints all my experiences of pleasure; a personal reserve that keeps me from expressing, or experiencing, joy; old wounds that I lack the faith for God to heal; the writer's "observer syndrome" that holds me at arm's length from life; a stubborn clinging to my identity as a renegade; an approach/avoidance pattern that I practice with God as well as other people.

I would like to report that God removed all those binding cloths during the week-long retreat. No, spiritual cures rarely come so quickly or so easily. I got a mere glimpse of what healing may look like, a preview of an identity reconstructed by God and not me—a makeover that would liberate, not deny, my true self.

———

MARK VAN DOREN, THE literature professor who once taught Thomas Merton, visited his former student at a Kentucky monastery after a thirteen-year separation. Van Doren and other friends of Merton still could not comprehend Merton's transformation from a New York party animal into a monk who cherished solitude and silence. Van Doren reported,

> Of course he looked a little older; but as we sat and talked I could see no important difference in him, and once I interrupted a reminiscence of his by laughing. "Tom," I said, "you haven't changed at all."
>
> "Why would I? Here," he said, "our duty is to be more ourselves not less." It was a searching remark and I stood happily corrected.

I believe God has a similar goal for all of us, that we become more ourselves by realizing the "selves" God originally intended for us. The Rabbi Zusya concluded, "In the world to come I shall not be asked: 'Why were you not Moses?' I shall be asked: 'Why were you not Zusya?'" Quietly, persistently, the Spirit coaxes me to be neither Moses nor Zusya, but Philip Yancey, a flawed personality in whom God himself has chosen to dwell. With infinite resources, God can assist every willing person on earth in that custom process. It begins with trust in God's best for me, a confidence that God will liberate my true self, not bind it.

"No one ever hated his own body, but he feeds and cares for it, just as Christ does the church—for we are members of his body," Paul wrote the Ephesians, adding, "This is a profound mystery," as if he too had trouble believing the depth of God's intimacy with his people. I think of all that I do on my body's behalf: take vitamin pills; jog and exercise; cut hair, toenails, and fingernails; sleep; visit the doctor and dentist; eat; bandage scrapes and spread lotion over dry skin; keep room temperature comfortable. I am never *not* conscious of my body: right now as I write I sense the pressure on my fingertips. That is the kind of intimate relationship God has with his people on earth, for he has chosen our bodies as his own.

"How great is the love the Father has lavished on us, that we should be called children of God! And that is what we are!" the apostle John exclaims in his first letter. Everything around us murmurs the opposite: we are unworthy, we have failed, we fall short. As if anticipating the objection, John adds, "Dear friends, now we are children of God, and what we will be has not yet been made known. But we know that when he appears, we shall be like him. . . ." A part of us now remains hidden and undeveloped, like an organ the function of which we've not yet ascertained. Yet the Spirit's work proceeds, invisibly and unendingly, to fashion our true selves. We cannot construct the personality that pleases God but God can and promises to do exactly that.

God makes clear that he accepts us—more, delights in us—as individual bearers of his image. We do not always sense that divine love, of course. Self-doubt and despair may steal in, as had happened among those the apostle John was addressing. Sometimes "our hearts condemn us," John acknowledges, but "God is greater than our hearts, and he knows everything." When the New Testament translator J. B. Phillips came across that passage from 1 John, it seemed to leap off the page. Phillips explains, "Like many others, I find myself something of a perfectionist, and if we don't watch ourselves this obsession for the perfect can make us arrogantly critical of other people, and in certain moods, desperately critical of ourselves." Phillips suffered from clinical depression, and when the dark moods descended he would wallow in condemnation and feel no mercy. Ever after, he clung to the words of that verse. "It is almost as if John is saying, 'if God loves us, who are we to be so high and mighty as to refuse to love ourselves?'"

For me too, accepting God's love involves a relentless hushing of voices that whisper otherwise. *You are unworthy. You failed again. God cannot possibly love you.* My conscience having formed under sermons portraying an Old Testament God of strict authority and punishment, I can barely grasp the reality that God has con-descended to live within me and now loves me from the inside out. I must ask the God who "is greater than our hearts" to halt that ruthless cycle of condemnation and to remind me of perhaps the hardest truth to grasp, that God desires and loves me.

Why does God love me? The Bible answers that profound question with one incomparable word: grace. God loves because of who God is, not because I have done anything to deserve it. God cannot help loving, for love defines his nature.

I remember few of the many sermons I have heard in my life, an exception being the only sermon I heard preached by Ian Pitt-Watson, a professor at Fuller Seminary. His sermon had one point, not three, which may explain why I still remember it: "Some things are loved because they are worthy; some things are worthy because they are loved."

Pitt-Watson began with examples of things we love because of their inherent worth: gorgeous super-models, gifted athletes, brilliant scientists, priceless works of art. Then he mentioned an object of no intrinsic worth that was greatly loved regardless. He told of his daughter Rosemary's rag doll—dirty, threadbare, but the most precious of all her possessions. Like Linus with his blanket, Rosemary could not bear to face life without her rag doll. When the Pitt-Watsons relocated from Scotland across the ocean to America, each member of the family carefully selected what possessions to bring along. Rosemary chose just one article: her rag doll. When she misplaced the rag doll in the airport, Rosemary became so distraught that the family considered postponing their flight. Found at last, the doll had magical powers to calm the little girl. It had little worth in itself but much worth in her eyes.

Pitt-Watson proceeded to make the biblical application. God's love, thankfully, is not based on our intrinsic worth. It comes by grace, a priceless yet free gift that bestows worth on the most unlovable object. Some things are loved because they are worthy and some are worthy because they are loved—theologically, we fit the latter category. In the words of St. Augustine, "By loving the unlovable, You made me lovable."

When I love someone, I take delight in that person. When friends visit us in Colorado, we shop for foods we know they like, clean the house and place fresh flowers in the guest room, and design an itinerary to give them maximum pleasure. I cannot keep myself from staring out the window as their arrival time approaches, as if my looking will somehow bring them to us quicker. Something of that delight, God feels toward each one of us.

Toward the end of his life, Henri Nouwen said that prayer had become for him primarily a time of "listening to the blessing." "The real 'work' of prayer," he said, "is to become silent and listen to the voice that says good things about me." That may sound self-indulgent, he admitted, but not if it meant seeing himself as the Beloved, a person in whom God had chosen to dwell. The more he listened to that voice, the less likely he was to judge his worth by how others responded to him or by how much he achieved. He prayed for God's inner presence to express itself in his daily life as he ate and drank, talked and loved, played and worked. He sought the radical freedom of an identity anchored in a place "beyond all human praise and blame."

I too have found that prayer means far more than telling God what I want him to do. Primarily, it means putting myself in a place where God can "renew my mind," where I can absorb my new identity as God's Beloved, which God insists is mine for the believing.

In a daring analogy, Kathleen Norris reverses the point of view we normally ascribe to God:

> One morning this past spring I noticed a young couple with an infant at an airport departure gate. The baby was staring intently at other people, and as soon as he recognized a human face, no matter whose it was, no matter if it was young or old, pretty or ugly, bored or happy or worried-looking he would respond with absolute delight.
>
> It was beautiful to see. Our drab departure gate had become the gate of heaven. And as I watched that baby play with any adult who would allow it, I felt as awe-struck as Jacob, because I realized that this is how God looks at us, staring into our faces in order to be delighted, to see the creatures he made and called good, along with the rest of creation. And, as Psalm 139 puts it, darkness is as nothing to God, who can look right through whatever evil we've done in our lives to the creature made in the divine image.
>
> I suspect that only God, and well-loved infants, can see this way.

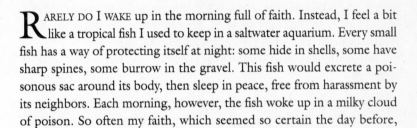

RARELY DO I WAKE up in the morning full of faith. Instead, I feel a bit like a tropical fish I used to keep in a saltwater aquarium. Every small fish has a way of protecting itself at night: some hide in shells, some have sharp spines, some burrow in the gravel. This fish would excrete a poisonous sac around its body, then sleep in peace, free from harassment by its neighbors. Each morning, however, the fish woke up in a milky cloud of poison. So often my faith, which seemed so certain the day before, disappears overnight and I wake up in a cloud of poisonous doubt.

"Don't you know that you yourselves are God's temple and that God's Spirit lives in you?" Paul asked the Corinthians, who were showing few outward signs of such knowledge. It appalls me how frequently I must give myself the same reminder. If God himself lives inside me, shouldn't I wake up with that knowledge and live in constant awareness all day long? Alas, I do not.

Paul says elsewhere that God "set his seal of ownership on us, and put his Spirit in our hearts as a deposit, guaranteeing what is to come." After an organ transplant, doctors must use anti-rejection drugs to suppress the immune system or else the body will throw off the newly grafted member. I have come to see the Holy Spirit as something like that agent, a power living inside me that keeps me from throwing off the new identity God has implanted. My spiritual immune system needs daily reminders that God's presence *belongs* within me and is no foreign object.

I remind myself of what I deeply know: that my worth comes from God, who has lavished love and grace upon me. In relating to an invisible God, though, without a determined effort, my thoughts of him slip away. Phone calls, distractions, fleeting images on the television or an Internet screen push aside God-consciousness. How can I keep from forgetting? How to cultivate the belief that God himself lives within me, even as I so regularly forget his presence?

While living in Africa, John V. Taylor observed how Africans experience a sense of personal presence. In the West, he says, we converse with friends with our minds partly on something else, and the friends soon notice. Whereas in Africa he would be working and a friend would enter the room, give a brief greeting, and squat down. After a few words of response, the missionary would get on with his chores while his visitor simply sat. A half an hour or so would pass, then the visitor would rise, say, "I have seen you," and move on. He had wanted no information, no conversation even; shared presence seemed enough.

Taylor remarks that *attention* is the key to retaining this sense of presence:

> Every good teacher knows the futility of rapping on his desk and calling: Pay attention, please! True attention is an involuntary self-surrender to the object of attention. The child who is absorbed is utterly relaxed. The adult mind, also, must be unstriving, receptive, expectant, before there can be any creative insight.
>
> Again and again this is the state of mind in which new truth dawns. We do not work it out or think it out; rather, we have the sense of waiting for the disclosure of something that is already there. Attention means being in attendance. . . . To be "in the Spirit" is to be vividly aware of everything the moment contains, the twigs of the thorn-bush as well as the presence of God.

Monastics have a practice they call *statio* that means, simply, stopping one thing before beginning another. Rather than rushing from one task to the next, pause for a moment and recognize the time between times. Before dialing the phone, pause and think about the conversation and the person on the other end. After reading from a book, pause and think back through what you learned and how you were moved. After watching a television show, pause and ask what it contributed to your life. Before reading the Bible, pause and ask for a spirit of attention. Do this often enough and even mechanical acts become conscious, mindful. I find that if I take time to pray for the recipient before beginning to compose a letter or before making a phone call, it makes the task less of a chore and more of an opportunity in which to receive or express God's grace.

If I do not consciously work at attending, I inevitably allow myself to conform to the world around me, a world that mainly honors achievement and competition. As a corrective, the apostle Paul recommends a process of mental purging, a *statio* time. "Set your minds on what the Spirit desires," he counsels the Romans. In Philippians he fills in the blanks: ". . . whatever is true, whatever is noble, whatever is right, whatever is pure, whatever is lovely, whatever is admirable—if anything is excellent or praiseworthy—think about such things." Absorbing a new identity requires an act of will. Take off your old self and put on your new self, Paul advises elsewhere, as if we "clothe our minds" in the way we make daily selections from a wardrobe.

"What do we want from our meditation?" asked Dietrich Bonhoeffer. "We want to rise up from our meditation in a different state from when we sat down."

The visible world forces itself on me without invitation; I must consciously cultivate the invisible. I wish the process were spontaneous and natural, but I have never found it so. Indeed, I have found that such a process, like anything of worth, requires discipline. "If I omit practice one day, I notice it. If two days the critics notice it, if three days the public notices it," said the pianist Arthur Rubinstein. The Christian life likewise involves daily acts of will, a deliberate reorientation to a new— and in some ways unnatural—personal identity.

Communion with God also involves more relaxed times of meditation. The father of cellist Yo-Yo Ma spent World War II in Paris, where he lived alone in a garret throughout the German occupation. In order to restore sanity to his world, he would practice violin pieces by Bach during the day and at night, during blackout hours, play them alone in the dark. His son Yo-Yo took up the father's advice to play a Bach suite from memory every night before going to bed. Yo-Yo Ma says, "This isn't practicing, it's contemplating. You're alone with your soul."

I have found that spirituality includes a bit of both: the deliberate practice of Rubinstein and the calm meditation of Yo-Yo Ma. I ask myself at the end of the day, Did I do anything today that would give God pleasure? Since God longs to feel delight in me, did I give him such opportunity?

No matter what answers I come up with, I still relax in God's love and ask him to enfold me in grace and forgiveness. I try to quiet the clamor of my own self and create space for the quiet of God to enter. What matters most to God in prayer, I am convinced, is my longing to know him.

———— ∾ ————

ROBERTA BONDI TELLS OF a sixth-century monk overseeing a community in turmoil. Our irritable brethren are getting in the way of a proper love for God, some of the monks complained. You have it wrong, Dorotheos informed them. Visualize the world as a great circle with God at the center and human lives out on the circumference. "Imagine now that there are straight lines connecting from the outside of the circle all human lives to God at the center. Can't you see that there is no way to move toward God without drawing closer to other people, and no way to approach other people without coming near to God?"

As my identity changes from within, my eyes then lift up to see others who need God's love and mercy. Paul follows up his advice in Romans to "be transformed by the renewing of your mind" with the first full mention of the body of Christ analogy, then gives a series of abrupt commands, such as, "Share with God's people who are in need" and "Live at peace with everyone." In other letters he asks readers to feed the hungry, to show hospitality to traveling ministers, to reach out in love to unbelievers around them. Renewed minds express themselves in relationship with other bodies. "The road to holiness," said Dag Hammarskjöld, "necessarily passes through the world of action."

I have often recalled the story of a man who came up to me after a speaking engagement and said, rather blusteringly, "You wrote a book titled *Where Is God When It Hurts,* didn't you?" When I nodded yes, he continued, "Well, I don't have time to read your book. Can you tell me what it says in just a sentence or two?" (A writer loves requests like that, after spending many months on a book.)

I gave it some thought and replied, "Well, I suppose I'd have to answer with another question, 'Where is the church when it hurts?'" You see, I explained, the church is God's presence on earth, his Body. And if the church does its job—if the church shows up at the scene of disasters, visits the sick, staffs the AIDS clinics, counsels the rape victims, feeds the hungry, houses the homeless—I don't think the world will ask that question with the same urgency. They will know where God is when it hurts: in the bodies of his people, ministering to a fallen world. Indeed, our consciousness of God's presence often comes as a byproduct of other people's presence.

For several years I walked alongside a friend in the midst of a very dark time. He was struggling with deep depression, and those struggles ultimately led to a divorce and loss of his career. For a time he committed himself to an asylum and survived at least three suicide attempts. I met with him, prayed with him, and spent long hours on the telephone. Most of the time, I felt helpless and useless. The answers I suggested made little difference, and after a while I decided he needed my love, not my advice. I simply made myself available, as much as I could.

Eventually my friend experienced a healing that brought him back to sanity. He said to me, "You were God to me. I had no contact with God the Father—he seemed vacant, withdrawn. But I kept believing in God because of you." I wanted to shove him away, to refute him, for I know who I am and how far that is from God. As I listened, though, I realized the profound meaning behind Paul's phrase "the body of Christ." For whatever reason, God had chosen me and a few others as "clay vessels" through which he poured his own presence. We make this journey not alone, rather joined to one another.

> These are only hints and guesses,
> Hints followed by guesses;
>   and the rest
> Is prayer, observance, discipline,
>   thought and action.
>
> T. S. ELIOT

OUT OF CONTROL

All religious experience at its roots is an experience of an unconditional and unrestricted being in love.

BERNARD LONERGAN

As PART OF A musical diversity week, the Chicago Cultural Center invited a local gospel choir representing the Christ Bible Center. Their noon concert, which I attended, attracted predominantly a well-dressed crowd of business people and shoppers from tony Michigan Avenue.

"Can you believe how God works?" crowed the choir director as he glanced up at the concert hall's elegant Tiffany dome. "Who would have thought the Holy Spirit would ever get invited into the old public library building!" Most of the audience smiled indulgently, applauded, then settled back to enjoy a rousing hour of lusty voices and swaying bodies.

We got more than we bargained for. The spirited singers had the audience wrapped around their fingers until suddenly, about twenty minutes into the concert, one of the choir members went into an ecstatic fit. Leaping from the last row of risers, he began hopping backwards on one foot across the stage, shouting "Hallelujah! Hallelujah!" and speaking in tongues.

The choir kept right on singing as if this sort of thing happened all the time. The audience, however, grew visibly restless. Two silver-haired ladies in fur stoles grabbed their shopping bags and bustled out. Men and women wearing office attire looked at their watches and fidgeted. A sudden epidemic of coughing broke out.

When a few of its members got "slain in the spirit" and fell to the floor like corpses in rigor mortis, the choir lost its audience completely. The choir director seemed almost apologetic at the end as he turned to the faithful few who remained in their seats and said, "Well, you know how it is, you just can't hem the Spirit in."

O N THE EVE OF his twenty-eighth birthday Martin Luther King Jr. stood behind the pulpit of a church in Montgomery, Alabama. His home had been firebombed and he was sleeping little, anxious about recent death threats against his family. The future of the Montgomery civil rights campaign looked bleak. King began to pray aloud in the pulpit, and for the first time in his public life a burst of spiritual ecstasy swept over him.

"Lord, I hope no one will have to die as a result of our struggle for freedom in Montgomery," he prayed. "Certainly I don't want to die. But if anyone has to die, let it be me." His mouth remained open, but no more words came from it. He swooned, and other ministers leaped up to help him to his seat. This audience, unlike the one in Chicago, roared enthusiastic approval. The Holy Ghost had come down on the young scholar from Boston University! *Amen, hallelujah! Thank you, Jesus!*

Ever after, King himself felt embarrassed by the episode.

W HEN AN INVISIBLE SPIRIT and a human being connect, strange things may happen. That prospect terrifies some people, embarrasses others, and captivates still others. While directing a series on religion for public television, *Mine Eyes Have Seen the Glory,* Randall Balmer captured on film some spectacular displays of the Spirit's activity, mainly in Southern churches, mainly African-American. As he later told me, he had to ask himself why we balk at showing spiritual ecstasy on television, a medium which features close-ups of physical ecstasy every night.

As a journalist, I have a tendency to distance myself, to observe my surroundings like some invisible person who does not enter into but glides in and out of the scene, taking notes all the while. That stance may help someone reporting on politics in Washington or covering a war or sporting event, but it definitely does not help someone trying to understand spiritual reality. "It's dark at the foot of the lighthouse," says a German proverb.

I sit in a charismatic-style meeting and look around. The music, a few repetitive phrases set to a mediocre composition, jars me but seems to have a mesmerizing effect on others. Their hands lift in the air palms up, their eyes squint shut, their bodies sway. They appear transported to an emotional plane unattainable to me, connecting to something that leaves me behind. Cautiously, I approach these worshipers afterward. "Exactly what happened out there?" I ask. "I want to understand. Can you break it down for me?"

In response to my questions I get blank stares, mumbled phrases, looks of irritation, pity, or condescension. I learn that such journalism is as intrusive as the TV camera that zooms to a close-up of the woman who has just lost her daughter in a house fire. For this reason, I have no desire to reduce spirituality to its constituent parts. Shine a spotlight on activity of the Spirit and it flees.

In the interest of full disclosure, I also must confess that I have little personal experience of the more dramatic manifestations of God's presence.* I have sat in prayer meetings in which everyone around me saw this as a grievous flaw and beseeched the Holy Spirit to come down and fill me. Mostly, I felt intense discomfort. I have also watched as a couple of zealous students tried to exorcise demons from my brother in a piano practice room. These encounters have been rare, however. When I now hear reports of churches making animal sounds and breaking out in fits of

---

* I attended a Christian college at a time when a sister school, Moody Bible Institute, posted instructions on what to do in case of "Emergencies," which they defined as fire, tornado and air raid, bomb threat, emotional upset and/or suicide, sickness or injury, and "charismatic activity."

laughter, I remember the discomfort I felt in the Chicago Cultural Center and in that demon-haunted practice room.

I have never spoken in tongues or barked in church, and not once have I been swept up in a public display of spiritual ecstasy like Martin Luther King's. This may relate to awkward experiences from the past, to my fear of losing control, to spiritual inadequacy, or to a squelching streak of rationality. I do not know. What I do know, however, is that the New Testament writers consistently speak of the "spirit of Christ" and in fact use the phrases "in the Spirit" and "in Christ" almost interchangeably. Therefore, when I want to visualize God's Spirit—an oxymoron, I realize—I turn to Jesus, in whom the unseeable takes on a face.

Jesus said this to the disciples at the Last Supper:

> But the Counselor, the Holy Spirit, whom the Father will send in my name, will teach you all things and will remind you of everything I have said to you. . . .
>
> He will bring glory to me by taking from what is mine and making it known to you.

Because of Jesus' life on earth, we have an actual and vivid representation of what a human being connected to God should look like. The "fruits of the Spirit" are in fact the qualities that Jesus showed on earth, and he promised to "abide," or make his home, in us to nurture those same qualities.

IF I WONDER *HOW* or in what style God's Spirit works in me, I need look no further than Jesus for the answer to that as well.

I read a psychiatrist's study of twenty-five Westerners, thirteen of them missionaries, who were imprisoned and brainwashed by Chinese communists early in Chairman Mao's regime. The communist jailers took on the task of purging out all wrong thoughts that had been implanted by imperialists and capitalists. To do so, they had to use torturous techniques of coercion. The Westerners were forced to stand, hands tied behind their backs, wearing chains on their legs, for days and even weeks without sleep while their cellmates barraged them with "correct thinking." A wrong response brought on a beating. It took up to three years to break strong-willed prisoners, but eventually every one of them admitted guilt and signed confessions. Most assisted in the brainwashing of new prisoners. When deported back to the West, the twenty-five former prisoners at first seemed confused, even paranoid, unsure of what to believe. Yet all but a few soon denounced the propaganda of their captors that they had been forced to believe.

Jesus never brainwashed anyone. To the contrary, he depicted the cost of following him in the most realistic terms imaginable ("Take up your cross and follow me"). He never imposed himself on another person but always left room for choice and even rejection. In that same style, any changes God works in a person will come about not as a result of coercion from the outside but by a Spirit working from within, summoning up new life, transforming from the inside out. The words used to describe God's Spirit—Comforter, Helper, Counselor—imply that change may involve a slow, internal process, with many fits and starts.

After considering the various words used of the Holy Spirit, both in Greek and in English, James Houston summarizes them in the simple word "friend." A true friend always has my best interest at heart. Sometimes the Spirit must, like a good friend, use tough love to remind me of what needs to change—knowing me from the inside out, God can bring to mind shortcomings I would prefer to overlook. Yet when I feel empty, misunderstood, and lonely, the Spirit offers comfort, calming my anxiety and fear. Most of all, the Spirit reminds me of God's love, his very presence a token of the fact that I have been graciously adopted as God's child.

Author Larry Crabb says that we Christians often communicate to each other one of these two solutions: "Do what's right" or "Fix what's wrong." Instead, the New Testament holds up a better way: "Release what's good." What's good is the Holy Spirit, already living in us, with all the resources of God at his command.

When I think of the fear and discomfort summoned up by mentioning the Holy Spirit, I have to laugh at the irony of being spooked by the Comforter. Sometimes I secretly yearn for the spectacular—fits of ecstasy, miraculous answers to prayer, resurrections, healings—when the Holy Spirit chiefly offers a slow, steady progression toward the end God desires all along: the gradual reconstruction of my fallen self.

As the new millennium rolled around and I was winding up work on this book, I went on a spiritual retreat. The director told me he leads such retreats several times a year, and not once has a participant failed to hear God speak during the four days. We would remain silent, reading only what he assigned, committing to pray at least four hours per day.

I arrived with much skepticism. I had, after all, been spending months on a book that delves into doubt and God's silence. I expected a full day of restlessness and boredom and maybe a second day of resistance before finally hearing anything like the voice of God, whatever form that might take. Nevertheless, I decided to go along with the program and try my best to listen attentively.

To my great surprise, God started speaking right away. The first afternoon, sitting outside on a moss-covered rock in a forest of evergreens, I started writing in a journal what God might say to me if he dictated a spiritual "action plan" for the rest of my life. The more I listened, the longer grew the list. Here is a mere sampling:

- *Question your doubts as much as your faith.* By personality, or perhaps as a reaction to a fundamentalist past, I brood on doubts and experience faith in occasional flashes. Isn't it about time for me to reverse the pattern?

- *Do not attempt this journey alone. Find companions who see you as a pilgrim, even a straggler, and not as a guide.* Like many Protestants, I easily assume the posture of one person alone with God, a stance which more and more I see as unbiblical. We have little guidance on how to live as a follower alone because God never intended it.

- *Allow the good — natural beauty, your health, encouraging words — to penetrate as deeply as the bad.* Why does it take around seventeen encouraging letters from readers to overcome the impact of one caustic, critical one? If I awoke every morning and fell asleep each night bathed in a sense of gratitude and not self-doubt, the hours in-between would doubtless take on a different cast.

- *For your own sake, simplify. Eliminate whatever distracts you from God.* Among other things, that means a ruthless winnowing of mail, giving catalogs, junk mail, and book club notices no more time than it takes to toss them in the trash. If I ever get the nerve, my television set should probably land there as well.

- *Find something that allows you to feel God's pleasure.* The sprinter Eric Liddell told his sister, "God made me fast. And when I run, I feel his pleasure." What makes me feel God's pleasure? I must identify it and then *run.*
- *Don't be ashamed.* "I am not ashamed of the gospel," Paul told the Romans. Why do I speak in generalities when strangers ask me what I do for a living and then try to pin down what kind of books I write? Why do I mention the secular schools I attended before the Christian ones?
- *Remember, those Christians who peeve you so much—God chose them too.* For some reason, I find it much easier to show grace and acceptance toward immoral unbelievers than toward uptight, judgmental Christians. Which, of course, turns me into a different kind of uptight, judgmental Christian.
- *Forgive, daily, those who caused the wounds that keep you from wholeness.* Increasingly, I find that our wounds are the very things God uses in his service. By harboring blame for those who caused them, I stall the act of redemption that can give the wounds worth and value, and ultimately healing.

"Exactly how did God speak?" you may ask. I never heard an audible voice or saw a vision. Admittedly, these insights did not come from outer space; they were inside me all along, a form of spiritual self-awareness. But here is the point: until I took the time to extract myself from daily routine and commit to long periods of silence, I missed hearing that internal voice. Although God may have been speaking all along, until I opened my ears it made little difference in my life.

ONCE IN ARIZONA I went jogging down a dirt road that wound through the sagebrush and saguaro cacti, and stumbled upon an eating disorder clinic that caters to the wealthy. I veered off my dusty desert trail onto a groomed cinder track which, I soon discovered, was a twelve-step trail. Signs with motivational slogans such as "Expect a miracle!" lined the trail, and as I continued to jog along I found myself proceeding through each step in the AA-based recovery plan. Placards on the trail urged me to confess that my body is out of control and that I am powerless to control my eating habits. For more than a mile, the trail looped through the further steps, on through the need to depend on friends and a Higher Power. Markers placed beside benches at each of the twelve steps encouraged the participants to rest and reflect on their progress.

The trail ended at a cemetery of tiny carved grave markers. I stopped to read each grave, dripping sweat and panting from the desert heat. "Here lies my fear of intimacy," someone named Donna had written on September 15, just three days before. She had decorated the tombstone in yellow, red, and blue paint. Others had buried such things as cigarettes, an obsession with chocolate, diet pills, a lack of self-discipline, the need to control others, a habit of lying.

I recognized in the graveyard an echo of Christian terminology: dying to self, crucifying the flesh. I also knew that Donna's fear of intimacy, three days buried, would someday resurrect. Spiritual powers that hold a person in their grip do not simply disappear, nor do they stay dead.

What do I need to bury? I asked myself. If I attended a *spiritual* disorder clinic and took this walk each day, how many tombstones would I leave along the trail? And how would it change me to comprehend, truly comprehend, that the Higher Power is actually an inner power, living inside me at this minute? Could that power, God's own Spirit, keep dead those things — pride, doubt, selfishness, insensitivity to injustice, lust — that I have tried to crucify and bury so many times before?

Richard Mouw of Fuller Seminary recalls being in a meeting with sociologist Peter Berger. Speaking as a seminary president should, Mouw said that every Christian is called to engage in radical obedience to God's program of justice, righteousness, and peace.

Berger responded with the observation that I was operating with a rather grandiose notion of radical obedience. Somewhere in a retirement home, he said, there is a Christian woman whose greatest fear in life is that she will make a fool of herself because she will not be able to control her bladder in the cafeteria line. For this woman, the greatest act of radical obedience to Jesus Christ is to place herself in the hands of a loving God every time she goes off to dinner.

Berger's point was profound. God calls us to deal with the challenges before us, and often our most "radical" challenges are very "little" ones. The call to radical micro-obedience may mean patiently listening to someone who is boring or irritating, or treating a fellow sinner with a charity that is not easy to muster, or offering detailed advice on a matter that seems trivial to everyone but the person asking for the advice.

C. S. Lewis was surprised to learn that his life after conversion consisted mostly in doing the same things he had done before, only in a new spirit. Eventually he concluded that being a practicing Christian "means that every single act and feeling, every experience, whether pleasant or unpleasant, must be referred to God." It was a matter of learning to live not for himself but for someone else, in the same way an athlete might devote a game to a coach dying of cancer—or to a lover.

In a play or a movie, the most ordinary events—walking out to buy a paper, getting into a car, answering the phone—may have momentous implications. The plot hinges on such details, and the audience watches carefully because it does not know which one may prove significant or hold an essential clue. Life with God is like that, for God's presence gives new potentiality to every single event.

Whether I battle incontinence, an eating disorder, a fear of intimacy, an attraction to lust and infidelity, or a spirit of bitterness and blame, the good news is that I need not "clean myself up" before approaching God. Just the opposite: in the Spirit, God has found a way to live within me, helping from the inside out. God has not promised a state of constant bliss or a problem-free existence but has promised to be present in the silence and in the dark, to exist alongside us, within us, and for us.

THE EVANGELICAL SUBCULTURE I grew up in emphasized God's power. As a child I lived in fear of a God who, like Jehovah of the Old Testament, would use lightning bolts, disease, or other weapons in his arsenal to punish my sin. Later I viewed the Christian life as a venue for God's more benign power. My brother, after winning a piano competition, would say piously, "It wasn't me, it was the Lord." (I, who practiced just as hard, with half the talent, always wondered why the Lord didn't guide my fingers so skillfully.) Sometimes at prayer meetings I would hear requests like this: "May we have no ideas of our own, no actions of our own. May you do it all through us." (A cynical friend noted that the prayers were often answered—those people indeed seemed to have no ideas of their own.)

Ultimately I saw that a constant emphasis on God's power may lead to the fatalism of extreme Muslims or Hindus, who conclude that we humans need do nothing because the will of God works itself out regardless. Far more impressive is the miracle of God's condescension, his humble willingness to share power and offer us full partnership in the mission of transforming the world.

I used to feel spiritually inferior because I had not experienced the more spectacular manifestations of the Spirit and could not point to any bona fide "miracles" in my life. Increasingly, though, I have come to see that what I value may differ greatly from what God values. Jesus, often reluctant to perform miracles, considered it progress when he departed earth and entrusted the mission to his flawed disciples. Like a proud parent, God seems to take more delight as a spectator of the bumbling achievements of his stripling children than in any self-display of omnipotence.

From God's perspective, if I may speculate, the great advance in human history may be what happened at Pentecost, which restored the direct correspondence of spirit to Spirit that had been lost in Eden. I want God to act in direct, impressive, irrefutable ways. He wants to "share power" with the likes of me, accomplishing his work through people, not despite them.

"Take me seriously! Treat me like an adult, not a child!" is the cry of every teenager. God honors that request. He makes me a partner for his work in and through me. He grants me freedom in full knowledge that I will abuse it. He abdicates power to such an extent that he pleads with me not to "grieve" or "quench" his Spirit. God does all this because he wants a mature lover as a partner, not a puppy-love adolescent.

I have already mentioned the analogy of marriage, the most "adult" relationship that most people ever have. (Deep friendships show these same qualities as well.) In marriage two partners can achieve a unity while preserving their freedom and independence. Something new takes shape, a shared identity in which husband and wife both participate. When my wife and I plan a trip, she makes some of the arrangements and I make others; we rarely haggle over who does what because we know that our efforts go toward something that benefits us both.

Even so, as every couple learns, combining two genders in a marriage introduces differences that may take a lifetime to work out. Joining a human being with God involves a whole new category of "incompatibilities." One partner is invisible, overwhelming, and perfect; the other is visible, weak, and flawed. How can the two possibly get along?

In some ways, the Holy Spirit acts as a kind of resident "marriage counselor" between myself and God. The analogy may seem far-fetched, but remember the New Testament's words to describe the Spirit: Comforter, Counselor, Helper. The Spirit comforts in moments of distress, calms me in times of confusion, and overcomes my fears. Consistently, the Bible presents the Spirit as the invisible inner force, the Go-Between God who assists us in relating to the transcendent Father.

Like every starry-eyed newlywed, Janet and I both learned that the wedding ceremony was just the beginning of the process of making love work. Our marriage has hardly been a place of serenity, void of negative emotions. To the contrary, we are more likely to express feelings of anger and disappointment to each other than to anyone else, even when "outside" forces prompt those feelings. A healthy marriage is not a problem-free place, but it can be a safe place. We know that we will still love each other the next day and the next, and that despite the strain, our love may well soothe the hurt that caused those feelings in the first place.

When I read the Psalms and Job and Jeremiah, I sense something of the same pattern at work. Notice the angry outbursts, the complaints, the wild accusations against God contained in those books. God offers a "safe place" to express ourselves, even the worst parts of ourselves. I heard little of that blunt honesty in church growing up, which I now see as a spiritual defect, not a strength. Christians, I have noticed, are not immune from the kinds of circumstances that provoked the outbursts in Job and Psalms. Why attempt to hide deep emotions from a God who dwells within, a Spirit who has promised to express on our behalf "groans" for which words fail us?

I will never be able to reduce life with God to a formula for the same reason I cannot reduce my marriage to a formula. It is a living, growing relationship with another free being, very different from me and yet sharing much in common. No relationship has proved more challenging than marriage. I am tempted sometimes to wish for an "old-fashioned" marriage, in which roles and expectations are more clearly spelled out and need not always be negotiated. I sometimes yearn for an intervention from outside which would decisively change one of the characteristics that bring my wife and me pain. So far, that has not happened. We wake up each day and continue the journey on ground that grows incrementally more solid with each step.

Love works that way, with partners visible or invisible.

> Those who say that they believe in God and yet neither love nor fear him, do not in fact believe in him but in those who have taught them that God exists. Those who believe that they believe in God, but without any passion in their heart, any anguish of mind, without uncertainty, without doubt, without an element of despair even in their consolation, believe only in the God-idea, not in God.
>
> MIGUEL DE UNAMUNO

PASSION AND THE DESERT

For the God who fills human hunger is at the same time the Unknown, the Stranger. Only his absence-presence allows a person to be oneself.

JEAN SULIVAN

I AM SEEKING TO give an honest accounting, to tell the truth about the Christian life and not oversell it. For this reason I must pause, step back from the grand prospect of God living within us and consider another vista. The devil Screwtape, in C. S. Lewis's mischievous fantasy, advised the demon Wormwood to get his subject to "flit to and fro between an expression like 'the body of Christ' and the actual faces in the next pew." When we inspect those faces, including our own, the sparkling images of the New Testament can lose their luster.

Consider the experience of one man whom many revere as a spiritual leader:

So what about my life of prayer? Do I like to pray? Do I want to pray? Do I spend time praying? Frankly, the answer is no to all three questions. After sixty-three years of life and thirty-eight years of priesthood, my prayer seems as dead as a rock. . . . I have paid much attention to prayer, reading about it, writing about it, visiting monasteries and houses of prayer, and guiding many people on their spiritual journeys. By now I should be full of spiritual fire, consumed by prayer. Many people think I am and speak to me as if prayer is my greatest gift and deepest desire.

The truth is that I do not feel much, if anything, when I pray. There are no warm emotions, bodily sensations, or mental visions. None of my five senses is being touched—no special smells, no special sounds, no special sights, no special tastes, and no special movements. Whereas for a long time the Spirit acted so clearly through my flesh, now I feel nothing. I have lived with the expectation that prayer would become easier as I grow older and closer to death. But the opposite seems to be happening. The words *darkness* and *dryness* seem to best describe my prayer today. . . .

Are the darkness and dryness of my prayer signs of God's absence, or are they signs of a presence deeper and wider than my senses can contain? Is the death of my prayer the end of my intimacy with God or the beginning of a new communion, beyond words, emotions, and bodily sensations?

Henri Nouwen wrote those words during the final year of his life. Due to Nouwen's untimely death, we have no answer to his final question, which in retrospect seems eerily prophetic. Because I knew Nouwen and have some idea how much time and energy he devoted to prayer—more than anyone I know—I cannot blithely dismiss this passage as a temporary aberration or a phase he would work through. It describes the frank reality of his spiritual experience. I suspect the popularity of this Catholic priest's writings among evangelical Protestants stems from the searing honesty of such passages. "Just when people were thanking me for bringing them closer to God, I felt that God had abandoned me," he wrote. "It was as if the house I had finally found had no floors."

Nouwen would have taken dark encouragement from the renowned mystic Thomas à Kempis, author of *The Imitation of Christ*, who lamented, "And I, unhappy one and poorest of men, how shall I bring you into my house, I who scarce know how to spend a half-hour devoutly? And would that I spent once, even one half-hour worthily!"

Nouwen might also have taken encouragement from the conclusions of Thomas Green, a specialist in prayer and the spiritual director of a seminary in the Philippines. Dryness, says Green, is the normal outcome of a life of prayer. Drawing a parallel with human love, Green charts out three stages in a healthy prayer life. In the courtship period, we get to know God; in the honeymoon period we move from knowing to loving; in the long years of day-by-day married life, we move from loving to truly loving. As any married person can tell you, the final stage of mature love involves more tedium than romance, and the same applies to a relationship with God. Thus a season of dryness in prayer may signify growth, not failure, says Green.

Raised in the upbeat evangelical tradition, I found such ideas mildly heretical at first. Perhaps dryness and darkness afflict mainly Roman Catholics, I mused. Since monks and nuns pray all day, no wonder they find it tedious. Yet I discovered a similar pattern in the Bible itself, especially the Old Testament. Many of the Psalms recount times of dryness and darkness, and Jesus quoted from some of the bleakest. Paul and other letter-writers of the New Testament may describe the Christian life in glowing terms, but reading between the lines you realize that few of their readers were experiencing anything like the victory toward which they were being exhorted.

Thérèse of Liseux, another Catholic saint, admitted that "prayer arises, if at all, from incompetence, otherwise there is no need for it." I now see that it is our neediness, our sense of incompleteness, that drives us to God. Grace comes as a gift, received only by those with open hands, and often failure is what causes us to open our hands.

When we receive God's grace and spiritual life begins, tension increases as well. A perfect saint would experience no tension, nor would a sinner untroubled by guilt. The rest of us must live somewhere between the two extremes, which complicates rather than simplifies life.

"Nothing is happier than the Christian," Saint Jerome wrote, "for to him is promised the kingdom of heaven: nothing is more toil-worn, for every day he goes in danger of his life. Nothing is stronger than he, for he triumphs over the devil: nothing is weaker, for he is conquered by the flesh. . . . The path you tread is slippery, and the glory of success is less than the disgrace of failure."

Asked whether he was filled with the Spirit, Dwight L. Moody replied, "Yes. But I leak."

———— ❧ ————

SO WHICH IS IT, fullness or dryness, light or darkness, victory or failure? If pressed to answer, I would suggest, "Both." Chart out a course that guarantees a successful prayer life, the active presence of God, and constant victory over temptation, and you will probably run aground. A relationship with an invisible God will always include uncertainty and variability.

I prefer to dodge the question, however, because I believe it is the wrong question. As I look back over the giants of faith, all had one thing in common: neither victory nor success, but *passion*. An emphasis on spiritual technique may well lead us away from the passionate relationship that God values above all. More than a doctrinal system, more than a mystical experience, the Bible emphasizes a relationship with a Person, and personal relationships are never steady-state.

I cringe at the homespun preachers I hear on radio and television, and wonder at their appeal, especially among the poor. Perhaps they appeal because they present a God whom someone can know and love. Jesus said we must enter the kingdom as little children. Children do not understand relationship; they simply live it.

"I used to think that the ideas of a God who fumed with rage, who was jealous, who burned with love and could be disillusioned were childish, human, alas, all too human," writes theologian Jürgen Moltmann. "The abstract god of the philosophers, purified of all human images, seemed to me nearer to the truth. But the more I experienced how much abstraction destroyed life, the more I understood the Old Testament passion of God and the pain which tore the heart of this God."

God's favorites responded with passion in kind. Moses argued with God so fervently that several times he persuaded God to change his mind. Jacob wrestled all night long and used trickery to grab hold of God's blessing. Job lashed out in sarcastic rage against God. David broke at least half the Ten Commandments. Yet never did they wholly give up on God, and never did God give up on them. God can handle anger, blame, and even willful disobedience. One thing, however, blocks relationship: indifference. "They turned their backs to me and not their faces," God told Jeremiah, in a damning indictment of Israel.

Adult Children of Alcoholics, an organization that works with families afflicted by alcoholism, identifies three coping mechanisms children learn in order to survive such a dysfunctional setting: Don't Talk, Don't Trust, and Don't Feel. Later, as adults, these same survivors find themselves incapable of sustaining an intimate relationship and must unlearn the pattern of indifference. Christian counselors tell me that wounded Christians may relate to God in the same way. Reacting against a strict upbringing or feeling betrayed by God, they squelch all passion and fall back on a more formal, less personal faith.

In contrast, a healthy relationship sustains passion through sad or happy times, through victory or failure, and even through physical separation. Absence provokes as much passion as presence. When a soldier leaves home on active duty or a teenager graduates from high school and heads for college, emotions do not fade away; they may intensify. Estrangement arouses passion too, as any divorcing family can testify.

From the spiritual giants of the Bible, I learn this crucial lesson about relating to an invisible God: Whatever you do, don't ignore God. Invite God into every aspect of life. For some Christians, the times of Job-like crisis will represent the greatest danger. How can they cling to faith in a God who appears unconcerned and even hostile? Others, and I count myself among them, face a more subtle danger. An accumulation of distractions—a malfunctioning computer, bills to pay, an upcoming trip, a friend's wedding, the general busyness of life—gradually edges God away from the center of my life. Some days I meet people, eat, work, make decisions, all without giving God a single thought. And that void is far more serious than what Job experienced, for not once did Job stop thinking about God.

IN A BIBLE STUDY I attended, a friend made this remark about King David's life: "If Saul proves that 'To obey is better than sacrifice,' then David proves that relationship is even better than obedience." Though some may quarrel with that wording, David's story does at least show that a relationship with God can survive the most appalling acts of disobedience. I keep thumbing back to the story of David because I know no better model for a passionate relationship with God than the king named David. His very name meant, appropriately, "beloved."

An unavoidable question dangles over the account of David's life. How could anyone so obviously flawed—he did, after all, commit adultery and murder—get the reputation as "a man after God's own heart"? We have much to draw from in answering that question, for the pages devoted to David give the fullest treatment of any person in the Bible, including Jesus. Apparently God felt this remarkable man has a lot to teach us.

As I review David's story in search of his spiritual secret, two scenes stand out. The first suggests an answer to that unavoidable question. In one of his first official acts as king, David sent for the sacred ark to install as a symbol of God's presence in Jerusalem, the new capital city he was building. When the ark finally arrived, to the accompaniment of a brass band and the shouts of a huge crowd, King David totally lost control. Bursting with joy, he cartwheeled in the streets—like an Olympic gymnast who has just won the gold medal and is out strutting his stuff. The sight of a king doing somersaults in a scanty robe scandalized his wife until David set her straight. "I will become even more undignified than this," he told her. "I will celebrate before the Lord." David cared not a fig about his royal reputation as long as that one-Person audience could sense his jubilation.

A man of passion, David felt more passionately about God than about anything else in the world, and during his reign that message trickled down to the entire nation. As Frederick Buechner writes,

> He had feet of clay like the rest of us if not more so—self-serving and deceitful, lustful and vain—but on the basis of that dance alone, you can see why it was David more than anybody else that Israel lost her heart to and why, when Jesus of Nazareth came riding into Jerusalem on his flea-bitten mule a thousand years later, it was as the Son of David that they hailed him.

The second scene occurred years later, at the peak of David's powers, and more than any other it shows the king's greatness. David had just acted out one of the world's oldest plot lines: man sees woman, man sleeps with woman, woman gets pregnant. Nothing unusual there. Substitute a politician, actor, millionaire—or evangelist—for the king, and a beauty queen for Bathsheba, and you can read the same story in any modern scandal sheet. What else is new?

The episode with Bathsheba reveals a Machiavellian side to David. When his plan to cover up the adultery failed, he turned to a ruthless scheme involving the husband's murder and needless slaughter on a battlefield. A classic case of "one crime leads to another" ensued as David, the nation's spiritual leader, broke the sixth, seventh, ninth, and tenth commandments in quick succession. When Bathsheba moved into the palace and married David, it appeared he had gotten away with the crime. No one raised a word of protest—except the prophet Nathan.

I love the scene told in 2 Samuel 12 because of what it demonstrates about the power of story. Nathan began with a tale of callous greed—a rich man with many sheep who stole his poor neighbor's single pet lamb—and after two paragraphs had David wrapped around his narrative finger. Then Nathan risked his life by making a direct application to the sin-drenched king. What happened next brought to light David's true greatness. David could have had Nathan killed. Or he could have laughed and thrown him out of the palace. He could have issued a string of denials—what evidence could Nathan produce? Would servants testify against their king?

Anyone who has lived through the sordid affairs of Watergate and Monica-gate has a sense for what David *could* have done. The Republican Richard Nixon lied and authorized hush money to cover up his crimes; a tape-recording, not a confession, brought him down. The Democrat Bill Clinton solemnly looked into a camera and deceived an entire nation; a stained dress, not a confession, led to his impeachment. Nixon could barely force himself to mutter, "Mistakes were made"; Clinton admitted only what had been proven and broadcast to the world.

The contrast of David's first words could not be greater: "I have sinned against the Lord." Not the cuckolded husband Uriah, not the mistress Bathsheba, not the spin-doctor Joab came to mind—God did. As he had danced before a one-Person audience, so David had sinned before the same audience.

A reflective poem he wrote, Psalm 51, may stand as the most impressive outcome of David's sordid affair. It is one thing for a king to confess a moral lapse in private to a prophet and quite another for him to compose a detailed account of that confession to be sung throughout the land

and ultimately around the world. This psalm exposes the true nature of sin as a broken relationship with God. "Against you, you only, have I sinned," David cried out. He saw that God wanted "a broken spirit, a broken and contrite heart"—qualities which David had in abundance.

Looking back on their greatest king, Israel remembered David more for his devotion to God than for his illustrious achievements. Lusty, vengeful King David had fully earned the reputation of "a man after God's own heart." He loved God with all his heart, and what more could be said?

David's secret? The two scenes, one a buoyant high and the other a devastating low, hint at an answer. Whether cartwheeling behind the ark or lying prostrate on the ground for six straight nights in contrition, David's strongest instinct was to relate his life to God. In comparison, nothing else mattered at all. As his poetry makes clear, he led a God-saturated life. "O God, you are my God, earnestly I seek you," he wrote once in a desiccated desert. "My soul thirsts for you, my body longs for you, in a dry and weary land where there is no water. . . . Because your love is better than life, my lips will glorify you."

Apparently, the relationship got to God as well. Years later, when the Assyrian army was about to overwhelm Jerusalem, God worked a miracle of rescue, "for my sake and for the sake of David my servant!" He told the Jews his love for them would never end: "I will make an everlasting covenant with you, my faithful love promised to David."

As I RECONSIDER MY own assumptions about relating to God, I now see them as misguided and simplistic. From childhood I inherited an image of God as a stern teacher passing out grades. I had the same goal as everyone else: to get a perfect score and earn the teacher's approval. Cut up in class and you'll be sent to the back of the room to stand in the corner or to a vacant room down the hall.

Almost everything about that analogy, I have learned, contradicts the Bible and distorts the relationship. In the first place, God's approval depends not on my "good conduct" but on God's grace. I could never earn grades high enough to pass a teacher's perfect standards—and, thankfully, I do not have to.

In addition, a relationship with God does not switch on or off depending on my behavior. God does not send me to a vacant room down the hall when I disobey him. Quite the opposite. The times when I feel most estranged from God can bring on a sense of desperation, which presents a new starting point for grace. Sulking in a cave in flight from God, Elijah heard a gentle whisper that brought comfort, not a scolding. Jonah tried his best to run from God and failed. And it was at Peter's lowest point that Jesus lovingly restored him.

I tend to project onto God my understanding of how human relationships work, including the assumption that betrayal permanently destroys relationship. God, however, seems undeterred by betrayal (or perhaps has grown used to it): "Upon this *rock*," Jesus said to Peter, "I will build my church." As Luther remarked, we are always at the same time sinners, righteous, and penitent. The halting, stuttered expressions of love we offer may not measure up to what God wants, but like any parent he accepts what the children offer.

I visited two friends who work in inner-city ministry and asked each of them the same question. "Typically, church folks tell us that when we sin, or 'backslide,' we disrupt our relationship with God. You work with people who live with failure every day. Have you found that 'backsliding' draws them further from God or presses them toward God?"

Bud, who works among drug addicts, had an immediate answer. "Without question, it pushes them toward God. I could tell you story after story of addicts who give in to their addiction, knowing what a terrible thing they are doing to themselves and their families. Watching them, I understand the power of evil in this world, evil they want above all else to resist but cannot. Yet those moments of weakness are the very moments when they are most likely to turn to God, to cry out in desperation. They have failed, terribly. Now what? Can they get up and walk again, or will they stay paralyzed? Through the grace of God, some of them do get up. In fact, I've decided there is one key in determining whether individual drug addicts can be cured: if they deeply believe they are a *forgivable* child of God. Not a failure-free child of God, a forgivable one."

David, who directs a hospice for AIDS patients, agreed. "I have met no more spiritual people than the men in this house who face death and know that in some ways they brought the disease on themselves. Most got the HIV virus through drug use and sexual promiscuity. Their lives are defined by failure. I cannot explain it, but these men have a spirituality, a connection with God, that I've seen nowhere else."

Francis de Sales wrote, "Now the greater our knowledge of our own misery, the more profound will be our confidence in the goodness and mercy of God, for mercy and misery are so closely connected that the one cannot be exercised without the other." De Sales decried those who stumbled and then wallowed in their wretchedness: "How miserable I am! I am fit for nothing!" True followers of God quietly humble themselves and rise again courageously.

I once heard a memorable sermon on Ananias and Sapphira, a frightening story from Acts 5 that most preachers studiously avoid. It's about a married couple who, after lying about their gift to the church, fall down dead. The passage makes clear, said John Claypool, that the pair did only one thing wrong to bring on their fatal punishment. Withholding some of the money was not the problem—Peter assured them they had that right. The couple went wrong by misrepresenting themselves spiritually. God can forgive any sin and can deal with any spiritual condition. We fall down, we get up, a pattern the Bible amply illustrated, as with David and Peter. God does require honesty, though. We dare not misrepresent ourselves to God, for by doing so, we close our hands to grace.

In my childhood I would have pointed to traveling evangelists, conference speakers, and devotional authors as those closest to God. Alas, I have gotten to know some of these "professionals," including myself. Now I would point to some of my friends who struggle sexually or battle alcoholism. This year, in fact, the person who has helped lead me to new levels in a relationship with God is a defrocked priest who battles an addiction both to alcohol and cigarettes. The terrifying struggle drives him to God daily, for he does not have the luxury of waking up and thinking himself righteous. "I'm just one sinner talking to another," he says when he meets with me. He has long since abandoned any false perfectionism that might lure him from grace.

Not everyone turns to God in a time of need, of course. Yet whenever I sense a *thirst*, a restlessness, I have hope for new life, the Creator's specialty. As long as we do not become inured to the pain around us and in us, and indifferent to the world's fallenness, as long as we do not feel too at home here, we allow space for God to enter.

Henri Nouwen wrote of a constant struggle to distinguish between the voice of his wounded self, which never went away, and the voice of God. His readers and listeners kept looking to him for the authoritative voice of God; meanwhile he looked within and found a badly wounded self. Gradually he came to see that the voice of God *only* speaks through wounded selves. He kept attending to God, out of need, regardless of apparent results:

> [It is] not a time in which I experience a special closeness to God; it is not a period of serious attentiveness to the divine mysteries. I wish it were! On the contrary, it is full of distractions, inner restlessness, sleepiness, confusion, and boredom. It seldom, if ever, pleases my senses. But the simple fact of being for one hour in the presence of the Lord and of showing him all that I feel, think, sense, and experience, without trying to hide anything, must please him. Somehow, somewhere, I know that he loves me, even though I do not feel that love as I can feel a human embrace, even though I do not hear a voice as I hear human words of consolation, even though I do not see a smile, as I can see in a human face. Still God speaks to me, looks at me, and embraces me there, where I am still unable to notice it.

God chooses jars of clay for his dwelling place. In this book you may hear thin strains of the voice of God—that is my deepest wish and my lifelong search. Like Nouwen, though, I mainly hear the voice of a wounded self trying to articulate the voice of God. I live in daily awareness of how much easier it is to edit a book than edit a life.

M y Lord God, I have no idea where I am going. I do not see the road ahead of me. I cannot know for certain where it will end. Nor do I really know myself, and the fact that I think I am following your will does not mean that I am actually doing so. But I believe that the desire to please you does in fact please you.

THOMAS MERTON

SPIRITUAL AMNESIA

*The burning of a little straw may hide the stars, but the
stars outlast the smoke.*

VOLTAIRE

O N A VISIT TO Yellowstone National Park, it jarred me to see posted
beside Old Faithful a large digital clock counting down to the next
eruption. Old Faithful's eruption should be a natural, not a staged phenomenon, I reasoned, though I did have to admit that the clock helped
build a crescendo of anticipation. Rings of Japanese and German tourists
surrounded the spot, their video cameras trained like weapons on the
famous hole in the ground as the steamy, sulfurous moment drew near.
The minutes ticked down, 10, 9, 8, 7, and I could not help thinking of
rocket launches at Cape Canaveral, which artificially reproduce the geyser's
clouds and noise.

After watching one eruption up close, my wife and I passed the second countdown in the dining room of Old Faithful Inn overlooking
the geyser. When the digital clock reached one minute, we along with

every other diner left our seats and rushed to the windows to observe the big wet event.

Immediately, as if on signal, a crew of busboys and waiters descended on the tables to refill water glasses and clear away dirty dishes. When the geyser shot up, we tourists oohed and aahed and clicked our cameras; a few spontaneously applauded. But glancing back over my shoulder I saw that not a single waiter or busboy—not even those who had finished their chores—looked out the huge windows. Old Faithful, grown entirely too familiar, had lost its power to impress them.

Religious faith can work the same way. Jews in nineteenth-century France had a saying to describe the decline of spiritual ardor over the generations: "The grandfather prays in Hebrew, the father reads the prayers in French, the son does not pray at all." A similar pattern may also play out within an individual. Spiritual passion erupts like a geyser in the early days following conversion, then settles into a lukewarm pool, and finally may evaporate of neglect or disillusionment.

The poem "Pascal" by W. H. Auden describes the great mathematician's spiritual geyser. An intense spiritual search had, says Auden, "doubt by doubt / Restored the ruined chateau of his faith; / Until at last, one Autumn, all was ready: / And in the night the Unexpected came." Auden refers to Pascal's mystical revelation that he could not express in words, an encounter that came to light only after his death when his family found the word "Fire!" and a few cryptic notes sewed on a scrap of paper in his coat. Auden adds these disquieting lines: "Then it was over. By the morning he was cool / His faculties for sin restored completely."

<hr>

THE CHRISTIAN LIFE DOES include times of close encounter with God, but in my experience these are not a norm we can count on. Evangelicals, whose very label carries the promise "good news," make fine marketers—much better, say, than Jesus in his warnings to the disciples or John in his dire diagnosis of the seven churches in Revelation. We sing hymns that celebrate, "O, the pure delight of a single hour, that before Thy throne I spend," and honor saints of Olympian mysticism.

Evangelicals pass down stories of spiritual ancestors like the Baptist pastor Charles Spurgeon, who claimed that he never passed a single quarter of an hour in his waking moments without a distinct consciousness of the presence of the Lord. The British activist George Müller set as his primary goal each morning to "have my soul happy in the Lord." After one of her husband's revivals, Jonathan Edwards's wife swooned for seventeen days, caught up in the presence of God, almost unconscious of her surroundings.

I do not doubt any of these giants of the faith; I merely suggest that comments like these indicate why they gained their reputations as giants of the faith. To hold them up as the norm for Christians to emulate may diminish the rest of us to a point of despair, not unlike the sun extinguishing a firefly. Charles Spurgeon felt the presence of God every fifteen minutes; to my shame I can easily go through a day without even thinking about God.

C. S. Lewis compared two experiences: walking along a beach with occasional glimpses of the ocean and a voyage across the Atlantic. Mystical experiences of God, he said, are real but fragmentary, like a walk on the beach. To cross the Atlantic requires a new set of skills and discipline and, perhaps most important, a map based on the experience of other sailors. I have felt, oh yes I have felt, times of wholeness, guilt-free peace, sweet communion, holy bliss. They are so rare, however, that I could probably record them all in one paragraph. I have learned not to strive to reproduce them, rather to put myself in a place where they can visit me, "grace" me. I remember the homey cottages of England; I remember the wild promise of a New Land in America; but mainly I pull myself on deck every day to face the flat blue expanse of the Atlantic Ocean.

I assumed that spiritual maturity would progress like physical maturation. A baby learns to crawl, then toddle like a drunk, and then run. Should not our walk with God progress the same way, so that we gradually strengthen, gain control of our early lurching motions, and then stride toward sainthood? Listen, though, to the sequence in a familiar passage from Isaiah:

> Those who hope in the Lord
>   will renew their strength.
> They will soar on wings like eagles;
>   they will run and not grow weary,
> they will walk and not be faint.

John Claypool, reflecting on that passage, notes that the order reverses what we might expect. As if to overturn our preconceptions, Isaiah begins with soaring and ends with walking. All Christians pass through various stages. At times—for many it comes early in the journey—we soar in a state of spiritual ecstasy; at times we run, expressing our faith with the boundless energy of activism; at times we can barely take a step without fainting.

Claypool made this observation, in fact, while sitting at the hospital bedside of his ten-year-old daughter. A prominent minister of national renown, he had certainly known the sensation of soaring. And for eighteen months he had run, frenetically seeking every prayer or healing technique that might bring his daughter relief from leukemia. Now, though, as her life slipped away, he could do nothing but sit by her side, hold her hand, soothe her lips with moisture, and weep. It took every ounce of spiritual energy to keep from fainting.

> Now I am sure that to those looking for the spectacular this may sound insignificant indeed. Who wants to be slowed to a walk, to creep along inch by inch, just barely above the threshold of consciousness and not fainting? That may not sound like much of a religious experience, but believe me, in the kind of darkness where I have been, it is the only form of the promise that fits the situation. When there is no occasion to soar and no place to run, and all you can do is trudge along step by step, to hear of a Help that will enable you "to walk and not faint" is good news indeed.

I HAVE MENTIONED THAT distractions can push God away from the center of my life—in truth, they push God out of my field of consciousness altogether. I work alone, as every writer must, so I cannot blame my God-forgetfulness on other people. Even more embarrassing to admit, I make my living writing books about God! I read devotional or theological books, check items off my to-do list, write a chapter or an article, and collect any thoughts that might someday make their way into my writing. It amazes me how I can sail through this daily routine without giving God much thought or putting into practice what I write.

I could write a beautiful paragraph about inner peace and serenity, but if some software error causes me to lose that paragraph, any inner peace and serenity will vanish faster than the electrons on my computer monitor. As John Donne confessed in a pre-technological era, "I neglect God for the noise of a fly, the rattling of a coach, the creaking of a door."

How can this be? How can the worshipful practice of pausing before a meal in gratitude devolve into "ThankyouforthisfoodAmen—Please pass the butter"? If my car breaks down, my mind fixates on that problem, pushing any thoughts of God to the margins. I "make time" for God most days, yes, but often as one of the items on my to-do list and often abbreviated if deadlines press in. When I am wrenched from my normal routine on a trip somewhere, it will suddenly occur to me that except for a cursory prayer before meals I have not thought about God all day. Forget the essence of the universe and the central focus of my life? Yes, I do.

"God certainly does not dominate my life," confesses Romano Guardini, a devout German theologian. "Any tree in my path seems to have more power than he, if only because it forces me to walk around it!" Guardini goes on to wonder:

> How is it that God permeates the universe, that everything that is comes from his hand, that every thought and emotion we have has significance only in him, yet we are neither shaken nor inflamed by the reality of his presence, but able to live as though he did not exist? How is this truly satanic deceit possible?

I marvel at a God who puts himself at our mercy, as it were, allowing himself to be quenched and grieved, and even forgotten. Reading the Old Testament convinces me that this human tendency—indifference taken to a lethal extreme—bothers God more than any other. Gracious to doubters and a pursuer of willful unbelievers, God finds himself stymied, and even enraged, by those who simply put him out of mind. God reacts like any spurned lover who finds his phone calls unreturned and his Valentines tossed aside unopened.

"Only be careful, and watch yourselves closely so that you do not forget . . . ," Moses warned the Israelites as he introduced some visual reminders of the covenant. A short time later, though, he faced up to the reality: "Your heart will become proud and you will forget the Lord your

God, who brought you out of Egypt, out of the land of slavery." The Israelites' forgetfulness developed just as Moses predicted, and here is God's doleful response:

> Does a maiden forget her jewelry,
>   a bride her wedding ornaments?
> Yet my people have forgotten me,
>   days without number.
> ... Does the snow of Lebanon
>   ever vanish from its rocky slopes?
> Do its cool waters from distant sources
>   ever cease to flow?
> Yet my people have forgotten me ...

In some of the most poignant words of the Bible, God concludes, "I am like a moth to Ephraim, like rot to the people of Judah." I imagine some of the people who first heard those words felt a twinge of remorse, maybe even a gaping wound of guilt. If they responded as I sometimes do, they addressed that guilt by avoiding God even more: by not praying, by shutting him out, by falling back on routine as a substitute for true relationship.

I know a woman who, raised by deaf parents, would simply close her eyes to shut off the relationship. It infuriated her parents, who had no way to communicate with her except by signing. As I think of that young girl, her eyelids sealed tight against the frantic hand motions of her parents, I get a picture of how God must feel when I shut him out.

———— ∞ ————

How can we avoid the amnesia of the Israelites? Over the years I have tried various ways to "remember" God. For me, the process divides into a daily habit of reorientation and conscious remembering.

Reorientation for me means beginning the day with a God-consciousness so that gradually the center of my thought moves from self to God. I used to jump out of bed as soon as I woke up. Now I lie there in the quiet and invite God into my day, not as a participant in my life or an item on a check list but as the hub of all that will happen that day. I want God to become the central reality, so that I am as aware of God as I am of my own moods and desires.

"What is concrete but immaterial can be kept in view only by painful effort," wrote C. S. Lewis. He continued,

> That is why the real problem of the Christian life comes where people do not usually look for it. It comes the very moment you wake up each morning. All your wishes and hopes for the day rush at you like wild animals. And the first job each morning consists in shoving them all back; in listening to that other voice, taking that other point of view, letting that other larger, stronger, quieter life come flowing in. And so on, all day. . . .
>
> We can do it only for moments at first. But from those moments the new sort of life will be spreading through our systems because now we are letting Him work at the right part of us.

The first great commandment requires us to love God, which we do best through awareness of his great love for us. Thomas Merton remarks, "The 'remembering' of God, of which we sing in the Psalms, is simply the rediscovery, in deep compunction of heart, that God remembers us." We remember God best by believing that we *matter*, personally and infinitely, to him. I must ask again and again for the faith to believe that God delights in me and desires to relate to me. For that reason as much as any, I study the Bible: not merely to master a work of great literature or to learn theology, but to let soak into my soul the inescapable message of God's love and personal concern.

Some find it helpful to kneel or to assume a different body posture. Always conscious of the barrier of invisibility, I seek ways to underscore God's reality. Often I drink coffee as I pray, for it seems somehow natural to converse with an invisible God in the same style in which I converse with my friends, who are visible. Or I take a walk. The surroundings give me much reason for praise: spring coaxing extravagant life from dead twigs or winter coating muddy roads with a glistening mantle of white. And as I pass neighbors' houses, theirs and others' needs come urgently to mind.

Throughout the day, I need aids for conscious remembering. For a while I tried setting my watch alarm to chime at the top of each hour.

I would stop what I was doing, reflect on the hour that had just passed, and strive to practice the presence of God during the next hour. Later I learned I had accidentally stumbled on an old technique of Benedictine monks, who would stop and say the hour prayer every time the clock chimed. With the help of such markers during the day, remembering God can gradually become something of a habit.*

Augustine's *Confessions* gives a fine model of how to involve God in the details of life. Both in style and content, the book came out of nowhere, with no literary precedent. Who would have thought of addressing a biography to God, of writing a long book in the form of a prayer? Augustine did exactly that, stitching together his confession of sins, his dalliance with heresies, his intellectual ramblings. His intentional review of life details and his personal soul-searching set a pattern for all Christians who seek a God-centered life.

I have also learned about conscious remembering from Brother Lawrence, a cook in a seventeenth-century monastery who wrote the devotional classic *The Practice of the Presence of God*. To Brother Lawrence the phrase "practicing the presence of God" meant something like the practice of medicine or law. To novices it more resembles practicing the piano: if I keep at it long enough, especially those scales and finger exercises, maybe I'll get it.

Brother Lawrence emphasizes our need for God's help and then asks bluntly, "But how can we ask him without being with him? And how can we be with him without often thinking of him? And how can we often think of him without forming a holy habit of doing so?" Brother Lawrence then suggests an answer:

> He does not ask much of us — an occasional remembrance, a small act of worship, now to beg his grace, at times to offer him our distresses, at another time to render thanks for the favors he has given, and which he gives in the midst of your labors, to

---

* In *A Serious Call to a Devout and Holy Life*, William Law sets out particular subjects of meditation for different hours in the day: 6:00 A.M., praise and thanksgiving; 9:00 A.M., humility; 12 noon, intercessions for others; 3:00 P.M., conforming to the will of God; 6:00 P.M., self-examination and confession of sins of the day; bedtime, Death. His regimen in relating to God seemed awfully strict when I read it, until I recalled that faithful Muslims pray five times per day, and many computer users check their e-mail at least that often.

find consolation with him as often as you can. At table and in the midst of conversation, lift your heart at times towards him. The smallest remembrance will always please him. It is not needful at such times to cry out loud. He is nearer to us than we think.

Brother Lawrence mentions practical ways to "offer God your heart from time to time in the course of the day," even in the midst of chores, "to savor him, though it be but in passing, and as it were by stealth." The depth of spirituality, said Lawrence, does not depend on changing things you do but rather in doing for God what you ordinarily do for yourself. Lawrence shied away from spiritual retreats because he found it as easy to worship God in his common tasks as in the desert.

Evidently, Lawrence practiced what he preached. In a eulogy his Abbé wrote that "The good Brother found God everywhere, as much while he was repairing shoes as while he was praying with the Community. . . . It was God, not the task, he had in view. He knew that, the more the task was against his natural inclinations, the greater was his love in offering it to God."

That last comment affected my wife deeply. She read the book while working with senior citizens in downtown Chicago, and sometimes her job called for tasks that would go against anyone's natural inclinations. As she cleaned up after an incontinent senior or scrubbed an apartment after a messy death, she would remind herself of Brother Lawrence's formula. With some effort, even cleaning a toilet can be presented as an offering to God.

A CHRISTIAN WHO LIVED in our own century strove throughout his life to put Brother Lawrence's principles into practice. Worldwide, Frank Laubach gained renown as the founder of the modern literacy movement, the person who has probably done more than anyone in history to teach people to read and write. His private journals, however, record a lifelong effort to make a different kind of mark: to live in constant awareness of God's presence.

Laubach began by trying to focus his mind upon God before rising out of bed, banishing other thoughts and distractions. "It is a will act.

I compel my mind to open straight out toward God. . . . I fix my attention there, and sometimes it requires a long time early in the morning to attain that mental state." He struggled at first, admitting,

> I am like an oarsman rowing against a current. My will-pressure must be gentle but constant, to listen to God, to pray for others incessantly, to look at people as souls and not as clothes, or bodies, or even minds. The moment the pressure on the oar ceases, I drift, and downward. . . . "Let go and let God" does not fit my experience. "Take hold and keep hold of God" is what it feels like to me. There is a will-act, and I can feel the spiritual muscles growing from rowing!

After a year he could report, "This simple practice requires only a gentle pressure of the will, not more than a person can exert easily. It grows easier as the habit becomes fixed. Yet it transforms life into heaven."

Later, Laubach proposed an experiment to himself: to bring God back into his mind-flow every few seconds, so that awareness of God would always exist in his consciousness as a kind of "after image." To achieve that goal, he played a "game with minutes," by "trying to line up my actions with the will of God about every fifteen minutes or every half hour. . . . I have started out trying to live all my waking moments in conscious listening to the inner voice, asking without ceasing, 'What, Father, do you desire said? What, Father, do you desire done this minute?'"

Laubach succeeded in bringing God to mind at least once each minute, and gradually increased the rate. Some of his journals estimate the actual percentages he experienced each day: "conscious of God 50 percent; willful refusal, a little." Sometimes he achieved 75 percent, occasionally 90 percent. He reported many failures as well, when distractions drove God out of mind altogether. Gradually, though, he found that the daily exercise transformed his spirit. Every time he met a person, he inwardly prayed for the other party. Answering the telephone, he would whisper to himself, "A child of God will now speak to me." Walking down a street or standing in line at a bus stop, he would pray silently for the people around him.

Laubach proves that one can combine a busy, modern life with mysticism; we need not seclude ourselves in a monastery or convent. He served as Dean of Education at a major university, helped found a seminary, worked among tribal people, served the poor, and traveled worldwide to promote his literacy techniques.

The morning after reading Laubach's book, I was scheduled to meet a friend for breakfast at 7:30. I sat and waited for ten, fifteen, twenty minutes, until finally I concluded he had forgotten. I know my normal response: irritation at being "stood up," frustration over the waste of time, anger at myself for not bringing something to read to fill the time. Instead, I remembered some of Laubach's discoveries. I prayed for my friend—perhaps he had car trouble or a family emergency? I prayed for the waitress, the staff around me, others in the restaurant. I asked God to calm my spirit and to help me enjoy a rare hour of nothingness at the beginning of my day. Even though my friend never showed up, I left the restaurant in a better frame of mind than when I had arrived, with a small dose of the power Laubach had learned to tap into consistently.

It does not do justice to Brother Lawrence or Frank Laubach to report snatches of a lifelong process. If their spiritual exercises seem like hard work performed under a sense of obligation, read their full accounts. For them, the discipline led to delight and joy. They simply recognized that the oddity of a personal relationship between an infinite, invisible being and a finite, visible one, requires certain adjustments.

As Laubach reports, the reward fully compensates the effort: "After months and years of practicing the presence of God, one feels that God is closer; His push from behind seems to be stronger and steadier, and the pull from in front seems to grow stronger.... God is so close then that He not only lives all around us, but all *through* us."

I now hear the phrase "practicing the presence of God" in a different way. Previously I sought an emotional confirmation that God is actually there. Sometimes I have that sense, sometimes I do not. I have changed the emphasis, though, to one of putting myself in God's presence. I assume God is present all around me, though undetectable by my senses, and strive to conduct my daily life in a way appropriate to God's presence. Can I refer back to God whatever happens today, as a kind of offering?

At a conference on evangelism sponsored by Billy Graham in Manila, a Cambodian man mesmerized the audience with his story of daily meditation. Under the Pol Pot regime he was held in a concentration camp like those depicted in the movie *The Killing Fields*. Believing he had little time to live, he wanted to spend time each day with God, preparing for death. "Even more than deprivation of food, even more than the torture, I resented having no time to meet with God. Always guards were yelling at us, forcing us to work, work, work." Finally he noticed that the guards could get no one to clean out the cesspits. He volunteered for the wretched job. "No one ever interrupted me, and I could do my work at a leisurely pace. Even in those stinking depths, I could look up and see blue sky. I could praise God that I survived another day. I could commune with God undisturbed, and pray for my friends and relatives all around me. That became for me a glorious time of meeting with God."

> The soul must long for God in order to be set aflame by God's love; but if the soul cannot yet feel this longing, then it must long for the longing. To long for the longing is also from God.
>
> MEISTER ECKHART

PART FIVE

Growth

Stages Along the Way

CHILD

We would rather be ruined than changed.

W. H. AUDEN

I HAVE KNOWN GOD's presence and God's absence, fullness and emptiness, spiritual intimacy and a dark void. The sequence as well as the
variety of these steps in my pilgrimage took me by surprise, and as I
looked around for a road map that might offer clues on what to expect,
I found much confusion.

Some groups of Christians equate spiritual maturity and asceticism:
whoever keeps the strictest rules gains intimacy with God. This cannot
be correct, I know, because Jesus himself had a loose reputation compared to John the Baptist or the Pharisees.

Other Christians devalue the search for intimacy with God. I have
friends serving on the front lines of justice issues who scorn spiritual disciplines as "too mystical." Although I admire their commitment and agree
with some of their causes, I cannot simply ignore the many biblical passages

on union with God and on the need for holiness. What then does a mature Christian look like? And how does my behavior affect a relationship with God?

With these issues in mind I slowly read the entire New Testament, marking on a yellow legal pad every passage that encouraged believers to grow spiritually. I tried to peer beneath the straightforward commands—Steal no more; Stop gossiping; Serve the poor—to the underlying motive. To what were Jesus, Paul, and the others appealing? I filled many pages of my legal pad with notes, which I then scoured in search of trends.

The New Testament presents life with God as a journey, with followers found at many different places along the way. For the sake of convenience I settled on three rough groupings—Child, Adult, and Parent—marking in the margins which level of development the author seemed to be addressing. These three categories summarized for me three overall stages in the spiritual life. First, I looked at all the passages directed to Christians who were just beginning their pilgrimage or who seemed stuck in the Child stage.

Anyone who has tried to rear a child knows that an appeal to high motives may not work so well. I know a couple who attempted to "self-actualize" their son by letting him make every decision. They would explain the potential consequences of his behavior and then let the little boy make the final choice. I witnessed one of these scenes on a wintry Chicago day, with the temperature below freezing and a foot of snow covering the ground. Drew, then four years old, thought it would be fun to go outdoors and play, wearing only his shorts and a T-shirt. The parents explained that the body has a lower resistance to infection in the cold and that prolonged exposure can lead to bad things like frostbite and hypothermia. Drew stamped his foot and declared, "But I want to go out *now*!" No appeal to higher motives worked, and eventually his parents let him outdoors, hoping the elements would soon drive him back inside.

A very different kind of scene transpired in the summer along the shoreline of Lake Michigan. There a child sat at the edge of a concrete breaker, his feet dangling, and stared at the cool, surging water below. "No, No, No!" he said, obviously repeating to himself the instructions his parents had drilled into him. He may not have been able to explain why the delights of Lake Michigan were forbidden him, but he did understand the rules. No doubt his parents had appealed to some lower motives, such as the threat of punishment.

When I went through the New Testament, a surprising number of passages earned a "Child" in the margin for their approach. Jesus himself did not hesitate to threaten dire punishment for the disobedient and promise rewards to the obedient. Some behavior is so harmful that we simply must avoid it. A counselor would never advise a proven alcoholic to cut back a bit on his drinking or only get drunk in the evenings. A judge would not tell a habitual thief, "Try to reign it in—how about if you only broke into houses on weekends?" The only appropriate message is the kind Paul gives: "Whoever is stealing, stop it!"

The apostle Paul's lectures on morality usually come with a large dose of exasperation. "Don't you know . . . Don't you realize?" he sputters, upset that people called by God to be saints are instead squabbling over whether to eat meat or get circumcised. He gives pep talks, much like a father who urges his child to eat green vegetables "for your own good."

New Testament writers cannot comprehend why some believers lag in perpetual adolescence when they should be acting like adults. Although they may prefer appealing to "higher" motives, these authors go ahead and spell out the scary consequences of wrong behavior, for they know that a wise choice out of immature motives beats a poor choice. If teenagers abstain from promiscuous sex and cigarette smoking for no other reason than fear of disease, their souls may not benefit but their bodies certainly will.

So FAR I HAVE avoided writing about a most difficult period of my life, a time of serious physical complications when I could not talk or walk. I lay in bed all day, barely able to move my arms and legs. My eyes did not focus. I could not feed myself and was incontinent. I had little comprehension of what was going on around me. Resigned to my state, I could not imagine any improvement.

I outgrew that condition and now look back on it as a necessary transition time: human infancy. No one reaches adulthood without undergoing such a period of immaturity. Equally, no healthy person wants to remain there. I know nothing sadder in life than a rupture in the maturing process:

a caterpillar that never becomes a butterfly, a tadpole that does not meta-morphose, a brain-damaged baby who lies in a crib for thirty years.*

A newborn baby has all the body parts it will ever need, yet it must grow up in order to use them as intended. The same principle applies spiritually in the life of faith. "I could not address you as spiritual but as worldly—mere infants in Christ," Paul scolded the Corinthians. "I gave you milk, not solid food, for you were not yet ready for it." Like many young believers, the Corinthians balked at moving past childhood immaturity to a more advanced stage.

On the other hand, Jesus plainly stated that, "unless you change and become like little children, you will never enter the kingdom of heaven." Somehow we must learn to distinguish between appropriate *childlike* behavior, a prerequisite for the kingdom of heaven, and inappropriate *childish* behavior, a mark of stunted growth.

Psalm 131, one of the shortest psalms, hints at the difference between childish and childlike trust in God:

> I do not concern myself with great matters
>> or things too wonderful for me.
> But I have stilled and quieted my soul;
>> like a weaned child with its mother,
>> like a weaned child is my soul within me.

Artur Weiser comments that the Christian is

> not like an infant crying loudly for his mother's breast, but like a weaned child that quietly rests by his mother's side, happy in being with her. . . . And just as the child gradually breaks off the habit of regarding his mother only as a means of satisfying his own desire and learns to love her for her own sake, so the worshipper after a struggle has reached an attitude of mind in which

---

* In a medical museum I once saw displayed an ossified fetus. The placard explained that a very obese woman had gotten pregnant and never noticed it. Something went wrong and the fetus did not deliver, remaining instead inside her womb, its cells gradually replaced over the years by minerals in the same process that petrifies trees. When the woman had an unrelated surgery at age sixty-five, doctors found inside her a hunk of bone, heavy as a bowling ball, in the shape of a perfectly formed fetus.

he desires God for himself and not as a means of fulfillment of his own wishes. His life's centre of gravity has shifted.

Sometimes I find myself yearning for the glorious self-indulgence of infancy, when the world revolved around me, when a whimper or cry brought attention, when others met my needs with no effort on my part. Sometimes I look back, too, on an early stage in my spiritual pilgrimage when God seemed close and faith seemed easy and irrefutable—a stage before testing and disappointment, a stage before weaning. And then at church or in the supermarket I come across a baby, helpless, immobile, with little comprehension, and I realize anew the wisdom of creation that presses us on toward maturity, our growth fueled by a diet of solid food, not milk.

While I still bear the scars of growing pains, I am learning to identify and avoid some seductions of childish faith: unrealistic expectations, legalism, and unhealthy dependence.

Several times I have alluded to the danger of unrealistic expectations. A child must, at some point, learn to accept the world as it is rather than as he or she wants it to be. "It's not fair!" the foot-stamping lament of a child, mellows into "Life is not fair," the wisdom of adulthood. People vary in beauty, family background, athletic skill, intelligence, health, and wealth, and anyone who expects perfect fairness in this world will end up bitterly disappointed. Likewise, a Christian who expects God to solve all family problems, heal all diseases, and thwart baldness, graying, wrinkling, presbyopia, osteoporosis, senility, and the other effects of aging is pursuing childish magic, not mature religion.

J. I. Packer explains that

God . . . is very gentle with very young Christians, just as mothers are with very young babies. Often the start of their Christian career is marked by great emotional joy, striking providences, remarkable answers to prayer, and immediate fruitfulness in their first acts of witness; thus God encourages them, and establishes them in "the life." But as they grow stronger, and are able to bear more, He exercises them in a tougher school. He exposes them to as much testing by the pressure of opposed and discouraging influences as they are able to bear—not more (see the promise,

1 Corinthians 10:13), but equally not less (see the admonition, Acts 14:22). Thus He builds our character, strengthens our faith, and prepares us to help others.

Writing this book, so many times I have wished I could promise more. I wish I could encourage Christians, as some do, to "name it and claim it!" I wish I could raise expectations that God will change the rules on our behalf and make life easier, not harder. Every time I wish that, I face the temptation of childish faith—the very temptation that Jesus resisted in the wilderness.

According to both Jesus and Paul, legalism represents another symptom of childish faith. As Paul explained it, the strictness of the Old Testament law was intended not to offer an alternative path to God, rather to prove that no amount of strictness can achieve what God desires. God wants perfection, and for that we need another way, the way of grace.

"To the faithful you show yourself faithful, to the blameless you show yourself blameless," wrote David in one of his psalms, reflecting the contract faith of the Old Testament. I wonder how David might have edited that psalm after his monumental failure with Bathsheba and the scandals that followed. To the unfaithful God showed himself faithful; to the blameworthy he showed himself blameless. David's performance-based faith had prepared him for justice, but not for grace.

Legalism has its place in spiritual development, as it surely does in child development, but perpetual legalism impedes growth. "Never cross a street by yourself!" "Keep out of rivers!" "Don't play with knives!" I heard all these commands while growing up and usually obeyed them. Now, as an adult, I jog in city traffic, go white-water rafting, and wield knives and even chain saws. Though I now recognize that the strictness of childhood helped prepare me for the responsible freedom of adulthood, I seldom look back on the earlier, regimented days with nostalgia or regret.

Paul, raised in the strictest Jewish tradition, knew firsthand the dangers of a faith based on rule-keeping. Indeed, he put his finger on a peculiar irony of human behavior: legalism often fosters disobedience, as the Old Testament amply demonstrates. As he told the Colossians, "Such regulations indeed have an appearance of wisdom, with their self-imposed worship, their false humility and their harsh treatment of the body, but they lack any value in restraining sensual indulgence." The apostle of grace could not imagine why anyone would want to return to a relationship with God marked by so much irritability and failure. He pointed to a freedom based not on rules but on love. "The entire law," he said, "is summed up in a single command: 'Love your neighbor as yourself.'"

Looking back on Old Testament times, Paul also saw a pattern of unhealthy dependence. Like children reared by a famous parent who provides for all their needs, the Israelites found their identity by resenting their dependence on God. They stayed in a state of childish rebellion whereas God wanted them to move steadily toward adulthood.

I know a man who at age seventy still lives with his mother, asks her permission before going out, and turns over his money to her each week. After she made him break up with his fiancée years ago, he has lived ever since under her thumb. I know other adults who continue to act like children because of smothering parents who never learned to let go. They defy a basic principle of nature: the goal of parenthood is to produce healthy adults, not dependent children. The female crocodile helps her young to hatch by gently cracking the eggs; the eagle stirs the nest to force her eaglets to fly; the father lets his son stumble and fall, for how else can he learn to walk? Growing up involves new birth, healthy pain, and a gradual autonomy.

A childish faith based on unrealistic expectations, legalism, and unhealthy dependence can work well for a while — until a person runs headfirst into a new reality. Job broke through that barrier, as did Abraham, the prophets, and Jesus' disciples. "Lazarus is dead," Jesus told his disciples, "and for your sake I am glad I was not there, so that you may believe." He was preparing them for a new reality that included resurrection, yes, but not before the necessary step of death.

───── ⌘ ─────

WHEN JESUS SAID, "UNLESS you change and become like little children, you will never enter the kingdom of heaven," he was not speaking of immature faith such as I have just described. Nor was he speaking of the traits of children all too evident on playgrounds: bullying, competition, whining, tattling. What, then, did he mean? Tucked away in a sermon by Frederick Buechner, I find three traits of childhood that may well hint at the meaning of childlike, as opposed to childish, faith.

Children, says Buechner, have no fixed preconceptions of reality. Several children, on hearing *The Chronicles of Narnia* read aloud as bed-time stories, have taken up hatchets and hacked away at wardrobes in search of the secret entrance. Many more children have peered with anxiety up a blocked chimney wondering how Santa Claus will make it through such a tight space. And in Steven Spielberg's movie, tellingly, it was the children, not adults, who accepted E.T. and invited him into their household.

"They don't know any better," we say of children who believe in magic and pretend playmates. Sometimes they do know better. It took childlike faith for a centurion to approach Jesus about healing his servant, for a paralytic to talk his friends into lowering him through a roof, for Peter to step out of a boat onto a lake, for disciples to recognize the man standing in their midst as the same Jesus they had watched die. Meanwhile, adults of the time who did "know better" rounded up wit-nesses to try to convince a once-blind man that he could not possibly see, hatched a conspiracy to kill poor Lazarus yet again, and paid hush money to Roman guards who had testified of Jesus' resurrection.

The faith that astonished Jesus had a disturbingly childlike quality, and as I read the Gospels I am convicted of my own lack of childlike faith. Too easily I settle for lowered expectations, holding out little hope of change, not believing that God can heal wounds in me that I have learned to live with. The balance between childlike and childish faith may be precarious, but we dare not tilt too far toward the one in trying to avoid the other.

Second, says Buechner, children know how to accept a gift. Dependent since birth, they receive gladly and unself-consciously. They do not debate whether they deserve the gift or worry about the etiquette of reciproca-tion. They tear off the wrapping paper with gusto and start to enjoy the gift. My grandmother, a wise woman, used to give me a lesser gift on my brother's birthday and vice versa. Not once did I think of correcting her, pointing out why my brother deserved all the attention on that day. I seized her offerings as my natural birthright.

God must share this "childlike" quality, for God has no problem accepting gifts, as the Old Testament makes clear. While on earth, Jesus also accepted gifts: expensive gifts from wise men as a baby, a gift of perfume from a woman who poured it over his feet, the gift of time and commitment from his disciples, the gift of adoration from Lazarus's sister Mary.

Children have taught me most of what I know about praise and thanksgiving. They have no problem giving thanks every day for the family dog and the squirrels who play outside. "Give us this day our *daily* bread," Jesus taught us to pray. Only a childlike spirit allows me to receive God's ordinary gifts each day without thinking them ordinary. And the same childlike spirit allows me to open my hands to God's grace, which comes to me free of charge, unrelated to my performance.

Third, children know how to trust. A busy street holds no terror for a child who has an adult's hand to grasp. Indeed, children must sternly be taught *not* to trust strangers, for distrust goes against their instincts.

When Jesus prayed in the Garden of Gethsemane, he used the term Jewish children used for daddy. "Abba, Father," he said, "everything is possible for you. Take this cup from me. Yet not what I will, but what you will." He made a conscious decision to trust God regardless of what lay before him, a childlike dependence that held true even on the cross, where he prayed, "Father, into your hands I commit my spirit."

Kathleen Norris tells of a long intellectual battle against the faith of her childhood, finding it impossible for a time to swallow much of Christian doctrine. Later, experiencing problems in her personal life, she felt drawn to a Benedictine abbey where, to her surprise, the monks seemed unconcerned about her weighty doubts and intellectual frustrations. "I was a bit disappointed," she writes. "I had thought that my doubts were spectacular obstacles to my faith and was confused but intrigued when an old monk blithely stated that doubt is merely the seed of faith, a sign that faith is alive and ready to grow." Rather than address her doubts one by one, the monks instead instructed her in worship and liturgy.

Norris learned that in its Greek root *belief* means simply "to give one's heart to," and she found that the act of worship can constitute a concrete form of belief. She did not find it strange to recite creeds she could not comprehend, for, as she says, "As a poet I am used to saying what I don't thoroughly comprehend." Gradually it dawned on her that to have a relationship with God, like any relationship, she must plunge into it without knowing where it might take her. She began with trust, and from there a mature faith developed.

Unrealistic expectations versus open-minded faith, legalism versus grace, unhealthy dependence versus childlike trust—I often feel I am walking a tightrope between childish and childlike faith. The difference is crucial though: one kind of faith keeps me in perpetual infancy while the other leads toward a mature relationship with God.

———— ◈ ————

THE REMARKABLE LITTLE BOOK *He Leadeth Me*, by Walter Ciszek, shows childlike faith exercised in the most demanding of circumstances. Ciszek, raised a devout Catholic in Pennsylvania, joined a Jesuit mission and volunteered for service in Soviet Russia at the height of its militant atheism. To Ciszek's consternation, his superior assigned him instead to a mission in Poland. A few years later, war broke out and Hitler's army invaded Poland. In the horde of Polish refugees fleeing toward Russia, Ciszek saw a providential opportunity. Disguising himself as a worker, he joined the refugees and sneaked into Russia, where he had always wanted to serve. His prayers had been answered, he believed.

Not long afterward, though, the Soviet secret police arrested Ciszek. The next five years, he was kept in Moscow's notorious Lubianka Prison, undergoing constant harassment and interrogation. In solitude throughout his time in Lubianka, Ciszek spent day and night questioning God. Where had he gone wrong? He had felt called as a priest, but how could he serve in solitary confinement? What use was all his training? Why was he being punished? Finally, he caved in to KGB demands and signed a written confession of spying activities. When he refused to cooperate further, he received a sentence of fifteen years hard labor in Siberia.

In the Gulag's much harsher conditions of fierce cold and fourteen-hour work days, Ciszek got at last the chance to serve as a priest, after gradually winning the confidence of Ukrainian Catholics. He took risks, endured punishment, and pursued God. One by one, all remnants of childish faith fell away. In their place grew a mature yet childlike faith, along the lines Frederick Buechner suggests.

First, Ciszek had to adjust to new realities. In the years of training for priesthood, not once had he envisioned the kind of career path that lay before him in Russia. First in Poland, then Lubianka, then a Siberian labor camp, and finally in exile working in a peasant village, he faced conditions he never would have chosen for himself. He had no theological or inspirational books to study, and scant Christian fellowship. He had to smuggle in wine and bread for the Eucharist. Authorities forbade all proselytism or evangelism. For a time, Ciszek felt a sense of betrayal because his calling to the priesthood had not worked out as he had expected.

Ciszek learned to accept God's will "not as we might wish it, or as we thought in our poor human wisdom it ought to be," but rather as "the twenty-four hours of each day: the people, the places, the circumstances he set before us in that time." He realized he had always approached life with an expectation of what God's will should be, and assumed God would help him fulfill that. Instead, he had to learn to accept as God's will the actual situations he faced each day, most of which lay outside of his control. Ciszek's vision narrowed to a twenty-four-hour time frame.

Second, Ciszek discovered new gifts coming to him from God. As he prayed, "Give us this day our *daily* bread," he began to accept those gifts presented before him:

> Each day to me should be more than an obstacle to be gotten over, a span of time to be endured, a sequence of hours to be survived. For me, each day came forth from the hand of God newly created and alive with opportunities to do his will. . . . We for our part can accept and offer back to God every prayer, work, and suffering of the day, no matter how insignificant or unspectacular they may seem to us. . . . Between God and the individual soul, however, there are no insignificant moments; this is the mystery of divine providence.

Finally, and above all, Ciszek learned to trust. His book records the agony involved in overcoming doubt and trusting God when everything in his life seemed to argue against it. He learned how by watching the old-fashioned peasant faith of his convict-parishioners. "To them, God was as real as their own father, or brother, or best friend." Probably they could not have articulated their beliefs, but at the core of their beings they believed in God's faithfulness. They trusted in God, turned to him in hard times, gave thanks in the few joyful times, stood ready to lose everything in the world rather than offend God, and fully expected to be with God for all eternity. (The character Alyosha in Solzhenitsyn's novel *One Day in the Life of Ivan Denisovich* perfectly captures the simple, child-like faith Ciszek encountered in Siberia.)

Ciszek had often puzzled over how to sense the presence of God. In a most unlikely place, a Siberian prison camp, he learned an important truth:

> By faith we know that God is present everywhere and is always present to us if we but turn to him. So it is we who must put ourselves in God's presence, we who must turn to him in faith, we who must leap beyond an image to the belief—indeed the realization—that we are in the presence of a loving Father who stands always ready to listen to our childish stories and to answer to our childlike trust.

When he chose consciously to abandon himself to God's will, Ciszek knew he was crossing a boundary of trust he had always feared. When he finally did cross it, however, "the result was a feeling not of fear but of liberation."

As I LOOK BACK on my own pilgrimage, I can see the grave dangers in childish faith. I had to learn that life is not fair and that God will not magically level the playing field for me. I learned that legalism does not necessarily produce virtue or maturity and may in fact lead the opposite direction. I learned that an unhealthy dependence can stunt growth.

I am still seeking a mature, childlike faith. I gain at least some idea of what it looks like from people like Walter Ciszek. Though our circumstances are very different, the challenge is similar: to trust that God's way is best, regardless. A childlike state represents my most accurate state in relating to God, for I am a fallen creature seeking contact with the perfect Creator.

> Who is the greatest in the kingdom of heaven?" The disciples asked this because they were trying hard, and Jesus showed them a child who in all probability neither knew nor much cared to know what the kingdom of Heaven was nor what such a question might mean. And then he told them to become like that little child—neither knowing in the sense of understanding nor caring in the sense of being anxious.
>
> FREDERICK BUECHNER

ADULT

> *What punishment is there, you ask, for those who do not
> accept things in this spirit? Their punishment is to be as
> they are.*

EPICTETUS

WISE PARENTS NUDGE THEIR children away from dependence toward freedom, for their goal is to produce independent adults. Lovers, however, choose a new kind of voluntary dependence: possessing freedom, they gladly give it away. In a healthy marriage, one partner yields to the other's wishes not out of compulsion but out of love. That adult relationship reveals, I believe, what God has always sought from human beings: not the clinging, helpless love of a child who has no real choice, but the mature, freely given commitment of a lover.

I keep falling back on marriage as a picture of this mature relationship because it is one I have lived in every day for thirty years and one the Bible itself relies on. (Close friendship between two single persons could serve much the same purpose.) How, exactly, do I "choose a new kind of voluntary dependence" within marriage? I think of two major decisions

Janet and I have made, both of which led us to uproot and move to a new location.

The first time, we moved from the far suburbs of Chicago to a downtown neighborhood. It seemed a risky move at the time for, like many suburbanites, we thought we would get mugged or assaulted at least once a week in the city. We went from worrying about dandelions on the lawn to jockeying for a parking place and hauling groceries up three flights of stairs. We heard other languages almost as often as English on the streets and learned to revel in the diversity of races and cultures surrounding us. And in thirteen years downtown, we never once got mugged.

After those enriching years of city life, we moved to a secluded site in Colorado, the opposite of Chicago in every way. We knew no one and had to begin again the complicated process of finding community, church, and friends. Through my office window I now look upon not the gravel roof of Winchell's Donuts, but a grove of aspen trees and, in the distance, the glint of snow off 14,000-foot mountains.

In retrospect it seems clear that we made the move into Chicago primarily for Janet's sake and the move to Colorado primarily for mine. Janet thrived in the city, building a fine church-based program that ministered to the practical needs of senior citizens, most of them poor, some of them homeless. Eventually, though, city life with its pressures, incessant car alarms, and frenetic pace gradually drained my creative energy, and we chose Colorado in search of a more nourishing environment for my introspective work of writing.

Both moves involved major adjustments, even sacrifices. Yet as anyone in a healthy marriage knows, a couple only undertakes these changes in a spirit of mutual consent. Because I work at home, we have more freedom to make such choices than some people. But a spirit of power ("I need a change of environment, and I'm moving whether you like it or not") or retaliation ("You had your fun, now I'm going to have mine") would spell doom. Neither of us would dare impose such a decision on the other.

Marriage offers only one sure check on freedom abuse: love. In any mature relationship, in fact, love sets the boundaries. I could point to many times in which Janet has set aside her own first preferences in favor of mine, and I have done the same for her. Neither of us "wins" all the time. Yet because we are committed to each other, we make the small and large adjustments necessary to live together in peace, and try to exercise power and freedom within the boundaries marked by love.

Thirty years of marriage has changed both Janet and me. We are vastly different people from the moonstruck lovers who said "I do" when barely out of adolescence. She has taught me social skills, an appreciation for plants, a compassion for the poor and lowly. I have taught her classical music, an awareness of natural beauty, a zest for travel and physical exercise. Our mutual surrenders have caused us to grow, rather than shrink.

Lovers understand that a lasting relationship grows in the soil of trust and grace and forgiveness, not law. Lovers know that love cannot be commanded or compelled. By nature a lover wants what the other person wants. When love requires personal sacrifice, it often seems more like gift: "Not my will but thine be done." Lovers praise: I talk about my wife to others and boast of her accomplishments not because I feel obligated but because I want others to know her as I do. In these and other ways, I have learned from marriage how a mature relationship with God may work. Augustine described a good spiritual life as, simply, "well-ordered love."

The state God wants only comes about as a result of a faithful relationship with him. We seek to please God, accept as our highest goal to know and love him, make necessary sacrifices — and in the process we ourselves change. Personal spirituality grows as a byproduct of sustained interaction with God. In the end, we find ourselves not just doing things that please God but wanting to do them.

———⌘———

ASK A THOROUGHLY SECULAR person to explain the behavior of committed Christians. Why do they avoid habits that harm the body, battle temptations toward lust and immorality, indulge others rather than themselves, insist on honesty and justice, seek out the unlovable and outcasts? You may hear one of these answers: "They're scared of hellfire, afraid of getting God mad at them." "Religion is a crutch — they rely on rules because they can't figure things out on their own." "It's peer pressure — they get together and reinforce each other's beliefs." Although any of these judgments may have some basis in reality, they do not reflect the motivations for behavior described in the Bible.

Jesus told of a merchant who found one pearl so incomparable that he sold everything he owned in order to buy it. The joy in what he gained swallowed up any remorse in what he lost. That is the Adult image of the Christian life: not a grim-faced regimen of self-discipline but an exuberant new life easily worth whatever sacrifice may be required.

Attaining that goal may take time and practice, of course. As C. S. Lewis said, "I must say my prayers today whether I feel devout or not; but that is only as I must learn my grammar if I am ever to read the poets." Just as Lewis studied Greek grammar not in order to parse verbs but to read poetry, I play scales on the piano only because of what they will enable me to play. The reward comes after the practicing and will not come without the practicing. To quote Lewis once more, "We act from duty in the hope that someday we shall do the same acts freely and delightfully."

Why should we be good? Why bother with all the commands in the New Testament? As I read through its pages, I marked many places describing the Adult relationship God longs for. I offer three illustrations, each of which points to a motivation with strong parallels in the Bible.

The first illustration, I heard from Arun Gandhi, grandson of Mahatma Gandhi and now a U.S. resident. Arun spent his teenage years in South Africa, where his father helped lead the campaign for civil rights started by his grandfather Mohandas (or "Mahatma") years before. Shortly after Arun had learned to drive, his father asked if he would drive him downtown to a lawyer's office for a strategy meeting, then take the car in for repair. "You can do anything you want as long as you pick me up at 6:00 P.M. sharp," he said. Like any teenager with a new license, Arun jumped at the chance to drive into the big city.

After dropping off the car at a garage, Arun went to a movie theater. The first picture, a Western from America, proved so entertaining that he sat through the double feature, losing all track of time. When he walked out into fading twilight he panicked, wondering if the garage had now closed. He dashed there, found the shop still open, and retrieved the car. Skidding to a halt in front of the lawyer's office at 6:30, he found his father waiting by the curb.

Aware of how his father valued punctuality, Arun spun a story about problems the garage had encountered while repairing the car. "We're lucky they finished it," he said. "I had to wait almost an hour, which is why I'm late."

Arun's father, though, had called the garage at 5:00 to check on progress and learned then the car was ready. When they got beyond the city limits, he asked Arun to pull to the side of the road. He explained that he had called the garage and that he knew Arun was lying. "I am deeply troubled," he said. "What would cause my son to lie to me? How have I failed as a father that my son would not trust me with the truth? I must reflect on this."

The father walked the rest of the way home, asking Arun to drive behind him so that the car's headlights could illuminate the lightly traveled country roads. Because they lived some distance from the city, it took six hours for him to walk, his head down, deep in thought. Arun drove at a snail's pace behind his father the entire way.

When I heard Arun tell that story, I wondered if he might use it as an example of a "guilt trip," a manipulative way for a father to make his son wallow in regret. He did not see it that way at all. Even in his teens he respected his father as a great leader who modeled integrity and justice. When his father said he must reflect on how he had failed as a father, he meant it sincerely, and Arun was stricken to the core. More than anything else, he wanted to please his father and to emulate him; the lie pointed out how far he had to grow. "After that," said Arun, "I never told another lie."

The second illustration comes from a movie, *Saving Private Ryan*. A squad of GIs, led by actor Tom Hanks, undertakes a daring mission to find Private Ryan, whose three brothers have already been killed in World War II. The rescuers gripe about their assignment, insult the general who ordered it, and fight skirmishes with the Nazis behind enemy lines. Several of them die on the quixotic mission. At the very end of the movie, Private Ryan, the main object of all their exploits, comes across the captain (Tom Hanks) lying mortally wounded. Looking around him at the devastation resulting from a battle fought on Private Ryan's behalf, the captain says these words, the final words of the film: "Earn this."

Earn it. You have been graced with the courage, the sacrifice, and finally the lives of those who died so that you might live. They have nothing more to offer. But you do. You can live in a way that proves worthy of their sacrifices. Respond not out of guilt but out of gratitude, honoring what they have done.

The third illustration comes from Edward Langerak, a philosophy professor at St. Olaf College in Minnesota, who said in a chapel address:

> I once knew a little boy. When he was seven years old, this boy made a mistake that left a deep impression on him. He walked into a drug store and tried to steal some penny candy. He was unsuccessful, but instead of being reported to the police was made to go home and tell his parents what he had done. This task was the most difficult he had ever faced. He had fleeting thoughts of breaking his arm on purpose, of running in front of a car, of doing anything that would relieve him of the dreadful conversation with his parents. But the conversation took place. The boy's father had one immediate reaction: "My son is a criminal." Those words cut to the heart. They were terrible, but they were true: seven years old — a criminal. But the boy's weeping mother took only a few seconds to respond to that verdict: "My son is not a criminal; he's going to be a preacher."
>
> I was that boy, and my mother's response was a lesson in love. My father loved me too, loved me enough to say what was true. I had done something that, at that moment, defined me as a thief. But he did not say the whole truth; my mother saw the *possibility* in me, saw what I could do, and not just what I had done. Now it turns out that both of them were wrong [I became neither a preacher nor a criminal, but a professor], but the way that my mother loved me then taught me much about how to love myself. . . .
>
> Suppose there were a person who always saw the possibilities in you, who always forgave you for what you are and who constantly, sympathetically challenged you to become what you should be. And suppose this person is not just anyone, but is a person to whom you and everyone else is ultimately responsible. Would not such a person enable you to discover the power of love, to realize the truth of the claim that only the loved can love? Would not such a person be loved in your love for yourself and for others? If so, then in devotion to that person you

would love yourself and your neighbor as you love yourself. And that would be something truly awesome. . . .

The desire to please someone you respect, as Arun Gandhi did, and gratitude like Private Ryan's for an extraordinary sacrifice both represent adult, not childish, motives for obedience, and both apply in a relationship with God. The philosophy professor, however, may have singled out the most important, overarching motive: to reflect our true identities as persons beloved by God. We love others, says the apostle John, because God first loved us. We please him as a lover pleases the beloved, not out of compulsion but out of desire.

Think about it: Can anyone fulfill the greatest commandment—to love God—from fear of punishment? Love can never be forced. It flows out of fullness, not fear. Jesus laid out the next step, "If anyone loves me, he will obey my teaching."

Reading the New Testament, I am struck by how consistently the authors appeal to my new identity as a motive for good behavior. As a temple of the living God, what business have I rooting around in what I know God disapproves of? Henri Nouwen calls this new identity "the inner voice of love," an indwelling reminder that frees me to act as God's beloved, beyond the reach of human praise or blame. Goodness, or "holiness," is not some egregious new routine that I must lace around myself like a hair shirt. It is the outworking of an inner transformation, the gradual but sure response of a person in whom God lives.

"On earth we are wayfarers, always on the go," said Augustine. "This means that we have to keep on moving forward. Therefore, be always unhappy about where you are if you want to reach where you are not. If you are pleased with what you are, you have stopped already. If you say, 'It is enough,' you are lost. Keep on walking, moving forward, trying for the goal."

I HAVE A VIVID memory of the practice of spiritual disciplines. While attending graduate school, having recently graduated from a Bible College that enforced a sixty-six-page rule book, I was exercising my freedom by avoiding anything that smacked of legalism or spiritual disciplines. One winter weekend we entertained a visitor named Joe, a Bible

College classmate who took spiritual matters much more seriously than I did, so seriously that he inadvertently woke the entire household at five o'clock in the morning.

I should mention that we had a miniature Schnauzer who had a strange aversion to people engaged in physical exercise. He would chase runners and lunge at cyclists, and when my wife tried jumping rope for aerobics, she sometimes ended up on the floor in a tangle of limbs, rope, and Schnauzer. And so it happened that at five o'clock we heard a loud, angry barking in the living room. Fearing a burglar, I grabbed a tennis racket as the only available weapon, bravely opened the door, and switched on the living room light. There I found Joe, wearing only boxer shorts, his eyes wide with terror, frozen in a pushup position with a small gray dog standing on his bare back, growling and biting Joe's hair.

Joe explained, after we calmed the dog, that before beginning a two-hour quiet time in the morning, he did a series of exercises in order to help wake up. At the time I judged Joe as legalistic, clinging to habits ingrained from Bible College. That snap judgment merely exposed my own spiritual immaturity, for as I followed Joe over the years I realized that no superego or guilty conscience was forcing his spiritual disciplines: he did them for his own sake, like an athlete in training. Though no one really enjoys getting up in a cold, dark house for prayer and Bible reading, Joe found he functioned better in every way if he began each day with that routine. A mature Christian need not act from a sense of duty but a sense of desire, for the very action that pleases God pleases self as well.

Today, I still feel unqualified to give anyone specific instructions in spiritual disciplines. Rather, I recommend recent works by Eugene Peterson, Dallas Willard, and Richard Foster; Thomas Merton's instructions of a generation ago; and the detailed programs set out by Benedict and Ignatius in past centuries. Simplicity, solitude, submission, service, confession, worship, meditation, prayer, fasting, study, spiritual direction, Sabbath-keeping, pilgrimage, small groups, stewardship, journal-keeping, purity, friendship, devotion, work, leadership, witness—all these may play a role in spiritual maturity, and all of them require a commitment that draws on the old-fashioned notion of discipline.

Church history yields many examples of people who took spiritual discipline to an unhealthy extreme, mortifying their bodies and shunning all pleasures. We rightly recoil from such extremes. Yet as I read their accounts now I note that these "spiritual athletes" were acting voluntarily, and few looked back on their experiences with much regret. We live in a society that cannot comprehend those who fast or carve out two hours for a quiet time, and yet honors professional football players who work out with weights five hours a day and undergo a dozen knee and shoulder surgeries to repair the damage they inflict on themselves in the sport. Our aversion to spiritual discipline may reveal more about ourselves than about the "saints" we criticize.

Thomas Merton drew a parallel between freedom and the wealth a rich man enjoys. A rich man can, if he chooses, light cigarettes with his money. Before conversion, Merton says, he squandered his freedom much the same way, living as a New York socialite famous for his partying and drinking. A wiser rich man finds ways to invest his money, to put it to good use so that he may reap the benefits later on. Merton ultimately chose to invest his freedom by entering a monastery, praying for hours at a time, and living in silence and solitude. Few who know his life would argue that he wasted it.

As I study people like Merton, Benedict, Francis of Assisi, John Wesley, Charles de Foucauld, Mother Teresa, I see in these disciplined souls not set-jaw determination but rather spontaneity and even joy. By investing their freedom in discipline, they secure a deeper freedom unavailable elsewhere.

St. Benedict counseled the need for "a little strictness in order to amend faults and safeguard love," and perhaps that formula provides the guideline to keep disciplines from tilting to the extremes.* Love is what God wants from a relationship with us, but we humans tend to experience love like any emotion: intermittently, waxing and waning. Discipline nurtures in us a spiritual staying power—the kind of love a couple enjoys on their golden anniversary, not at their wedding. As part of his spiritual conditioning, Jonathan

---

* Joan Chittister, a modern Benedictine prioress, describes the Rule of Benedict as a "guidepost" or "railing," something to hang on to in the dark, something that leads in a given direction, something that gives us support as we climb. The Rule of Benedict, in other words, is more wisdom than law. The Rule of Benedict is not a list of directives. The Rule of Benedict is a way of life. And that's the key to understanding the Rule. It isn't one.

Edwards compiled a list of seventy "Resolutions" to review on a regular basis. Number twenty-five reads, "To examine carefully and constantly, what that one thing in me is, which causes me in the least to doubt the love of God; and so direct all my forces against it."

Those who write about the Christian life often report that it gets harder, not easier, as the years go by. At such times the spiritual disciplines offer the only effective remedy. Someone who climbs Mt. Everest must rely on years of conditioning; a crash course before the ascent will not suffice.

FOR TWENTY YEARS I have run, biked, or done other aerobic conditioning at least three times a week. I do so not because someone forces me, and surely not because it feels good — it seldom does — but rather because of what it allows me to enjoy. I can climb mountains and ski the Rockies without gasping for breath or pulling muscles. That is the reward for physical discipline. (The apostle Paul drew the obvious parallel: "Train yourself in godliness, for, while physical training is of some value, godliness is valuable in every way, holding promise for both the present life and the life to come.")

I have run a number of moderate-length races, but only one marathon. For the one-time amateur, at least, the marathon seemed a different kind of athletic event altogether. It took me so long — three and a half hours, compared to forty minutes for a ten-kilometer race — that I struggled with mental focus. In the shorter races, I always managed to stay aware of how I was doing, how much distance remained, how I measured up to my desired time. In the marathon, I felt like I was wearing blinders, unable to concentrate on the race as a whole. I fixated on the pain in my left big toe or my bladder's fullness or the quivering muscle on my right calf. Running on a cold, rainy day in Chicago, I could feel blisters developing on my feet from the friction of wet socks. I put on a windbreaker, then took it off. I hit moods of exaltation and despair, with no apparent reason. *Keep moving,* I told myself. *It will end sometime. The only way to get to the finish line is to keep going.*

A friend had agreed to meet me at the ten-mile mark, and when he failed to appear, I sank into a depression that lasted five miles. I forced myself to look at the runners around me, to notice the Chicago neighborhoods, to listen to the bands posted along the route, and as I did so once again I lost track of the race and my place in it. As I passed seventeen miles, a roar went up from the crowd who had just heard on the radio that the first runners had crossed the finish line. I had nine miles to run.

At the twenty-mile mark I hit the fabled Wall and was tempted to slow to a walk. Then my friend finally appeared, and for the first time I had someone to talk to. Chicago had closed off so many streets that he couldn't make the ten-mile rendezvous, he explained as he jogged beside me. In an unforgettable act of friendship, Dave, sensing my weakness, ran alongside me in street clothes the remaining six miles, offering me encouragement.

In five places the New Testament likens the Christian life to a race, and I have little doubt that were Paul writing today he would specify a *marathon* race. The twenty-six miles I ran encompassed every human emotion. The transitory ones, peaks of excitement or despair, faded quickly. What kept me going was patience, endurance, and finally the encouragement of my friend. Later, as I looked back on the race, my whipsaw moods fit into a predictable pattern that the running magazines describe as normal. At the time, though, I had no perspective, simply the step-by-step decision to keep going until the end.

"If you can't fly, run. If you can't run, walk. If you can't walk, crawl, but by all means keep moving," Martin Luther King Jr. used to tell the civil rights workers. His advice applies equally to marathon runners and Christian pilgrims. Life with God advances like any relationship: unsteadily, with misunderstandings and long periods

> I think all Christians would agree with me if I said that though Christianity seems at first to be all about morality, all about duties and rules and guilt and virtue, yet it leads you on, out of all that, into something beyond. One has a glimpse of a country where they do not talk of those things, except perhaps as a joke. Every one there is filled full with what we should call goodness as a mirror is filled with light. But they do not call it goodness. They do not call it anything. They are not thinking of it. They are too busy looking at the source from which it comes.
>
> C. S. LEWIS

of silence, with victories and failures, testings and triumphs. To achieve the perfection that drew us on the quest, we must wait until the race has ended, until death, and the waiting itself is an act of extraordinary faith and courage.

NINETEEN

PARENT

Love, I believe, descends. Parents love their children more than children can their parents, so that children can only enter into the fulness of the parents' love by becoming parents themselves.

BISHOP KING

As a nonparent, I stand in awe of parents. Our friends save for years to bring their children to Colorado, spend thousands of dollars on the vacation of a lifetime, and then get little apparent return on their investment. The ten-year-old wants to play video games all day. The teenager sulks in the back seat, plugged into a portable CD player, head buried in a sports or fashion magazine, refusing even to glance at the majestic views outside the van window. Younger children squabble about who gets which seat, feign motion sickness at every curve, and whine about how much time they must spend in a car. It's too cold for a picnic—or too hot. Why do we have to hike this stupid trail? I thought we were supposed to see wild animals—where are they? Can't we just stay home and watch a movie?

Amazingly, these reactions faze the parents not at all. They are well accustomed to shelling out dollars, prodding their children to get dressed, scraping uneaten food off the plate, cleaning up messes, and receiving in return reactions ranging from diffidence to sullenness. As parents, they expect nothing more.

JUST AS WE PROGRESS through the physical stages of child, adult, and parent, so do we also move through parallel stages in the spiritual life, though not in such a tidy sequence.

Every person has three great "cries from the heart," says Jean Vanier, who founded the l'Arche homes for the profoundly disabled. First, we cry to be loved by a father and mother who can hold us in our weakness. Each of us begins life as a helpless infant, and even in adulthood we never outgrow the need for parental love and comfort. That longing may ultimately turn us to God, as children in need of a heavenly Father.

Next, says Vanier, we feel an adult cry for a friend—someone with whom we can share our deepest secrets, whom we can trust without fear, whom we can love. That cry also may turn us to God, who surmounted the barrier of invisibility first by joining our species, then by promising to live inside us. "I no longer call you servants . . . but friends," Jesus said.

Finally, we have a cry to serve those weaker than ourselves. For many people, physical parenthood satisfies this need. Others—like Vanier the priest, like Jesus himself—seek out service to the poor, the lonely, the forgotten, the sick or disabled, in response to this cry from the heart.

Like any human parent, the mature Christian lives not for himself or herself, but for the sake of others. John lays out this principle most directly:

> This is how we know what love is: Jesus Christ laid down his life for us. And we ought to lay down our lives for our brothers. If anyone has material possessions and sees his brother in need but has no pity on him, how can the love of God be in him? Dear children, let us not love with words or tongue but with actions and in truth.

When I went through the New Testament marking Child, Adult, or Parent in the margin beside each appeal to goodness, I found many such passages directed to "parental" instincts. Gradually, gently, the writers press their readers to move beyond self-fulfillment. For example, some passages urge Christians to avoid lawsuits, in effect waiving their legal rights, in order to set an example that may attract others to the faith. And though the apostle Paul himself had no qualms about certain controversial practices, he modified his own behavior for the sake of weak and immature Christians. "Though I am free and belong to no man, I make myself a slave to everyone, to win as many as possible," he said.

The New Testament persistently presses us upward, toward higher motives for being good. A child wants to know what she can get away with; an adult understands that boundaries exist for his own good; a parent voluntarily sacrifices her freedom for the sake of others. "Such ever was Love's way," wrote Robert Browning: "to rise, it stoops."

And here is a curious fact: When my friends pack their suitcases and head back in cars or airplanes to their homes, none regret what they have just endured. The glimpse of wonder in their children who watch fox kits peeking out of their den across the ravine, the momentary lapse from teenage sulkiness when their son scrambles to the top of a mountain and lifts his hands Rocky-style in the air, the cuddle of a ten-year-old body against their own at the end of an exhausting day outdoors—these memories displace the frustration. They have seen progress toward maturity, confidence, and independence, and what else is the reward of parenthood?

GOD KNOWS WE ARE but children, which is why the Bible so often draws on that human parallel. At the same time, God yearns for us to grow toward the Parent stage of sacrificial love, which most accurately reflects God's own nature. We draw near to God in likeness when we give ourselves away. In fact, as Jean Vanier insists, we *need* this further stage as an essential part of spiritual development; it teaches what we might otherwise never learn.

As one example, a human parent learns something of the unconditional love that most resembles God's love. Ronald Rolheiser remarks,

> Perhaps there is nothing in this world as powerful to break selfishness as is the simple act of looking at our own children. In our love for them we are given a privileged avenue to feel as God

feels—to burst in unselfishness, in joy, in delight, and in the desire to let another's life be more real and important than our own.

In nearly every other human relationship, we earn our way. Employers judge us by skills and intelligence; banks and retail stores treat us according to credit-worthiness; even friends choose us based on common interests. In a family, though, only one thing matters: birth. Try to imagine parents who would trade in their son when his IQ tests at only 90 or who disown their daughter after she fails to make the school soccer team. Although the rest of the world may operate like that, families do not. In a healthy family, love comes without conditions. The son with a birth defect or the Down's syndrome daughter merits the same love and affection as the star athlete and potential Rhodes Scholar.

Even without birth-children we can gain some sense of loving others unconditionally, as God loves us. When my wife ran a senior citizens' program in Chicago, I used to answer people who asked how many children we had, "Dozens, but they're mostly twice our age." For many seniors in public housing and flophouse hotels, Janet served a parental role, battling welfare agencies, Medicaid, hospital workers, and the public housing authority on their behalf. She became an advocate, which in its Latin root means one who gives a voice to those who have none.

When Sarah had her electricity, gas, and phone cut off through a misunderstanding, Janet became her fiery advocate, advancing payment and shaming the utilities for acting so ruthlessly at the expense of a confused senior citizen. When Hank lost his leg to diabetes and gangrene, Janet stayed by his side, explaining why he still felt his "phantom limb" and teaching him to walk with crutches. When Zelda lost circulation in her feet, Janet sat by her hospital bed massaging them and drew up a chart to make sure the negligent nurses turned her frequently enough to prevent bedsores.

Janet did these things not because the seniors had somehow earned her care, but because she believed that every neglected senior citizen in Chicago was loved by God, yet might only sense that love through the hands of one of God's servants. One day Janet came across this quote: "The poor express their gratitude not by saying thanks but by asking for more." She had just spent an exhausting day and felt besieged by whiny, insistent demands for ever more help. That quote proved oddly comforting.

A curious thing happened during my wife's time at the senior citizens' center. Watching her and the others involved in outreach to the poor, I saw the personal sacrifice involved. Social workers get little pay for their long hours and receive few accolades. It surprised me, though, that despite the personal toll on her, Janet seemed to benefit as much as the seniors did. The missionary-martyr Jim Elliot once observed that many Christians are so intent on doing something for God that they forget God's main work is to make something of them. I saw that principle lived out in my wife. As she showered her own skills and compassion on people judged undeserving by most of society, she grew stronger in the ways that matter most.

In a fundamental human paradox, the more a person reaches out beyond herself, the more she is enriched and deepened, and the more she grows in likeness to God. On the other hand, the more a person "incurves," to use Luther's word, the less human she becomes. Our need to give is as great as anyone's need to receive.

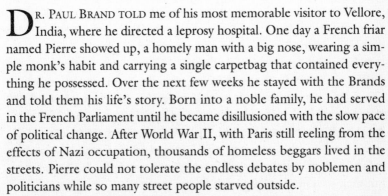

D R. PAUL BRAND TOLD me of his most memorable visitor to Vellore, India, where he directed a leprosy hospital. One day a French friar named Pierre showed up, a homely man with a big nose, wearing a simple monk's habit and carrying a single carpetbag that contained everything he possessed. Over the next few weeks he stayed with the Brands and told them his life's story. Born into a noble family, he had served in the French Parliament until he became disillusioned with the slow pace of political change. After World War II, with Paris still reeling from the effects of Nazi occupation, thousands of homeless beggars lived in the streets. Pierre could not tolerate the endless debates by noblemen and politicians while so many street people starved outside.

During an unusually harsh winter, many of the Parisian beggars froze to death. In desperation, Pierre resigned his post and became a Catholic friar to work among them. Failing to interest politicians or the community in the beggars' plight, he concluded his only recourse was to organize the beggars themselves. He taught them to do menial tasks better.

Instead of sporadically collecting bottles and rags, they divided into teams to scour the city. Next, he led them to build a warehouse from discarded bricks and then start a business in which they sorted and processed vast quantities of used bottles from hotels and businesses. Finally, Pierre inspired each beggar by giving him responsibility to help another beggar poorer than himself. The project caught fire, and in a few years an organization called Emmaus was founded to expand Pierre's work into other countries.

But now he had come to Vellore, Pierre told the Brands, because the organization was facing a point of crisis. After years of this work, there were no beggars left in Paris. "I must find somebody for my beggars to help!" he declared. "If I don't find people worse off than my beggars, this move-ment could turn inward. They'll become a powerful, rich organization, and the whole spiritual impact will be lost. They'll have no one to serve."

At a leprosy colony in India, five thousand miles away, Abbé Pierre found at last the solution to the crisis in Paris. He met hundreds of lep-rosy patients, many from the Untouchable caste, worse off in every way than his former beggars. As he met them, his face would break into a huge grin. Returning to his beggars in France, he mobilized them to build a ward at the hospital in Vellore. "No, no, it is you who have saved us," he told the grateful recipients of his gift in India. "We must serve or we die."

Abbé Pierre had mastered the principle of servant leadership, an essential part of the spiritual role of parent. "For even the Son of Man did not come to be served, but to serve, and to give his life as a ran-som for many," Jesus said about himself. I know no message more urgent for the wealthy countries of the West, who share a planet with three bil-lion people earning less than two dollars per day, a world in which 40,000 children die each day from malnutrition and easily preventable diseases. As Abbé Pierre himself has said, the solution to such problems will not come from massive programs administered by international agencies, helpful as they may be; it will come from many individuals who com-mit themselves in a willing spirit of servant love.

———— ✿ ————

THE PARENT STAGE REPRESENTS an advanced state of maturity. Sooner or later, parents find themselves alone, facing stern trials without much guidance on how to proceed—a fact of life that applies to spiritual parents as well as physical. I have met Christians in difficult places such as Lebanon, Russia, and Somalia who were totally unprepared for this advanced state. They volunteered to serve others in a spirit of idealism. As trials increased, they anticipated a closer sense of God's presence, more support, stronger faith. Instead they found the opposite.

The devil Screwtape, in C. S. Lewis's fantasy, grasped this pattern of faith-building perfectly. He advised his minions that at the beginning of spiritual life a believer may sense the closeness of God's presence, a dangerous state that demons will have few weapons to counter. Later, though, many opportunities against the Enemy (God) arise:

> It is during such trough periods, much more than during the peak periods, that it is growing into the creature He wants it to be. Hence the prayers offered in the state of dryness are those that please Him best.... He wants them to learn to walk and must therefore take away His hand; and if only the will to walk is really there He is pleased even with their stumbles. Do not be deceived, Wormwood. Our cause is never more in danger than when a human, no longer desiring, but still intending, to do our Enemy's will, looks round a universe from which every trace of Him seems to have vanished, and asks why he has been forsaken, and still obeys.

A friend of mine who researched thousands of saints in order to select 365 for a daily devotional guide told me that almost all of them climbed slopes of increasing difficulty. As God entrusts us with more responsibility, the hardships may increase as well. Feelings of abandonment intensify, any sense of the presence of God fades, and temptations and doubts multiply.

Henri Nouwen coined a daring phrase, "the ministry of absence," and advised that we do a disservice if we witness only to God's presence and do not prepare others to experience the times when God seems absent. The worship service itself, says Nouwen, expresses the fact of God's absence:

> We eat bread, but not enough to take our hunger away; we drink wine, but not enough to take our thirst away; we read from a book, but not enough to take our ignorance away. Around these "poor signs" we come together and celebrate. What then do we celebrate?

The simple signs, which cannot satisfy all our desires, speak first of all of God's absence. He has not yet returned; we are still on the road, still waiting, still hoping, still expecting, still longing. . . .
The minister is not called to cheer people up but modestly to remind them that in the midst of pains and tribulations the first sign of the new life can be found and a joy can be experienced which is hidden in the midst of sadness.

We need look no further than the Bible for examples of God's absence. "You have hidden your face from us," said Isaiah. "Why are you like a stranger in the land, like a traveler who stays only a night?" demanded Jeremiah. Any relationship involves times of closeness and times of distance, and in a relationship with God, no matter how intimate, the pendulum will swing from one side to the other.

I experienced the sense of abandonment just as I was making progress spiritually, advancing beyond childish faith to the point where I felt I could help others. Suddenly, the darkness descended. For an entire year, my prayers seemed to go nowhere; I had no confidence that God was listening. No one had prepared me with "the ministry of absence." I found myself turning for comfort to poets like George Herbert, frank about his times of spiritual desolation, and also Gerard Manley Hopkins, who wrote:

> God, though to Thee our psalm we raise
> No answering voice comes from the skies;
> To Thee the trembling sinner prays
> But no forgiving voice replies;
> Our prayer seems lost in desert ways,
> Our hymn in the vast silence dies.

My prayers too seemed lost, my hymns dead in the vast silence. When no "techniques" or spiritual disciplines seemed to work for me, in desperation I bought a Book of Hours used in high-church liturgy. Throughout that year I simply read the prayers and Bible passages, offering them to God as my prayers. "I have no words of my own," I told God. "Maybe I have no faith. Please accept these prayers of others as the only ones I can offer right now. Accept their words in place of my own."

I now look back on that period of absence as an important growth time, for in some ways I had pursued God more earnestly than ever before. I came away with renewed faith and an appreciation of God's presence as gift rather than entitlement.

I have learned to view the times of God's absence as a kind of absent presence. If a college student leaves home for school or for a short-term mission project, his parents sense his absence every day. Yet it does not feel like a void, for it has a shape, the shape of his former presence. They find reminders of him all through the house, dozens of times a day coming across some token that brings him to mind. They also have the hope of his return. That is the kind of absence created by God's withdrawal.

I have been through dry times since that year, but nothing like that time of barrenness, even dereliction. In the Bible I see that God's absence may represent a time of testing, from which Jesus himself was not exempt ("My God, my God, why have you forsaken me?"). It may, on the other hand, represent a phase of relationship with no great underlying significance. I am not the first to experience dark times and will not be the last. If I respond by shutting God out, by giving up, I may well forfeit a necessary stage in growth toward a mature relationship. If God grants us the freedom to draw close and pull away, should not God have that same freedom?

———— ⌘ ————

IN A POEM ABOUT his maturing son, C. Day Lewis wrote,

> I have had worse partings, but none that so
> Gnaws at my mind still. Perhaps it is roughly
> Saying what God alone could perfectly show—
> How selfhood begins with a walking away,
> And love is proved in the letting go.

Although not a parent myself, I have sat with many parents and listened to their heartaches. *We did all we could. We gave her everything she wanted, loved her in every way we knew how—and now this. She wishes she had never been born. She blames us for all her problems. She says she hopes she never sees us again.*

Parents learn the uses of power, and also its limits. They can insist on certain outward behavior but cannot change inner attitudes. They can require obedience, but not goodness, and certainly not love. How, then, do you build character in a child? How do you nurture such qualities as patience, kindness, gentleness, and compassion? How do you forgive obnoxious behavior without sanctioning it?

In effect, the human parent struggles with the same delicate issues of power and self-limitation that define God's relationship with us. Through parenthood we get a glimpse of the "problems" God introduced by creating human beings with the freedom to rebel against him. Reading the book of Jeremiah recently, I heard in God's words echoes of the pain that parents feel. *After all I've done for you, all the love I've poured into you, how can you treat me this way? Why are you turning your back on the one who gave you birth?*

You need not give birth to learn such lessons. Ask any pastor whether his experience with the congregation matches the ideals that first attracted him into ministry. Or simply read Paul's letters to the Corinthians and listen to his frustration over puerile spiritual offspring. Love relinquishes control over others, lets go and bears the consequences.

"Whoever tries to keep his life will lose it, and whoever loses his life will preserve it," Jesus said, in a statement repeated six times in the Gospels.* Jesus' own life bears out that principle, for he experienced the loss as soon as he committed himself to public ministry. Crowds stalked him with ever-increasing demands. Opposition arose. Ultimately he lost his life.

Bernard of Clairveaux set forth four stages of spiritual growth: (1) Loving ourselves for our own sake; (2) Loving God for our own sake, in view of what God does for us; (3) Loving God for God's sake,

---

* I must add a caution that the church often misrepresents self-denial. It does not mean denying one's own value or worth: Jesus never did that. Nor does it mean discounting one's gifts or abilities: Paul seized on these as our main contributions to the body of Christ. And not every person is ready for the message of self-denial. We must first receive before we can give, must possess in order to give up, must have a place before leaving it. Many Christians, diminished by misguided theology, need a healing emphasis on self-possession before they can think about self-sacrifice. Wounded children must be healed before becoming capable parents.

unselfishly; and (4) Loving ourselves for God's sake, in awareness of God's great love for us. I would add one more, representing the Parent stage of spiritual maturity: Loving others for God's sake.

Christians best influence the world by sacrificial love, the most effective way truly to change a world. Parents express love by staying up all night with sick children, working two jobs to pay school expenses, sacrificing their own desires for the sake of their children's. And every person who follows Jesus learns a similar pattern. God's kingdom gives itself away, in love, for that is precisely what God did for us.

Inspection stickers used to have printed on the back 'Drive carefully—the life you save may be your own.' That is the wisdom of men in a nutshell. What God says, on the other hand, is 'The life you save is the life you lose.' In other words, the life you clutch, hoard, guard, and play safe with is in the end a life worth little to anybody, including yourself; and only a life given away for love's sake is a life worth living. To bring his point home, God shows us a man who gave his life away to the extent of dying a national disgrace without a penny in the bank or a friend to his name. In terms of men's wisdom, he was a perfect fool, and anybody who thinks he can follow him without making something like the same kind of fool of himself is laboring under not a cross but a delusion.

FREDERICK BUECHNER

In an era that stresses self-fulfillment and self-actualization, not everyone would agree with Jesus' formula that we must deny the self to follow him. Gloria Steinem writes in *Revolution from Within,* "The bottom line is that self-authority is the single most radical idea there is." I disagree. Accepting a higher authority, and denying self in service of that authority, is far more radical.

Jesus did not disparage self-love: Love your neighbor *as yourself*, he commanded. Rather, he proposed that the highest fulfillment results from service to others, not narcissism. We develop or "actualize" ourselves in order that we may share those gifts with others less blessed.

Some college students strike out for the wilderness or take up meditation in order to "discover themselves." Jesus suggests that we discover that self not by staring inward but by gazing outward, not through introspection but through acts of love. No one can grasp how to be a parent by reading books before the birth of a child. You learn the role by doing a thousand mundane acts: calling the doctor during illness, preparing for the first day of school, playing catch in the back-yard, consoling hurts and defusing tantrums. A spiritual parent goes through the same process. In the end, Jesus' prediction—"Whoever loses his life will preserve it"—proves true, for the downward surrender leads upward.

PART SIX

Restoration

The Relationship's End

PARADISE LOST

*At the bottom of the heart of every human being, from
the earliest infancy until the tomb, there is something that
goes on indomitably expecting, in the teeth of all experience of crimes committed, suffered, and witnessed that
good not evil will be done.... It is this above all that is
sacred in every human being.*

SIMONE WEIL

O N THE DAY BILL CLINTON got elected to his first term, I moved to
paradise. My wife and I had punched through absentee ballots,
littering the car seat with small paper dots, as our Toyota, burdened with
a U-haul trailer, struggled across Iowa and Nebraska toward our new
home in Colorado. At dusk on the second day we pulled in, barely making it up the steep driveway, and unloaded a mattress, computer, two
place settings of dishes and utensils, and a few other essentials to see us
through until the moving van arrived. The next morning we awoke to
find Ponderosa pine trees coated with five inches of fresh snow and a
tableau of mountains glowing soft pink in the morning sun. Ah, paradise.

Over the next few weeks I organized books, arranged my office, and
resumed work on a book I had begun writing in Chicago. What a difference
outside my window! In Chicago I had worked in a basement with a slit of

a window affording a glimpse of people's knees walking past. As for wildlife, I saw only pigeons, squirrels, and the neighborhood dogs that left droppings for us to clean up. In Colorado we had almost daily visits from mule deer and red fox, as well as an exotica of birds that quickly converted me to bird watching. Hearing a strange sound one morning, I jumped up and dashed outdoors in my underwear to find a magnificent bull elk bugling for his harem of sixty cows. Some nights we heard the eerie caterwauling of a mountain lion on the prowl.

Each season brought new delights. In the winter I would clomp through the snow behind our house, trying to identify animal prints and tracking them to the animals' homes among the rocks and trees. Springtime and summer, the hills burst into a profusion of wildflowers: harebells, toadflax, columbine, Indian paintbrush, rare Calypso orchids. In fall the small animals scurried about to gather a storehouse before winter, and quaking-leaf aspens turned a luminous gold in the slanting rays of sun.

Before long, however, we discovered another side to paradise. After driving to Wyoming for a friend's wedding, we returned to find fifteen holes in the side of our house, some large enough to push a fist through. The holes bored through wood siding, insulation, and drywall; standing inside the house, we could look out and see sky. When we checked, neighbors said they had seen nothing unusual but had heard hammering sounds and wondered if we were building a deck. We solved the mystery next morning at five o'clock when we caught woodpeckers (actually, red-shafted flickers) pounding away on our house.

That first spring, we planted a small grove of aspen trees, tilling the soil, mixing in nutrients, and faithfully watering. They flourished until a herd of elk bedded down in our driveway and breakfasted on the fresh young aspen branches.

Squirrels climbed down our chimney and sewer pipes, raccoons tore up roof shingles, chipmunks feasted on the flowers we planted, moles and gophers finished off the roots underneath. Our corner of paradise turned out to be blemished just like the rest of the world. I imagined a meeting of the animals as the workmen began building our house in the forest. "Hey, here come the humans! Squirrels and raccoons, you take the roof; woodpeckers, the siding is yours; now, let's divide up the plants...."

In Colorado, I discovered the story of the universe. The world is good. The world is fallen. The world can be redeemed. I learned the first lesson as soon as I moved here, simply by looking out the window. I learned the second lesson gradually, as paradise conspired against human habitation. Ever since, I have worked to redeem my surroundings: by hanging rubber snakes, ceramic owls, and plastic garbage bags to scare the woodpeckers, by screening in chimneys and vents to deter squirrels, by setting traps for moles and gophers, by spraying deer deterrents (none of which work) on flowers, plants, and trees.

That same cycle of goodness, fallenness, and redemption applies to everything on this planet. Sex, family, church, economics, government, corporations—everything, in fact, that we humans touch gives off both the original scent of goodness and the foul odor of fallenness, and requires the long, slow work of redemption. That is the "plot" presented in the Bible, the plot of all history.

THE WORLD IS GOOD. For this claim we have no less an authority than God himself. After each act of creation, Genesis 1 records the heartening refrain, "And God saw that it was good." His task finished, "God saw all that he had made, and it was very good."

From my vantage point at this moment, in a glass-lined room in the foothills of the Rockies, with music playing softly in the background, I have little trouble believing in that goodness. Within the hour a red fox in a gorgeous winter coat made a halfhearted pass at a black Abert squirrel, who still sits in a tree chattering indignation. Birds flit from the evergreens to a birdfeeder, then return to the branches to crack their seeds. I could turn to the book of Psalms, locate hymns of praise written in similar surroundings of natural beauty, and echo their spirit of worship.

Last weekend on a trip to Chicago I attended a concert in which the orchestra performed two masses, one by Mozart and one by Anton Bruckner. An Italian soprano stood next to a German mezzo-soprano, a Dutch tenor, and a baritone from Iceland. Daniel Barenboim, an Argentinian Jew, conducted these soloists in a spirited performance, backed by instruments and voices of the Chicago Symphony Orchestra and Chorus. Following the Latin text, the chorus sang glory to God in the highest and lifted praise to the One who came down from heaven, the Lamb of God who takes away the sins of the world. As the musicians sang and played, the gates of heaven swung open. Sitting in an elegant concert hall, hearing in both Classical and Romantic versions the great themes that have inspired composers and performers through the centuries, I had no trouble believing in the goodness of this world.

Ten seconds outside the symphony hall, my latent doubts resurrected. Panhandlers lined the sidewalk, hoping to hit up the wealthy concertgoers. Last night's snow had turned to gray-brown slush. Taxi drivers honked and gestured angrily at each other, jostling for position. Welcome back to reality. If I had suddenly started singing, "Holy, holy, holy, God of power and might," a Chicago cop might have taken me in for observation.

It is human evil, I must remind myself, that mars the inherent goodness of this world. People go homeless in Chicago for lack of compassion, not lack of resources. Likewise, the world grows plenty of food to nourish its citizens; people starve as a result of greed and injustice.

From Augustine onward, Christian theology has insisted that what we call bad things are actually good things perverted. A lie warps truth; sexual immorality sullies the beauty of physical love; gluttony abuses food and drink. A parasite, evil must live off good, and has no ability to create anything new. As C. S. Lewis's Screwtape put it, "[Pleasure] is His invention, not ours. He made the pleasures: all our research so far has not enabled us to produce one."

Many things in this world do not *seem* good, of course. I have learned, though, to look beyond apparent negatives to the underlying good, starting with the human body. From Dr. Paul Brand, my coauthor on three books, I learned to "befriend" many bodily processes normally regarded as enemies. Virtually every activity of our body that we view with irritation or disgust—blister, callus, swelling, fever, sneeze, cough, vomiting, and especially pain—demonstrates the body's protective response. Without these warning signs and crucial steps in the healing process, we would live at great peril.

My emotional pains reveal an underlying good as well. What's good about fear? I try to imagine mountain climbing or downhill skiing without the safeguard of fear that keeps me from acting even more recklessly. Or I think of a world without loneliness, a form of pain that Adam felt even before the Fall. Would friendship and even love exist without the inbuilt sense of need, the prod that keeps us all from being hermits? We need the power of loneliness to nudge us toward other people.

Negative emotions can have positive value if responded to well. In the words of psychiatrist Gerald May, "In reality, our lack of fulfillment is the most precious gift we have. It is the source of our passion, our creativity, our search for God. All the best of life comes out of *our human yearning*—*our not being satisfied*." We suffer most when we love most. We recoil from death because we want to keep on living.

I have learned an abiding appreciation for the goodness in this world, good that can be seen even in the residue of bad. When something bad happens—a disagreement with my wife, a painful misunderstanding with a friend, an ache of guilt over some responsibility I have let slide—I try to view it as I would view a physical pain, as a signal alerting me to attend to a matter that needs change. I strive to be grateful not for the pain itself but for the opportunity to respond, by mining good out of what looks bad.

---

*T*HE WORLD IS FALLEN. The movie *Grand Canyon* articulates the world's fallenness in words that might have been adapted from Augustine. A tow truck driver (played by Danny Glover), who is threatened by five troublemakers as he attempts to rescue a terrified motorist, says, "Man, the world ain't supposed to work like this. Maybe you don't know that, but this ain't the way it's supposed to be. I'm supposed to be able to do my job without askin' you if I can. And that dude is supposed to be able to wait with his car without you rippin' him off. Everything's supposed to be different than what it is here."

Whatever we humans touch goes wrong. In more optimistic times Christians had to struggle to make the case for a fallen world. No longer. The people who had the most optimistic view of human nature, those who envisioned a steady progression toward emergence of "the new socialist man," fell the hardest, littering the Siberian tundra and Chinese plains with perhaps a hundred million corpses. And now the United States, once the shining hope of a weary Europe, leads the world by many measures of violence and social chaos.

What the tow truck driver observed, the Christian doctrine of the Fall merely codifies: "Man, the world ain't supposed to work like this. . . ." If indeed a good God created a good world, something has gone awry. The word *Fall,* never used in the Bible to describe what happened to Adam and Eve, has achieved a central place in theology because it seems so apt. Earth's original couple reached too high, lost their balance, and landed on hard ground with a loud thud.

The Greeks had similar stories, of a man named Prometheus who stole fire that belonged to the gods; and a boy named Icarus who soared too high on feather wings and came crashing to earth; and a woman named Pandora who opened a secret box from the gods. In each of these stories, the characters advanced in a way but fell in a much steeper way. Adam and Eve fell the furthest, gaining the knowledge of good and evil by welcoming evil into the world, thus losing the chance to live as God intended.

In our own times, technology repeats the cycle of Adam and Eve, Prometheus, Icarus, and Pandora. We master the atom and nearly obliterate ourselves. We learn the secrets of life only to develop techniques to destroy the unborn and the aging. We unlock the genetic code and open a Pandora's box of ethics. We tame the Great Plains with agriculture and cause dust bowls, harvest rain forests and create floods, harness internal combustion and melt the icecaps. We link the world on an Internet only to find that the most downloaded items are pornographic. Every advance introduces yet another fall.

"It is not given to man to enjoy uncontaminated happiness," wrote Primo Levi, a survivor of Nazi concentration camps. Indeed it is not. Nor can we know uncontaminated love or goodness or anything else. Thanks to Adam's Fall, the entire planet is contaminated. All options have something wrong in them, and at best we seek out the least damaging.

"And yet . . ."—those two words, according to Elie Wiesel, always apply—even in a badly fallen world we catch glimpses of the original goodness. The artist Vincent Van Gogh wrote in a letter to his brother Theo, "I feel more and more that we must not judge of God from this world, it's just a study that didn't come off. What can you do with a study that has gone wrong?—if you are fond of the artist, you do not find much to criticize—you hold your tongue. But you have a right to ask for something better."

Later Van Gogh added, "The study is ruined in so many ways. It is only a master who can make such a blunder, and perhaps that is the best consolation we can have out of it, since in that case we have a right to hope that we'll see the same creative hand get even with itself." The flaws and imperfections in the world, and in himself, served Van Gogh as stimuli for hope.

---

*T*HE WORLD CAN BE *redeemed*. "It is as true of Christendom as of humankind that its fall came so briskly on the heels of its creation as to make the two events seem like one," remarks the novelist Marilynne Robinson. "The great recurring theme of biblical narrative is always rescue, whether of Noah and his family, the people of Israel, or Christ's redeemed. The idea that there is a remnant too precious to be lost, in whom humanity will in some sense survive, has always been a generous hope, and a pious hope."

I choose the word *redeemed* with care, knowing how it has devalued over time. In a slave culture, translators of the first English Bibles rightly settled on redemption as the most powerful image of what God has in store for individual persons and all creation. Could any image more aptly express God's grace than a buyer purchasing a slave in order to set him free? Nowadays we redeem mortgages, trading stamps, and pawned watches, not slaves, and carry bags of aluminum cans and glass bottles to a "redemption center." The word has badly shrunk.

Yet no other word quite fits. *Restore* and *reclaim* or *re-create*, which hint at the original good that God has promised to reinstate, lack a layer of meaning. A redeemed slave is not truly "restored": he still bears scars from the whip and carries within the trauma of being wrenched from home, family, and continent and sold in chains to a human master. Precisely because of that trauma, freedom means more to the redeemed slave than ever it did before. In spite of all the hardship, or perhaps because of it, something has advanced, progressed. The Bible's glimpses of our eternal state all indicate that what we endure on earth now, and how we respond, will inform that state, help bring it about, and be remembered there. Even the resurrected Jesus kept his scars.

Redemption promises not replacement—a wholly new creation imposed on the old—but a transformation that somehow makes use of all that went before. We will realize God's design as reclaimed originals, like a priceless oil painting restored after a fire or a cathedral rebuilt after a bombing. Redemption involves a kind of alchemy, a philosophers' stone that makes gold from clay. In the end, evil itself will serve as a tool of good.

Jews and Christians share this view of history with one important difference. Jews accept the goodness and fallenness of the world and, along with Christians, see history as achieving an end much like its beginning. When the book of Revelation paints a picture of that redeemed world, it simply borrows scenes from the Hebrew prophets and ends up with the same landscape as the book of Genesis: a garden, trees, a river, *shalom*, the unfiltered presence of God. The difference, of course, is that for thousands of years, in the midst of excruciating suffering that has darkened their long history, Jews have cried out for the redemption promise of a Messiah. Christians believe Messiah has already come, achieving in fact what has not yet been fulfilled in time.

In his book *The Creators*, former Librarian of Congress Daniel Boorstin contrasted this Jewish-Christian view with other ways of looking at the world. Buddhists have little interest in beginnings or ends and strive instead to escape the problems of this world. Hindus and Muslims submit to it. Science and art, suggests Boorstin, flourished in Jewish and Christian soil because of our instinct to struggle against this deformed world, stemming from our belief that we have a role to play in its redemption. Time matters, history matters, individuals matter. We are moving somewhere: toward redemption.

Even movements that deny the Christian story borrow elements from it. The Enlightenment promised a redemptive movement beyond ignorance toward a new consciousness; Romanticism sought to recover original innocence; communism promised a way to reverse the Fall without the need for redemption. Women, minorities, the disabled, environmental and human rights activists—all these draw their moral force from the power of the Christian story that promises redemption for the oppressed and enslaved.

To be complete, though, the Christian story requires all three elements. Remove any link, and the chain snaps. Many today deny that the world was created by a good God with human beings playing a central role, and as a result they have great difficulty distinguishing good and evil, worth and meaninglessness. (Animal rights activists maintain that a human has no more value than a pig; a prominent Princeton ethicist suggests a healthy chimpanzee has more rights than a Down syndrome baby.) Ironically, as I have mentioned, optimists who deny the Fall and paint the rosiest picture of human potential end up creating the greatest tragedies the world has ever seen. And those who have no hope of redemption end up with a view of history like Macbeth's: "It is a tale told by an idiot, full of sound and fury, signifying nothing."

The Christian story insists that history is, in lurches and detours, moving to a resolution. Every spark of beauty, worth, and meaning that we experience in this strange existence glimmers as a relic of a good world that still bears marks of its original design. Every twinge of pain, anxiety, cruelty, and injustice is a relic of the fall away from that design. And every demonstration of love, justice, peace, and compassion is a movement toward its ultimate redemption, the day when, in Paul's words, "the creation itself will be liberated from its bondage to decay and brought into the glorious freedom of the children of God."

> The heart itself is but a small vessel, yet dragons are there, and also lions. There are poisonous beasts and all the treasures of evil. But there too is God, the angels, the life and the kingdom, the light and the apostles, the heavenly cities and the treasuries of grace — all things are there.
>
> MACARIUS

GOD'S IRONY

The field had to be broken, the iron molten, the orchard lopped, the wheat winnowed, the stream imprisoned above the mill. Perhaps it was the same with man's life. From defeat greater endeavor must be born, from tears increased purpose, from despair hope. Why should a man fall but to rise again, die but to live?

GEORGE DELL

CLIMBING MOUNTAINS PRESENTS A constantly shifting point of view. At the beginning I face a sheer wall of granite thousands of feet high. *I'll never make it*, I think. But as I get closer I see a thin path following seams in the rock, and by taking that path I hike comfortably up what looked like an insurmountable cliff. As the path zigs and zags, the view below changes as well. At first I hike through a copse of aspen trees. Climbing higher, I notice that the aspens actually encircle an alpine lake, previously hidden though situated not far from the trailhead. Later I find that both forest and lake nestle in a lush valley dotted with lakes, meadows, and other groves of trees. Later still I see that this valley fits into a cut on the side of the mountain and that streams of water spilling from its lakes tumble down several thousand feet to feed a river that runs through a canyon near my home twenty miles away. Only when I reach the summit does the entire landscape fit together. Until then, any conclusions I might draw would prove mistaken.

The world is good. The world is fallen. The world can be redeemed. If this sequence describes the story of the universe, then I must learn to look at the world, and myself, through that lens. Faith means developing an ability to accept that point of view, which I will never fully grasp until I reach the summit, no matter how things look along the trail. I learn to trust that God's mysterious style of working on this planet, and of relating to us his creatures, will one day fit into a pattern that makes sense.

Philosopher Nicholas Rescher likens communicating with God to talking over an old-fashioned telephone system. Other conversations bleed in, static drowns out the voice, the line breaks abruptly—and still we call out, "Hello! Hello! Are you there?" According to the apostle Paul, though, these difficulties in knowing God are a temporary condition: "Now we see but a poor reflection as in a mirror; then we shall see face to face. Now I know in part; then I shall know fully, even as I am fully known." When God finally restores creation to its original design, any gulf between visible and invisible worlds will disappear. The goal of history, a goal God has staked his existence on, is to bring the two worlds together once more, to reconcile them.

Beginning with the first chapters of Genesis and ending with the last chapters of Revelation, I detect two main power streams in the history of this planet. First, evil seizes what is good and despoils it. Since the Fall we have lived in a world dominated by powers that are not morally neutral but rather tilted toward evil, as any history book or daily newspaper makes evident. Violence and injustice should not surprise us for we belong to an age in which evil rules.

In opposition, God unleashes a stream of power to redeem what evil has spoiled. For now, God has chosen to exercise his power through the most unlikely foot soldiers: flawed human beings. Because of these tactics, it may sometimes appear that God is losing the battle. The final victory will be won only when, in power and glory, God ends forever the reign of evil.

The day will come, I believe, when one set of powers vanquishes the other; we have Jesus' resurrection as a bright promise of that day. Until then, I experience these conflicting power streams every day, all day long. The powers work subtly, invisibly, and always I find myself caught in the two great power streams of history, one defacing the good and the other seeking to redeem what has been despoiled.

———— ✺ ————

I THINK OF GOD'S style as "ironic." A more straightforward approach would respond to each new problem with an immediate solution. A woman gets sick; God heals her. A man is falsely imprisoned; God releases him. Rarely does God use such an approach, however. An author of great subtlety, he lets the plot line play out in perilous ways, then ingeniously incorporates those apparent detours into the route home. Thus Paul gives thanks for his "thorn in the flesh" because it advances, rather than impedes, God's work through him; and Joseph can look back on his harrowing life and say to his cruel brothers, "You intended to harm me, but God intended it for good." Although Joseph never denied his horrible past, nor minimized the trauma, he ultimately saw it as part of a meaningful story that served purposes greater than he could imagine at the time. Only at the mountain's summit did the landscape make sense.

It should not surprise us that a sovereign God uses bad things as the raw material for fashioning good. The symbol of our faith, after all, which we now stamp in gold and wear around our necks or chisel in stone and place atop our churches, is a replica of a Roman execution device. God did not save Jesus from the cross but "ironically" saved others through Jesus' death on the cross. In the Incarnation, God's power stream of redeeming good from evil was stealthily underway. God overcomes evil with good, hate with love, and death with resurrection.

"Story-writers," said Flannery O'Connor, one of the best, "are always talking about what makes a story 'work'":

> From my own experience in trying to make stories "work," I have discovered that what is needed is an action that is totally unexpected, yet totally believable, and I have found that, for me, this is always an action which indicates that grace has been offered. And frequently it is an action in which the devil has been the unwilling instrument of grace. This is not a piece of knowledge that I consciously put into my stories; it is a discovery that I get out of them.

————

As my faith grows, so does my confidence that my individual life is contributing in some small way to a larger story. My own story contains details that I regret and may even resent: pain from childhood, illness and injury, times of poverty, wrong choices, broken relationships, missed opportunities, disappointment in my own failures. Can I trust, truly trust, that God can weave these redemptively into my overall story, as "unwilling instruments of grace"?

Teilhard de Chardin expands on O'Connor's analogy of God as the artist:

> Like an artist who is able to make use of a fault or an impurity in the stone he is sculpting or the bronze he is casting so as to produce more exquisite lines or a more beautiful tone, God, without sparing us the partial deaths, nor the final death, which form an essential part of our lives, transfigures them by integrating them in a better plan—*provided we lovingly trust in him*. Not only our unavoidable ills but our faults, even our most deliberate ones, can be embraced in that transformation, provided always we repent of them. Not everything is immediately good to those who seek God; but everything is capable of becoming good.

In high school, I took pride in my ability to play chess. I joined the chess club and during lunch hour could be found sitting at a table with other nerds poring over books with titles like *Classic King Pawn Openings*. I studied techniques, won most of my matches, and put the game aside for twenty years. Then, in Chicago, I met a chess player who had been perfecting his skills long since high school. When we played a few matches, I learned what it is like to play against a master. Any classic offense I tried, he countered with a classic defense. If I turned to more risky, unorthodox techniques, he incorporated my bold forays into his winning strategies. Even apparent mistakes he worked to his advantage. I would gobble up an unprotected knight, only to discover he had planted it there as a sacrificial lure, part of some grand design. Although I had complete freedom to make any move I wished, I soon reached the conclusion that none of my strategies mattered very much. His superior skill guaranteed that my purposes inevitably ended up serving his own.

Perhaps God engages our universe, his own creation, in much the same way. He grants us freedom to rebel against its original design, yet even as we do so we end up "ironically" serving his eventual goal of restoration. If I accept that blueprint—a huge step of faith, I confess—it transforms how I view both good and bad things that happen. Good things, such as health, talent, and money, I can present to God as offerings for his use. And bad things too—disability, poverty, family dysfunction, failures—can be "redeemed" as the very instruments that drive me to God.

"I have learned to be content whatever the circumstances," wrote the apostle Paul from prison. Naturally he preferred comfort over agony and health over weakness (his prayer to remove the "thorn in the flesh" proves that), but Paul had gained confidence that God could use circumstances both good and bad to accomplish his will.

Once again, a skeptic might accuse me of flagrant rationalization, arguing backwards to make evidence fit a prior conclusion. Yes, exactly. A Christian begins with the conclusion that a good God will restore creation to its original design and sees all history as proceeding toward that end. When a Grand Master plays a chess amateur, victory is assured no matter how the board may look at any given moment.

THE BIBLE ITSELF CELEBRATES God's ironic use of bad events to serve a desired result. For example, three-fourths of the Bible records the spectacular failure of God's covenant with the Israelites. At the end of the Old Testament the dream of bringing light to the Gentiles dissolves as Gentile armies all but annihilate the chosen vessels of that light. Yet as the apostle Paul looks back on that history, his own ethnic history, he sees a major advance. Apart from Israel's "no," the Christian church would have remained a minor Jewish messianic sect; rejection freed the Gospel to spread across the known world.

Paul used whatever was available—good, bad, or neutral—to further his mission. On Roman roads built by the Caesars to facilitate rule over subject people, he carried the message of God's love across the empire. He appealed to Roman justice for protection at crucial times. Even when he, most of the twelve disciples, and Jesus himself died at the hands of that "justice," God's ironic pattern prevailed. Jesus' execution accomplished

the salvation of the world; "Your grief will turn to joy," he had promised. Meanwhile, the early martyrs' deaths only accelerated church growth.
"The blood of Christians is the seed of Christianity," said Tertullian, in
a summary of this fact. Ever since, attempts to eliminate the faith have,
ironically, led to its greatest advances.

God's irony helps explain deep paradoxes in the Christian faith. The
Beatitudes present suffering and poverty as good things: Jesus calls
"blessed" the poor, the persecuted, and those who mourn. At the same
time we are urged to relieve poverty, fight injustice, and alleviate suffering. Do not these maxims work at cross-purposes? If the poor and persecuted are blessed, why doesn't the church strive to *increase* poverty and
pain?

Only the sequence of goodness, fallenness, and redemption explains
the paradox. Having given us a good world, God wants us to enjoy its
fruits. "The God of all comfort" desires that we be comfortable in every
sense of the word. Yet because we live in a fallen world full of evil and
injustice, many people will end up in circumstances of poverty and suffering. Even those undesirable circumstances, however, God can use for
his own purposes, wringing good out of bad. As Mother Teresa insisted, poor countries are often spiritually wealthy, and rich countries spiritually impoverished. She and the Missionaries of Charity chose a
redemptive way of voluntarily accepting personal hardship for the sake of
relieving others.

In a miracle of grace, our personal failures can become tools in God's
hands as well. Many people find that a persistent temptation, even an
addiction, is the very wound that causes them to turn in desperation to
God, so that the wound forms a beginning point for new creation. Paul
Tournier summed up the pattern well:

> The most wonderful thing in this world is not the good that we
> accomplish, but the fact that good can come out of the evil that we
> do. I have been struck, for example, by the numbers of people who
> have been brought back to God under the influence of a person to
> whom they had some imperfect attachment. . . . Our vocation is,
> I believe, to build good out of evil. For if we try to build good
> out of good, we are in danger of running out of raw material.

Although Tournier would surely prefer for people never to commit evil in the first place, that is an unattainable state in this fallen world. Here, the ironic response works best, for it never runs out of raw material.

———— ๛ ————

I HAVE KEPT CIRCLING around the age-old question of "Why do bad things happen, even to good people?" because this issue more than any other introduces confusion, and even a sense of betrayal, into a relationship with God. How can we trust in a loving God who allows such bad things to happen? Are the many terrible things that happen on earth God's will? Why must God use an "ironic" style—why not just prevent tragedy in the first place?

The British bishop Leslie Weatherhead makes helpful distinctions in the phrase "the will of God." A sovereign God interacting with a free creation involves at least three kinds of "wills," he says. First, there is God's intentional will. We know what God intends, for the first two chapters of Genesis spell out a world of perfect goodness, and Revelation ends with a similar landscape. God intends for human beings to be healthy and live with companions in pleasant and abundant circumstances. Anything else—poverty, loneliness, hatred, pain, sickness, violence, hunger—goes against God's intentional will for his creation.

The Fall, however, changed the rules of the planet. In the wake of a decisive victory by the power stream of evil, many bad things appeared on earth. God must then have a "circumstantial will" that adapts to the evil conditions of earth. Its original goodness having been spoiled on this planet, God must instead salvage good from bad. Many factors defy God's original plan, causing him much grief. Did God "will" for Joseph, Daniel, Jeremiah, Paul, and others to molder in prison? Certainly not in the sense of his intentional will. Yet evil circumstances, such as jealous brothers, political tyrants, and threatened religious leaders, caused each of them to spend time in prison.

Nevertheless, because each of these men trusted, God's plan went forward despite the evil circumstances, albeit in very different ways. Joseph triumphed and rose to power, Daniel experienced supernatural deliverance, Jeremiah left a lasting testimony as the "weeping prophet," and Paul formulated much of his theology behind bars. This last pattern Weatherhead calls God's "ultimate will." To those who trust him, God promises to use any circumstances to serve his ultimate will.

Nicholas Wolterstorff, a Christian philosopher who lost his son Eric in a climbing accident, sought to bring the strands of God's will into some sort of alignment. "How can we treasure the radiance while struggling against what brought it about?" he asked in his book *Lament for a Son*. "How do I receive my suffering as blessing while repulsing the obscene thought that God jiggled the mountain to make *me* better?" He filled his book with more questions than answers, and our limited point of view guarantees that we will always come away with unanswered questions. Wolterstorff found a narrow ledge of trust by recognizing that "to redeem our brokenness and lovelessness the God who suffers with us did not strike some mighty blow of power but sent his beloved son to suffer *like* us, through his suffering to redeem us from suffering and evil. Instead of explaining our suffering God shares it." God previewed in his own Son the ultimate triumph of his ironic style of redemption.

In an image that harks back to my opening illustration of mountain climbing, Leslie Weatherhead proposes that we picture a stream running down the side of a mountain. We can dam up that stream

> Our life is a short time in expectation, a time in which sadness and joy kiss each other at every moment. There is a quality of sadness that pervades all the moments of our life. It seems that there is no such thing as a clear-cut pure joy, but that even in the most happy moments of our existence we sense a tinge of sadness. In every satisfaction, there is an awareness of limitations. In every success, there is the fear of jealousy. Behind every smile, there is a tear. In every embrace, there is loneliness. In every friendship, distance. And in all forms of light, there is the knowledge of surrounding darkness.... But this intimate experience in which every bit of life is touched by a bit of death can point us beyond the limits of our existence. It can do so by making us look forward in expectation to the day when our hearts will be filled with perfect joy, a joy that no one shall take away from us.
>
> HENRI NOUWEN

and prevent its flow toward the valley below, but only temporarily. The law of gravity requires that water at high elevation will eventually make its way down. Similarly, God's ultimate will cannot be thwarted. Though human history with all its evils may place many blockages in the way, in the end these will be overcome. God will get his family back, on an earth restored to something resembling its original state.

On this planet, for this time, God allows us to be put in harm's way. Buildings collapse, tectonic plates shift, viruses proliferate, evil people resort to violence. From what we know about the character of God, none of these things reflect his intentional will. Nor, if we believe God's promises, do they reflect his ultimate will. In the meantime, though, the time in which we spend all our days on planet earth, bad things will inevitably happen.

In creation God works through matter. In redemption he acts through personality—through ourselves. In the face of tragedy, I can respond either by blaming and turning against God or by turning toward him, trusting him to fashion good out of bad. One option focuses on the past and closes off the future. The other option opens the future, allowing an Artist to use whatever happens as the raw material for a new story, different than it would have been without the tragedy or failure, but in some ways even richer, redeemed.

AN ARRANGED MARRIAGE

*In everything worth having, even in every pleasure, there
is a point of pain or tedium that must be survived, so that
the pleasure may revive and endure. The joy of battle comes
after the first fear of death; the joy of reading Virgil comes
after the bore of learning him; the glow of the sea-bather
comes after the icy shock of the sea bath; and the success of
the marriage comes after the failure of the honeymoon.*

G. K. CHESTERTON

LISTEN TO ANY POP music station or watch MTV and try to find a song
that does *not* feature the theme of romantic love. And is there a television soap opera without a steamy romance woven into the plot? Phrases
like "catching a man" and "hunting a woman" describe a basic law of life
and love, we think—until we travel to other parts of the world.
Remarkably, most marriages worldwide conjoin men and women who have
never felt a twinge of romantic love and may not recognize the sensation
if it hit them. Teenagers in much of Africa and Asia take for granted the
reality of marriages arranged by their parents in the same way we take for
granted romantic love.

A modern couple from India, Vijay and Martha, explained to me how
their arranged marriage came about. Vijay's parents surveyed all the young
girls in their village before deciding their son should marry Martha. Vijay

was fifteen then, and Martha had just turned thirteen. Although the two teenagers had met only once, their parents reached agreement and set a wedding date eight years away. Only then did the parents inform both teenagers whom they would be marrying and when. During the next eight years, Vijay and Martha were permitted to exchange one letter a month and saw each other on two closely chaperoned occasions. Although they moved in together as virtual strangers, their marriage today appears to be as secure and loving as any I know.

In fact, societies that practice arranged marriages tend to have much lower divorce rates than those that emphasize adolescent love. I doubt seriously that the West will ever abandon the notion of romantic love, no matter how poorly it serves as a basis for family stability. But through my conversations with Christians from different cultures I have begun to see how an arranged marriage might serve as a helpful model in relating to God.

In the U.S. and other Western-style cultures, people tend to marry because they are attracted to another's appealing qualities: a fresh smile, wittiness, a pleasing figure, athletic ability, charm. Over time these qualities may change, with the physical attributes, especially, deteriorating with age. Meanwhile, unexpected surprises will surface—slatternly housekeeping, bouts of depression, dissimilar sexual appetites—which disrupt the romance. In contrast, the partners in an arranged marriage do not center their relationship around mutual attractions. After your parents' decision, you accept that you will live for many years with someone you now barely know. The overriding question changes from "Whom should I marry?" to "Given this partner, what kind of marriage can we construct together?"

A similar pattern applies in a relationship with God. I have no control over God's qualities, such as his invisibility. God is free, with a "personality" and features that exist whether I like them or not. I have no choice about many of the details of my own makeup either: my facial features and uncontrollable curly hair, my handicaps and limitations, aspects of my personality, my family background. Taking the Western romantic approach, I can resent this quality or that one of God's and wish he ran the world differently. I can demand that God change my circumstances before I trust him with my life. Or I can take a very different approach. I can humbly accept God as he is revealed in Jesus and also accept myself, flaws and all, as the person God has chosen. I do not go in with a list of demands that must be met before I take the vow. Like a spouse in an arranged marriage, I pre-commit to God regardless.

Faith means taking a vow "for better or for worse, for richer or for poorer, in sickness and in health," to love God and cling to him no matter what. That involves risk, of course, for I may discover that what God asks of me conflicts with my selfish desires. Happily, the spirit of arranged marriage works two ways: God also pre-commits to me, promising a future and eternal life that will redeem the circumstances I now struggle with. God does not accept me conditionally, on the basis of my performance, but bestows his love and forgiveness freely, despite my innumerable failures.

Some people anticipate life with God to be a solution to their problems and choose God much as one would choose a spouse in a romantic-love culture, by seeking desirable results. They expect God to bring them good things; they tithe because they believe money will come back tenfold; they try to live right in hopes that God will prosper them. No matter what the problem—unemployment, a retarded child, a crumbling marriage, an amputated leg, an ugly face—they expect God to intervene on their behalf by arranging a job, patching together the marriage, and curing the retarded child, amputated leg, and ugly face. As we all know, though, life does not always work out so neatly. Indeed, in some countries becoming a Christian guarantees a person unemployment, family rejection, societal hatred, and even imprisonment.

Every human marriage has crisis times, moments of truth when one partner (or both) is tempted to give up. Older married couples will admit that during these times they questioned the entire relationship. Now, though, they retell the stories with humor and even nostalgia, for the crises fit together into—indeed, they helped form—a pattern of love and trust. Looking back from the vantage point of a few decades, it seems clear that the couple's mutual response to stormy times was what gave their marriage its enduring strength. A relationship with God can work the same way.

The apostle Paul took the spirit of arranged marriage to extremes that would be considered pathological in modern thinking. Paul told the Philippians he actually rejoiced in his imprisonment, for the chains helped advance the progress of the gospel. In a letter to the Corinthians, he boasted about the failures and hardships he had endured. He mentioned floggings, stonings, shipwrecks and other natural disasters, hunger, thirst, physical discomfort, unanswered prayers. "If I must boast, I will boast of the things that show my weakness," he declared. "For Christ's sake, I delight in weaknesses, in insults, in hardships, in persecutions, in difficulties. For when I am weak, then I am strong."

I read such words, then wander into my local Christian bookstore where I find racks of books telling me how to save my marriage, how to raise godly children, how to experience God's blessings, how to resist temptation, how to find happiness. Every year more "how-to" books appear, and every year the need for them grows. If a book really could save a marriage, divorce rates should be shrinking among book-buying Christians, a trend I have yet to observe. Likewise, a relationship with God requires something more than a problem-solution approach.

DOROTHY SAYERS SUGGESTS ANOTHER way of viewing God's personal involvement with us. She points to the analogy of an artist, who "does not see life as a problem to be solved, but as a medium for creation." Perhaps, says Sayers, God has invested each of us with the freedom of an artist, allowing us to work with different materials. A sculptor works with clay or metal but not much color; a painter works with many colors but only in two dimensions. Although these raw materials of creation have built-in limitations, a skilled artist can make from any of them a magnificent work of art.

As individuals, we each begin with a different medium. Some of us are ugly, some beautiful, some brilliant, some dense, some charming, some shy. We may choose to fixate on the raw materials, the "stuff" of life. We may, for example, spend our lives resenting God for a physical flaw or a facial shape or the family that reared us. We may demand that God solve those problems on our behalf (how, exactly—by changing the genetic code or reinventing a family?). Yet those same raw materials, which provoke such resentment in some people, may also be the very ingredients used to shape us in the ways that matter most to God.

Indeed, in an odd sort of way, human beings need problems more than we need solutions. Problems stretch us and press us toward dependence on God. As the Bible reiterates, success represents a far greater danger. Samson, Saul, Solomon, and scores of others show that success leads toward pride and self-satisfaction, a path away from dependence and often a prelude to a fall.

God does not promise to solve all our problems, at least not in the manner we want them to be solved. (I find no characters in the Bible who lived a problem-free existence.) Rather, God calls us to trust him and to obey—whether we live in affluence and success or whether, like some Christians, we spend our days in a concentration camp. What matters most to God is what we create from the raw material.

Dorothy Sayers' life, in fact, bore out the very principles she wrote about. She had great native intelligence but little in the way of physical beauty. The man she loved in her youth never returned her affection. In frustration she, the Oxford scholar, turned to an uneducated mechanic who introduced her to boating, drinking, smoking, dancing, and sex. Although he took her on as a party companion for a while, unlike Sayers he had no interest in marriage. He did leave her with a son, however, and now Sayers found herself burdened with the responsibilities and stigma of an illegitimate child. Eventually she married an older, divorced man who proved very hard to love.

In retrospect, Sayers credited these very experiences of failure and humiliation, even her sins and mistakes, as what drove her to God. Readers of her books today, whether the Lord Peter Wimsey detective stories or the bracing theological works, profit from what she fashioned out of the raw materials of her difficult life. Her problems may not have been solved in the way she wanted, but from them she created an enduring work of art.

In this hard task we have the pattern of Jesus himself who, when he came to earth, could have chosen any set of "raw materials" and deliberately settled on poverty, family shame, suffering, and rejection. He did not exempt himself from the annoyances of life on this planet, as if to prove that none of these circumstances need cancel out a healthy relationship with the Father. Perhaps we should say "Christ is the pattern" rather than "Christ is the answer," because Jesus' own life did not offer the answers most people are looking for. Not once did he use supernatural powers to improve his family, protect himself from harm, or increase his comfort and wealth.

———— ⌖ ————

I KNOW A FAMILY who grew concerned over bad influences in the high school their daughter attended. After praying about the issue and seeking the counsel of others, they transferred her from the bad school to a school called Columbine, where the next year she got shot and nearly died. I knew a man my age who believed God had given him the vocation of his dreams, the presidency of a seminary, and made great plans for its future until a brain tumor struck him down and he died within the year. I know a woman who as a parent lived out the drama of Jesus' prodigal son story, celebrating her daughter's return from a spell of drug addiction and prostitution, only to see the daughter run away yet again and go back to life in the "far country."

How to make sense of these stories from real life? No simple problem-solution formula can account for them. But then, neither can such a formula account for what happened to Paul or Peter or Jesus himself. Life is not a problem to be solved but a work to be made, and that work may well utilize much raw material that we would prefer to do without. God's goodness does not mean we will not get hurt, not in this fallen world at least. His goodness goes deeper than pleasure and pain, somehow incorporating both.

When Paul wrote, "In all things God works for the good of those who love him," he spelled out in the same passage some of those "things" God had used in his life: trouble, hardship, persecution, famine, nakedness, danger, sword. In all three families that I mentioned, I can see the ongoing redemptive work of God. None of them would have chosen what happened, nor do they blame God for the tragedies; yet all would agree that God is working great good in their lives through the sad things that happened to them.

Flannery O'Connor, who suffered from lupus and died at the age of thirty-nine, wrote to a friend, "I have never been anywhere but sick." In the same letter, she reflected on the two uninvited teachers that descended on her late in life: sickness and success. "In a sense sickness is a place, more instructive than a long trip to Europe," she wrote. She then added a sentence that strikes awe in those who knew how much she suffered, "Sickness before death is a very appropriate thing and I think those who don't have it miss one of God's mercies." Success, in contrast, she regarded as almost wholly negative: it isolates, breeds vanity, and distracts from the real work that brought it on in the first place.

In comparison with Flannery O'Connor I have hardly suffered. The pain I felt in childhood lacerated my soul more than my body: pain from a father's death by polio and the poverty that resulted; pain inflicted by angry churches who should have known better but probably didn't; the shame, alienation, and inferiority that defined my adolescence. I meet teenagers now who remind me of who I was then: shy, socially inept, physically uncoordinated, with a self-image so low it barely registers. They live in a world that glamorizes beauty, sports, and confidence. If they pray at all, they probably pray for God to change them, to make them more like the model on the cover of *Glamour* or the athlete in *Sports Illustrated*. No matter how earnest, that prayer will not likely be answered in the way they desire.

If only they could see—if only I could see—how differently God views this earth. We have a clue in the companions Jesus preferred: tax collectors, women of ill repute, those with leprosy, the unclean, half-breeds, fishermen. Paul too had to admit, "Not many of you were wise by human standards; not many were influential; not many were of noble birth. But God chose the foolish things of the world to shame the wise; God chose the weak things of the world to shame the strong. He chose the lowly things of this world and the despised things—and the things that are not—to nullify the things that are, so that no one may boast before him." God never commissioned us to remove all bad things from the world, to undo the Fall; God calls us to redeem the bad, transforming it into something good.

Reflecting on her pain from childhood, especially pain from a religious heritage, poet Kathleen Norris says, "Converting a painful inheritance into something good requires all the discernment we can muster, both from what is within us, and what we can glean from mentors. The worst of the curses that people inflict on us, the real abuse and terror, can't be forgotten or undone, but they can be put to good use in the new life that one has taken up." Much of what we struggle with today, we will still struggle with tomorrow and the next day. Some pains, whether the precisely-shaped pain of loss or the formless pain of unfulfilled longing, never go away. The wound will never heal completely, the problem never find a pure solution. We are offered instead the less satisfying but more realistic hope that God can redeem even the wound.

Those who attempt to use God as a means of self-realization almost always come away disappointed. God has in mind something like the reverse: to use us, the least likely vessels of his grace, as his self-realization on earth.

THE CZECH-BORN AUTHOR MILAN Kundera once wrote that he had always objected to Goethe's notion that "a life should resemble a work of art." Instead, Kundera wondered if perhaps art arose because life is so shapeless and unpredictable, art thus supplying the structure and interpretation that life lacks. But he had to make an exception, he admitted, in the case of his friend Vaclav Havel, who began as a writer like Kundera and went on to become president of the Czech Republic and one of the strong moral voices of our time. Havel's life, to Kundera, showed a thematic unity, a gradual, continuous progression toward a goal.

Having read some of both authors, I wonder if the difference lies in their underlying point of view. For Kundera, as for most postmodern thinkers, life has no "meta-narrative," no structure of meaning to explain where it comes from and where it is going. For Havel, it does. He laments, "I have become increasingly convinced that the crisis of the much-needed global responsibility is in principle due to the fact that we have lost the certainty that the Universe, nature, existence and our lives are the work of creation guided by a definite intention, that it has a definite meaning and follows a definite purpose."

The Christian—and Havel has never fully described himself as such—sees not just all of life but every individual life as a potential work of art. We are participating with God to fashion from raw materials something of enduring beauty. We are writing a small story with our lives, part of a larger story whose plot line we know in the sketchiest of details. Both the large and the small unfold like any story: with a beginning and end, with purpose and yet action that resists it, with consequences that cannot be avoided, with accidents and unexpected interruptions. In the end, the narrative incorporates all these details in a story line that achieves a satisfying fullness.

"It is not up to you to finish the work, but neither are you free not to take it up," goes an old Talmudic saying. The work is God's work, the work of reclaiming and redeeming a planet badly damaged. For the Jew and Christian both, that work means bringing a touch of peace, justice, hope, healing, *shalom* wherever our hands touch. For the Christian it means doing so as a follower of Jesus, who made possible the redemption we could never accomplish on our own.

High up in England's Winchester Cathedral sits a stained-glass window unique to its era. It neither tells a Bible story nor memorializes a saint, and its kaleidoscope of colors has a peculiarly modern design, as if Marc Chagall had time-traveled back into the seventeenth century to install it. The window is a relic from a violent time, when troops from Oliver Cromwell's army used iron bars to shatter the cathedral's ancient windows and break up its statuary. The troops left the ground outside littered with fragments of glass, which the people of the town picked up and stored until the time of frenzy had passed. Years later, a cathedral worker volunteered for the difficult task of re-installing the window. High on a scaffold above the nave, the workman assembled the pieces into an abstraction of color. It resembled nothing in Europe at the time, and even today seems oddly out of place. And yet no one can deny that the reconstructed bits of glass form a work of great beauty, a work of art. The play of light from sun and clouds filters through the window to illumine the cathedral in a constantly changing mosaic.

That illustration of redemption, of restoration, speaks to me with a personal message of hope because so many of my own wounds resulted from the same kind of religious zealotry that fueled Cromwell's soldiers. Often the church destroys even as it seeks to redeem, and a new and virulent kind of fallenness must be redeemed again. That ongoing process recapitulates itself in the world, the church, and in every individual soul committed to God's story on earth.

> And God who gives beginning gives the end . . .
> A rest for broken things too broke to mend.
>
> JOHN MASEFIELD

THE FRUIT OF
FRIDAY'S TOIL

In all the tragic dramas of antiquity, whether lived or staged, we detect the same pattern: the hero, be he Alexander or Oedipus, reaches his pinnacle only to be cut down. Only in the drama of Jesus does the opposite pattern hold: the hero is cut down only to be raised up.

THOMAS CAHILL

EARLY IN THIS BOOK I told of a friend who said to me, "I have no trouble believing God is good. My question is, more, What good is he? I cry out to God for help, and it's hard to know just how he answers. Really, what can we count on God for?" That question has lurked in the background of every chapter and is my true motivation in writing the book. In all other personal relationships we have some idea what to expect and count on. What about with God?

I find at least the hint of an answer in a phrase from Dallas Willard, whose book *The Divine Conspiracy* includes these words tucked away in a subordinate clause: "Nothing irredeemable has happened to us or can happen to us on our way to our destiny in God's full world." The world is good, the world is fallen, the world can be redeemed—in effect, Willard affirms that this same plot applies not only to the universe as a whole but to every one of God's followers. Nothing we encounter lies beyond the range of God's redemptive power.

In God's ironic method, what we regard as disadvantage may work to advantage, a truth that Jesus emphasized in nearly all his stories and human contacts. He held up the good Samaritan, not the privileged religious leaders, as an example of mercy. As his first missionary he chose another Samaritan, a woman with five failed marriages in her résumé. He pointed to a pagan soldier as a model of faith and transformed a greedy tax-collector named Zacchaeus into a model of generosity. On leaving, he turned over his mandate to a group of mostly uneducated peasants led by the traitor Peter. Each of these choices underscores the irony of redemption.

After trying many faulty cures, the cofounder of Alcoholics Anonymous, Bill Wilson, finally understood that irony. He reached the unshakable conviction, now a canon of twelve-step groups, that an alcoholic must "hit bottom" in order to climb upward. Wilson wrote his fellow strugglers, "How privileged we are to understand so well the divine paradox that strength rises from weakness, that humiliation goes before resurrection: that pain is not only the price but the very touch-stone of spiritual rebirth."

The irony continues throughout recovery. Although an alcoholic may pray desperately for the condition to go away, very few alcoholics or other addicts report sudden, miraculous healing. Most battle temptation every day of their lives. They experience grace not as a magic potion, rather as a balm whose strength is activated daily by conscious dependence on God.

EVERY PERSON ON EARTH lives out a unique script of hardship: singleness when marriage was always a goal, or a physical disability, or poverty, childhood abuse, racial prejudice, chronic illness, family dysfunction, addiction, divorce. If I envision God as Zeus-like, aiming thunderbolts on the wretched humans below, then naturally I will direct my anger and frustration at God, the immediate cause of my hardship. If, on the other hand, I perceive God as working from below, under the surface, calling out to us through each weakness and limitation, I open the possibility of redemption for the very thing I resent most about my life.

"Good and evil, in the moral sense, do not reside in things, but always in persons," wrote Paul Tournier. "Things and events, whether fortunate or unfortunate, are simply what they are, morally neutral. What matters is the way we react to them. Only rarely are we the masters of events, but (along with those who help us) we are responsible for our reactions.... Events give us pain or joy, but our growth is determined by our personal response to both, by our inner attitude." As a medical doctor Tournier opposed suffering and did his best to alleviate it in his patients. As a counselor, however, he made use of it, gently pointing his patients toward a response that would allow them to grow through the affliction.

Tournier, in fact, wrote the book *Creative Suffering* in order to explore a phenomenon that had always puzzled him: The most successful people are often the products of difficult and unhappy families. A colleague investigating leaders with the greatest influence on world history had discovered that almost all—his list of three hundred included Alexander the Great, Julius Caesar, Louis XIV, George Washington, Napoleon, and Queen Victoria—had one thing in common: they were orphans. It baffled Tournier that whereas he spent his time lecturing on the importance of a mother and father cooperating to produce a nourishing family environment, these leaders all emerged from a state of emotional deprivation. An orphan himself, Tournier began to look at hardship as something not simply to be eliminated, but rather harnessed for redemptive good.

In his book *Great Souls*, journalist David Aikman surveyed the twentieth century in search of individuals with the greatest spiritual and moral power. The list of six he settled on included Mother Teresa, who worked at the extreme edge of human suffering; Alexander Solzhenitsyn, chronicler of the Gulag; Elie Wiesel, Holocaust survivor; Nelson Mandela, imprisoned for twenty-seven years; Pope John Paul II, who grew up under Nazi and Communist regimes; and evangelist Billy Graham. Of the six, only Billy Graham had anything resembling a "normal" middle-class existence. Yet these six developed into towering spiritual leaders of the century.

Although we have no right to impose cheery formulas of redemptive suffering on others, neither can we ignore witnesses who insist on that truth. As a journalist I too have seen up close the redemptive potential of hardship. I remember meeting Joni Eareckson as a teenager, a few months after her accident, when she was still contemplating her future through a fog of despair and confusion. How could she serve God from a wheelchair, unable to feed herself, get dressed, or make it through a day without intimate personal assistance? "You can't imagine the shame and humiliation," she told me. What possible good could come from such a tragedy? Now, thirty years later, Joni looks back on the day she broke her neck diving into Chesapeake Bay and calls it the best day of her life. She allowed God to work with her to redeem a tragedy, to produce something good out of bad.

I also remember visiting Sadan, one of Dr. Paul Brand's former leprosy patients, in India. He looked like a miniature version of Gandhi: skinny, bald, perched cross-legged on the edge of a bed. In a high-pitched, singsong voice he told me wrenching stories of past rejection: the classmates who tormented him in school, the driver who kicked him—literally, with his shoe—off a public bus, the many employers who refused to hire him despite his training and talent, the hospitals that turned him away out of unwarranted fear. Sadan then recounted the elaborate sequence of medical procedures—tendon transfers, nerve strippings, toe amputations, and cataract removal—performed by Dr. Brand and his ophthalmologist wife. He spoke for half an hour, recounting a life that was a catalogue of human suffering. But as we sipped our last cup of tea in his home, Sadan made this astonishing statement: "Still, I must say that I am now happy that I had this disease."

"Happy?" I asked, incredulous.

"Yes," replied Sadan. "Apart from leprosy, I would have been a normal man with a normal family, chasing wealth and a higher position in society. I would never have known such wonderful people as Dr. Paul and Dr. Margaret, and I would never have known the God who lives in them."

One last example. I, along with many others who followed his career, was saddened to hear in 1984 of the spinal cord cancer that struck Reynolds Price, one of the South's leading lights in fiction, literary criticism, and spiritual reflection. Ten years later, I read this paragraph in the memoir of his illness and paralysis:

So *disaster* then, yes, for me for a while—great chunks of four years. *Catastrophe* surely, a literally upended life with all parts strewn and some of the most urgent parts lost for good, within and without. But if I were called on to value honestly my present life beside my past—the years from 1933 till '84 against the years after—I'd have to say that, despite an enjoyable fifty-year start, these recent years since full catastrophe have gone still better. They've brought more in and sent more out—more love and care, more knowledge and patience, more work in less time.

Price credits the "now appalling, now astonishing grace of God." A relationship with God does not promise supernatural deliverance from hardship, but rather a supernatural use of it.

IN MOST HUMAN ENDEAVORS, we determine the value of a "way" by looking at the result of all the effort. A researcher who fails to find a gene after searching thirty years feels his time has been wasted. A chemist who assembles compounds does not feel truly successful until someone finds a use for those compounds. A novelist wants above all to be published. A prospector digs with one object in mind: locating the gold.

Relationships proceed along a different path. Thinking of some of my best friends, in no case did I calculate, "I believe I'll become friends with Tim, Scott, and Reiner. Let's see, I need a plan to accomplish my goal." Those friendships grew up around me almost unexpectedly, with Tim and Scott as colleagues and Reiner as a college roommate. In relationships, the "way" itself is the goal. Shared meaning and common experience create the intimacy—and often, difficult times bond the relationship most securely.

"I am the way, the truth, and the life," Jesus said. Truth and life may supply the motives for following, yet in the end a relationship with God, like any relationship, boils down to the "way," the daily process of inviting God into the details of my existence. Søren Kierkegaard likened some Christians to schoolboys who want to look up solutions to the math problems in the back of the book. Only by doing the math, step by step, can you learn the math. Or in John Bunyan's analogy, only by pursuing the way, progressing through its joys, hardships, and apparent detours, can the pilgrim arrive at the destination.

I have an unmarried friend who prays earnestly for God to lessen or even remove his sexual drive. It causes him constant temptation, he says. Pornography distracts him, plunges him into a failure spiral, and ruins his devotional life. As gently as I can, I tell him that I doubt God will answer the prayer as he wants, by recalibrating his testosterone level. More likely, he will learn fidelity the way anyone learns it, relying on discipline, community, and constant pleas of dependence.

For whatever reason, God has let this broken world endure in its fallen state for a very long time. For those of us who live in that broken world, God seems to value character more than our comfort, often using the very elements that cause us most discomfort as his tools in fashioning that character. A story is being written, with an ending only faintly glimpsed by us. We face the choice of trusting the Author along the way or striking out alone. Always, we have the choice.

In my own spiritual life, I am trying to remain open to new realities, not blaming God when my expectations go unmet but trusting him to lead me through failures toward renewal and growth. I am also seeking a trust that "the Father knows best" in how this world is run. Reflecting on Old Testament times, I see that the more overt way in which I may want God to act does not achieve the results I might expect. And when God sent his own Son — sinless, non-coercive, full of grace and healing — we killed him. God himself allows what he does not prefer, in order to achieve some greater goal.

IN *PARADISE LOST* JOHN Milton wrote of Adam seeing a preview of all history to come. At last he lifts his head from guilt and despair and sings out:

> O goodness infinite, goodness immense,
> That all this good of evil shall produce
> And evil turn to good, more wonderful
> Than that by which creation first brought forth
> Light out of darkness! Full of doubt I stand,
> Whether I should repent me now of sin
> By me done and occasioned, or rejoice
> Much more that much more good thereof shall spring . . .

O felix culpa, or "Oh, happy guilt," was a staple of medieval theology, one still celebrated in the Holy Saturday liturgy. It means, simply, that in a mysterious way we are better off now than before Adam's

"Fortunate Fall." The final chapter of the story, redemption, achieves a state superior to the first chapter, creation. As Augustine expressed it, "God judged it better to bring good out of evil than to suffer no evil at all." The final result will prove worth the cost.

Surely we are better off in at least one way: we have Jesus, who in his life and death accomplished for the entire cosmos the same story of redemption promised to each of us individually. I have focused on a relationship with God from the human point of view, the only point of view I have. Yet I am aware that just as we must make adjustments to "know God personally"—a God invisible and utterly unlike us—so God must make adjustments in order to know us. Indeed, God had to subject himself to the very same plot. The early Christian writers spoke of Jesus as the "recapitulation" of the human drama.

The world is good. God pronounced it as such after each day's creative work. Even in its fallen state, God judged the world—judged us—worth the rescue effort, worth the condescension to the bounds of time and space, worth dying for.

The world is fallen. God has promised to abolish suffering, poverty, evil, and death. His means of doing so, however, involved absorbing those very things in strong doses. Though God may not prevent the hardships of this free and dangerous world, neither did God seek personal immunity from them. Deliberately, God's Son Jesus submitted to the worst of this fallen world.

Finally, *the world can be redeemed.* That was the whole point in Jesus' coming to earth. In the height of irony, God transformed ultimate evil into ultimate good, working through humanity's violence and hatred to accomplish our redemption. As Paul expressed it, "And having disarmed the powers and authorities, he made a public spectacle of them, triumphing over them *by the cross.*"

History changed forever as a result of Jesus' time on earth. And God's overall plan for the universe will ultimately prevail; history merely fills in the details. Again, Paul: "If God is for us, who can be against us? He who did not spare his own Son, but gave him up for us all—how will he not also, along with him, graciously give us all things? . . . Who shall separate us from the love of Christ?"

Today, we refer to the day Jesus died as Good Friday, not "Dark Friday" or "Tragic Friday." It is by his stripes, after all, that we are healed.

After the tears comes the silence:
The slow night, the still sad time,
Rinsed, empty, scoured and sore with salt,
Spent, waiting without hope.
After the night comes the Lamb:
Bright morning star, with living water free
And fresh, the fruit of Friday's toil.

N. T. Wright

M Y WIFE LEADS A weekly "Christian circle" at a nursing home. An
Alzheimer's patient named Betsy faithfully attends, led there by
a staff worker, and sits through the hour. Betsy is slender, with snow-
white hair, blue eyes, and a pleasant smile. Every week Janet introduces
herself, and every week Betsy responds as if she's never seen her before.
When other people interact in the group or laugh at some little joke,
Betsy smiles a distant, disarming smile. Mostly she sits quietly, vacant-
eyed, enjoying the change of scenery from her room but comprehending nothing of the discussion going on around her.

After a few weeks, Janet learned that Betsy has retained the ability
to read. Often, she carries with her a postcard her daughter sent her
several months before, which she pores over as if it came in yesterday's
mail. She has no comprehension of what she is reading and will repeat
the same line over and over, like a stuck record, until someone prompts
her to move on. But on a good day she can read a passage straight
through in a clear, strong voice. Janet began calling on her each week
to read a hymn.

One Friday the senior citizens, who prefer older hymns they remember from childhood, selected "The Old Rugged Cross" for Betsy to read.
"On a hill far away stands an old rugged cross, the emblem of suffering and shame," she began, and stopped. She suddenly got agitated. "I
can't go on! It's too sad! Too sad!" she said. Some of the seniors gasped.
Others stared at her, dumbfounded. In years of living at the home, not
once had Betsy shown the ability to put words together meaningfully.
Now, obviously, she did understand.

Janet calmed her: "That's fine, Betsy. You don't have to keep reading if you don't want to."

After a pause, though, she started reading again, and stopped at the same place. A tear made a trail down each cheek. "I can't go on! It's too sad!" she said, unaware she had said the same thing two minutes ago. She tried again, and again reacted with a sudden shock of recognition, grief, and the exact same words.

Since the meeting had drawn to a close, the other seniors gradually moved away, heading for the cafeteria or their rooms. They moved quietly, as if in church, glancing over their shoulders in awe at Betsy. Staff workers who had come to rearrange the furniture stopped in their tracks and stared. No one had ever seen Betsy in a state resembling lucidity.

Finally, when Betsy seemed tranquil, Janet led her to the elevator to return her to her room. To her amazement Betsy began singing the hymn from memory. The words came in breathy, chopped phrases, and she could barely carry the tune, but anyone could recognize the hymn.

> On a hill far away stood an old rugged cross
> The emblem of suff'ring and shame.

New tears fell, but this time Betsy kept going, still from memory, gaining strength as she sang.

> And I love that old cross where the dearest and best
> For a world of lost sinners was slain.
> So I'll cherish the old rugged cross,
> Till my trophies at last I lay down;
> I will cling to the old rugged cross,
> And exchange it some day for a crown.

Somewhere in that tattered mind, damaged neurons had tapped into a network of old connections to resurrect a pattern of meaning for Betsy. In her confusion, two things only stood out: suffering and shame. Those two words summarize the human condition, the condition she lives in every day of her sad life. Who knows more suffering and shame than Betsy? For her, the hymn answered that question: Jesus does.

The hymn ends, and the Christian story ends, with the promise that redemption will one day be complete, that God will vindicate himself with

We know of that Good Friday which Christianity holds to have been that of the Cross. But the non-Christian, the atheist, knows of it as well. This is to say that he knows of the injustice, of the interminable suffering, of the waste, of the brute enigma of ending, which so largely make up not only the historical dimension of the human condition, but the everyday fabric of our personal lives. We know, ineluctably, of the pain, of the failure of love, of the solitude which are our history and private fate. We know also about Sunday. To the Christian, that day signifies an intimation, both assured and precarious, both evident and beyond comprehension, of resurrection, of a justice and a love that have conquered death. . . . The lineaments of that Sunday carry the name of hope (there is no word less deconstructible).

But ours is the long day's journey of the Saturday.

GEORGE STEINER

a burst of re-creative power, that personal knowledge of God will be as certain as the most intimate relationships we know on earth. "For now we see through a glass, darkly; but then face to face: now I know in part; but then shall I know even as also I am known."

The Christian story ends with the promise that Betsy will one day get a new mind which retains suffering and shame, if at all, only as some dim recollection of a former time. The poet Patrick Kavanagh describes the promise set loose at Jesus' resurrection as "a laugh freed for ever and ever."

For some, like Betsy, Saturday's long day's journey seems too long, its burden too heavy. The fact of Good Friday may offer some solace of companionship. And yet for one trapped in suffering and shame and a mind too clouded to understand anything else, the promise of Sunday seems hazy and hopelessly insubstantial. Unless, of course, it's true.

NOTES

1. Born Again Breech

15. *Updike:* John Updike, *A Month of Sundays* (New York: Fawcett Crest, 1975), 203.

18. *Buechner:* Frederick Buechner, *Wishful Thinking* (New York: Harper & Row, 1973), 14.

19. *Augustine:* Saint Augustine, *The Confessions of St. Augustine* (Garden City, N.Y.: Image/Doubleday, 1960), 138.

19–20. *Peterson:* Eugene Peterson, *The Wisdom of Each Other* (Grand Rapids: Zondervan, 1998), 29.

20. *Lewis:* C. S. Lewis, *The World's Last Night* (New York: Harcourt Brace Jovanovich, 1959), 77.

22. *Gregory of Nyssa.* Quoted in Jürgen Moltmann, *History and the Triune God* (New York: Crossroad, 1992), 89.

2. Thirsting at the Fountainside

25. *Ionesco:* Eugene Ionesco, *Diaries.* Quoted in Helmut Thielicke, *How to Believe Again* (Philadelphia: Fortress, 1972), 199.

28. *Aquinas:* Thomas Aquinas. Quoted in Frederick Buechner, *Wishful Thinking* op. cit., 65.

28. *Lewis:* C. S. Lewis, *Miracles* (New York: MacMillan, 1947), 96.

31. *"God is love":* 1 John 4:16

31. *Marty:* Martin Marty, *A Cry of Absence* (Grand Rapids: Eerdmans, 1997), 25.

31–32. *Buechner:* Frederick Buechner, *The Alphabet of Grace* (New York: Seabury, 1970), 6.

32. *"I want to know":* Chorus from "In the Secret." Andy Park (Mercy Vineyard), 1995.

32. *Wilbur:* Richard Wilbur. Quoted in Dan Wakefield, *Returning* (New York: Penguin, 1988), 152.

3. Room for Doubt

37. *Dickinson:* From a letter to Otis Lord, April 30, 1882; Thomas H. Johnson, ed., *The Letters of Emily Dickinson* (Cambridge: Belknap, 1958), 728.

37. *De Vries:* Peter De Vries, *The Blood of the Lamb* (New York: Penguin, 1961), 237.

38. *"This is a hard teaching":* John 6:60

38. *"You do not":* John 6:67

38. *"Lord, to whom":* John 6:68

39. *"Your faith":* Matthew 9:22

40. *"I have not found":* Luke 7:9

40. *"Woman":* Matthew 15:28

40. *"I do believe":* Mark 9:24

41. *O'Connor:* Flannery O'Connor. In a letter to a friend, in Sally Fitzgerald, ed., *Letters of Flannery O'Connor: The Habit of Being* (New York: Vintage, 1979), 476.

42. *Luther:* Martin Luther. Quoted in Thomas G. Long & Cornelius Plantinga, eds., *A Chorus of Witnesses* (Grand Rapids: Eerdmans, 1994), 114.

42. *Mather:* Ibid., 114.

42. *Underhill:* Evelyn Underhill. Quoted in Hugh T. Kerr & John M. Mulder, eds., *Conversions* (Grand Rapids: Eerdmans, 1983), 187.

42–43. *Buechner:* Frederick Buechner, *Alphabet of Grace,* op. cit., 47.

44. *Carey:* William Carey. Mark Galli, "The Man Who Wouldn't Give Up," in *Christian History,* Issue 36 (Vol. XI, No. 4), 11.

45. *Milton:* John Milton, *Paradise Lost* (New York: Mentor Books/New American Library, 1961), 44.

45. *Pascal:* Blaise Pascal. Quoted in Kelly James Clark, *When Faith Is Not Enough* (Grand Rapids: Eerdmans, 1997), 38.

45. *"You will know":* John 8:32

46. *Donne:* John Donne, "Hymn to Christ at the Author's Last Going into Germany," *Donne: The Complete English Poems* (London: Penguin, 1987), 346.

47. *Hawthorne:* Nathaniel Hawthorne. Quoted in Lockerbie, *Dismissing God* (Grand Rapids: Baker, 1998), 89.

48. *O'Connor:* Flannery O'Connor. Quoted in Clark, *When Faith,* op. cit., 94.

4. Faith under Fire

52. *Newbigin:* Lesslie Newbigin, *The Household of God* (New York: Friendship, 1954), 29.

52. *"My Father":* Matthew 26:39.

52–53. *Ross:* George Everett Ross. Quoted in Leonard I. Sweet, *Strong in the Broken Places* (Akron: University of Akron, 1995), 109.

52. *"To this very hour":* 1 Corinthians 4:11.

54–55. *Kierkegaard:* Søren Kierkegaard, *Fear and Trembling/Repetition* (Princeton, N.J.: Princeton University, 1983), 18.

56. *"Do you have":* Job 40:9f.

57–58. *"Look at the birds":* Matthew 6:26.

58. *"Are not two sparrows":* Matthew 10:29.

58. *Ellul:* Jacques Ellul, *What I Believe,* trans. Geoffrey Bromiley (Grand Rapids: Eerdmans, 1986), 156.

58. *Betts:* Doris Betts. Quoted in interview with W. Dale Brown, *Of Fiction and Faith* (Grand Rapids: Eerdmans, 1997), 21.

59. *Capon:* Robert Farrar Capon, *The Parables of Judgment* (Grand Rapids: Eerdmans, 1989), 92.

59. *"In him all things":* Colossians 1:17.

59. *"Neither this man":* John 9:3.

60. *Herbert:* George Herbert, C.A. Patrides, ed., *The English Poems of George Herbert* (Totowa, N.J.: Rowman & Littlefield, 1974), 159.

61. *Guyon:* Madame Jeanne Guyon, *Spiritual Torrents* (Augusta, Maine: Christian Books, 1984).

5. Two-Handed Faith

63. *Hammarskjöld:* Dag Hammarskjöld, *Markings.* Quoted in Brennan Manning, *Lion and Lamb* (Old Tappan, N.J.: Revell, 1984), 123.

66. *Safire:* William Safire, *The First Dissident* (New York: Random House, 1992), xxii.

67. *"Prince of the Persian":* Daniel 10:13.

67–68. *Lewis:* C. S. Lewis, *World's Last Night,* op. cit., 23.

68–69. *Lewis:* C. S. Lewis. In C. S. Lewis and Don Giovanni Calabria, *Letters* (Ann Arbor, Mich.: Servant, 1988), 53.

69. *de Caussade:* Jean-Pierre de Caussade, *The Sacrament of the Present Moment* (San Francisco: HarperSanFrancisco, 1989), 72.

69. *de Caussade:* Ibid., 77.

70. *"If we are thrown":* Daniel 3:17.

70. *"My God,":* Matthew 27:46.

70. *"Father, into":* Luke 23:46.

70. *"I have learned":* Philippians, 4:12.

70–71. *"Never send to know":* John Donne, "Meditation XVII" in *Devotions* (Ann Arbor, Mich.: University of Michigan, 1959), 109.

71. *"Surely it is not":* Ibid., 15.

72. *"For I am convinced":* Romans 8:38.

72. *Donne:* John Donne, *Devotions,* op. cit., 41.

72. *Tolstoy:* Leo Tolstoy, "A Confession," John Bayley, ed., *The Portable Tolstoy* (New York: Penguin, 1978), 704.

6. Living in Faith

73. *Percy:* Walker Percy, *Lancelot* (New York: Farrar, Straus & Giroux, 1977), 235.

74. *"Blessed is the man":* Jeremiah 17:8.

76. *Byrd:* Richard E. Byrd, *Alone* (New York: Putnam, 1938), 104, 280.

76. *"Here is a trustworthy":* 1 Timothy 1:15.

77. *"Now to the King":* 1 Timothy 1:17.

77. *Moltmann:* Jürgen Moltmann, *Experiences of God* (Philadelphia: Fortress, 1980), 7–8.

78. *Herbert:* George Herbert, *English Poems,* op. cit., 155.

78–79. *Mandela:* Nelson Mandela, *Long Walk to Freedom* (New York: Little, Brown), 495–496.

80. *"Lord, to whom":* John 6:68.

80. *Tolstoy:* Leo Tolstoy, *Fables & Fairy Tales* (New York: Signet Classics, 1962), 87.

80. *"Thy will be done":* Matthew 6:10.

81. *"Quit playing God ...":* Quoted in Ernest Kurtz, *Not-God: A History of Alcoholics Anonymous* (Center City, Mo.: The Hazelden Foundation, 1991), vii.

81. *"There is no fear":* 1 John 4:18.

81. *"We love because":* 1 John 4:19.

82. *Merton:* Thomas Merton, *The Seven Story Mountain* (New York: Harcourt, Brace & Co., 1948), 370.

83. *Mother Teresa:* Quoted in David Aikman, *Great Souls* (Nashville: Word, 1998), 233.

83–84. *Saint Ignatius of Loyola.* Quoted in Alan Paton, *Instrument of Thy Peace* (New York: Seabury, 1968), 41.

84. *Pascal:* Blaise Pascal, *Pascal's Pensees,* Pensee #507 (New York: Dutton, 1958), 139.

84. *Donne:* John Donne, *Poems,* "Holy Sonnet XIV" (New York: Dutton, 1931), 254.

84. *Blake:* William Blake, "Milton." Quoted in David F. Ford, *The Shape of Living* (Grand Rapids: Baker, 1997), 157.

7. Mastery of the Ordinary

85. *Eliot:* T. S. Eliot, "Four Quartets," in *The Complete Poems & Plays* (New York: Harcourt, Brace & Co., 1952), 127.

86. *Lamott:* Anne Lamott, *Traveling Mercies* (New York: Pantheon, 1999), 82.

86. *Carl Jung:* Quoted in M. Scott Peck, *Further Along the Road Less Traveled* (New York: Simon & Schuster, 1993), 138.

88. *"My teaching":* John 7:16.

88. *Van Doren:* Mark Van Doren. Quoted in interview with Dan Wakefield in *Mars Hill Review* (Winter/Spring, 1996), 11.

89. *"What does the Lord require?":* Micah 6:8.

89. *Vanauken:* Sheldon Vanauken, *A Severe Mercy* (New York: Harper & Row, 1977), 99.

90. *Merton:* Thomas Merton, *No Man is an Island* (New York: Harcourt, Brace & Co., 1955), 241.

91. *Loyola:* Saint Ignatius Loyola. Quoted in Gerard Manley Hopkins, *The Sermons and Devotional Writings of Gerard Manley Hopkins* (London: Oxford University, 1959), 203–204.

92. *Greeley:* Andrew Greeley. In *The New York Times Book Review,* n.d.

92. *Chesterton:* G. K. Chesterton, *Orthodoxy* (New York: Image, 1959), 95.

93. *Jewish Rabbi:* Rabbi Bunam. In Clark, *When Faith,* op. cit., 158.

93. *Peck:* M. Scott Peck, *The Road Less Traveled* (New York: Simon & Schuster, 1978), 15.

94. *Trueblood:* Elton Trueblood, *The Yoke of Christ* (Waco, Tex.: Word, 1958), 17.

94. *"Come to me":* Matthew 11:28.

94. *"Take my yoke":* Matthew 11:29.

94. *"Peace of God":* Philippians 4:7.

94. *"Pondering":* Luke 2:19.

95. *"Hope that is seen":* Romans 8:24.

95. *"Suffering produces":* Romans 5:3.

95–96. *Covington:* Dennis Covington, *Salvation on Sand Mountain* (New York: Penguin, 1995), 204.

96. *Bunyan:* John Bunyan, *Pilgrim's Progress* (New York: Washington Square, 1957), 210.

96. *Niebuhr:* Reinhold Niebuhr. Quoted in Thomas Cahill, *The Gifts of the Jews* (New York: Doubleday, 1998), 169.

8. Knowing God, or Anyone Else

99. *Pascal:* Blaise Pascal, *Pensees,* #230, op. cit., 64–65.

102. *Berkeley:* George Berkeley. Quoted in Alvin Plantinga, *God and Other Minds: A Study of the Rational Justification of Belief in God* (Ithaca: Cornell University, 1967), viii.

104. *"We have this treasure":* 2 Corinthians 4:7.

105. *Tennyson:* Alfred Lord Tennyson,"The Higher Pantheism," *The Poetic and Dramatic Works of Alfred Lord Tennyson* (Boston: Houghton, Mifflin, 1898), 273.

105. *"When the counselor":* John 16:13.

105–106. *"The man without":* 1 Corinthians 2:14.

106. *"Now this is eternal":* John 17:3.

106. *"Being sure of":* Hebrews 11:1.

106. *"Saw him who":* Hebrews 11:27.

106. *Underhill:* Evelyn Underhill. Quoted in Richard Foster, *Streams of Living Water* (San Francisco: HarperSanFrancisco, 1998), 235.

106. *"Children of light":* Ephesians 5:8.

106. *"Dear friends,":* 1 John 3:1.

107. *Augustine:* Saint Augustine, *Confessions,* op. cit., 335.

108. *"The days of long ago":* Psalm 143:5.

108. *"Do not hide":* Psalm 143:7.

109. *Von Hugel:* Baron Von Hugel. Quoted in Alister Hardy, *The Biology of God* (New York: Taplinger, 1976), 155.

109. *Ezra Stiles.* Quoted in Alfred Kazin, *God and the American Writer* (New York: Vintage, 1997), 5.

110. *Orthodox writer:* Evagrius of Pontus. Quoted in *Christian History,* Issue 54, (Vol. XVI, No. 2), 36.

110–111. *Viktor Frankl:* Viktor Frankl, *Man's Search for Meaning* (New York: Simon & Schuster, 1984), 48.

111. *Thomas Green:* Thomas Green, S.J., *Drinking From a Dry Well* (Notre Dame: Ave Maria, 1991), 18.

112. *"The secret things":* Deuteronomy 29:29.

112. *Norris:* Kathleen Norris, *Amazing Grace* (New York: Penguin, 1998), 214.

9. Personality Profile

113. *Hansen:* Ron Hansen, *Mariette in Ecstasy* (New York: HarperPerennial, 1991), 174.

114. *"Certain of what":* Hebrews 11:1.

115. *"Am I only":* Jeremiah 23:23.

115. *"With the Lord":* II Peter 3:8.

116. *Updike:* John Updike, *Self-Consciousness* (New York: Knopf, 1989), 229.

116. *Buber:* Martin Buber. Quoted in Clark, *When Faith,* op. cit., 4.

116. *"Truly you are":* Isaiah 45:15.

116. *Lane:* Belden C. Lane, "A Hidden and Playful God," in *The Christian Century* (September 30, 1987), 812.

116. *Eckhart:* Ibid.

116–117. *Lane:* Ibid.

117. *"And will not God":* Luke 18:7.

117. *"This is the victory":* 1 John 5:4.

117. *"However, when the Son":* Luke 18:8.

118. *"Surely the Lord":* Genesis 28:16.

119. *"Whenever it seizes him"*: Mark 9:18 to 21.

119. *"Quench not the Spirit"*: 1 Thessalonians 5:19 (KJV).

119. *"Grieve not"*: Ephesians 4:30 (KJV).

119. *"Father, forgive"*: Luke 23:34.

120. *Taylor:* John V. Taylor, *The Go-Between God* (London: SCM, 1972), 33.

120. *"How faint"*: Job 26:14.

121. *Julian:* Julian of Norwich, *Revelations of Divine Love* (London: Methuen, 1901), 34–35.

121. *"Does whatever pleases him"*: Psalm 115:3.

121–122. *Lewis:* C. S. Lewis, *Christian Reflections* (Grand Rapids: Eerdmans, 1967), 168–169.

121. *Edwards:* Jonathan Edwards, *The Works of Jonathan Edwards* (Edinburgh: Banner of Truth Trust, 1992), vol. 1, 368b.

10. In the Name of the Father

123. *Dostoevski:* Fyodor Dostoevski. Quoted in Luigi Giussani, in "Religious Awareness in Modern Man," *Communio: International Catholic Review*, 25 (Spring 1998), 121.

125. *"I am"*: Exodus 3:7 (KJV).

125. *"The Son is"*: Hebrews 1:3.

125. *"He is the image"*: 1 Corinthians 11:7.

125. *"And by him we cry"*: Romans 8:15.

126. *"Who was with God ..."*: John 1:1 ... 1:14.

126. *"Lord, show us"*: John 14:8.

126. *"Anyone who"*: John 14:9.

126. *"Make disciples"*: Matthew 28:19.

127. *"The fear of the Lord"*: Psalm 111:10.

127. *"I no longer"*: John 15:15.

128. *Stafford:* Tim Stafford, *Knowing the Face of God* (Colorado Springs: NavPress, 1996), 20.

129. *Herbert:* George Herbert, *Poems,* op.cit., 113.

130. *MacDonald:* Gordon MacDonald, *Forging a Real World Faith* (Nashville: Nelson, 1989), 58.

130. *"Immanuel"*: Matthew 1:23.

131. *"When they heard"*: Exodus 4:31.

131. *Scholem:* Gershom Scholem. Quoted in Eleanor Munro, *On Glory Roads* (New York: Thames and Hudson, 1987), 112.

131. *"We will die"*: Numbers 17:12.

131. *"Let us not hear"*: Deuteronomy 18:16.

132. *Milton:* John Milton, *Paradise Lost,* op. cit., 332.

132. *Lessing:* Doris Lessing. Quoted in Eugene Peterson, *Reversed Thunder* (San Francisco: HarperSanFrancisco, 1988), 162.

132. *"But my people"*: Psalm 81:11.

132. *"Inquire among"*: Jeremiah 18:13.

132–133. *Heschel:* Abraham Heschel, *The Prophets, Vol. 1* (New York: Harper & Row, 1962), 110–112.

133. *"Then the fire"*: 1 Kings 18:38.

133. *"The Lord"*: 1 Kings 18:39.

133. *"I have had enough":* 1 Kings 19:4.

133–34. *"Then a great and powerful":* 1 Kings 19:12.

11. Rosetta Stone

135. *Price:* Reynolds Price, *A Palpable God* (New York: Atheneum, 1978), 14.

136. *"He was in":* John 1:10.

136. *Augustine:* Saint Augustine. Quoted in Garry Wills, *Saint Augustine* (New York: Penguin Putnam, 1999), 139–140.

136. *Milton:* John Milton, *Paradise Lost,* op. cit., 335.

137. *Tournier:* Paul Tournier, *Creative Suffering* (San Francisco: Harper & Row, 1981), 89–90.

138. *"Learned obedience" . . . "made perfect":* Hebrews 5:8.

138. *"For we do not have":* Hebrews 4:15.

138. *"Able to deal gently":* Hebrews 5:2.

139. *Niebuhr:* H. Richard Niebuhr, *The Meaning of Revelation* (New York: MacMillan, 1941), 154.

140. *"God of all comfort":* 2 Corinthians 1:3.

140. *"Thy will be done":* Matthew 6:10 (KJV).

140. *Ambrose:* Bishop Ambrose. Quoted in Fenelon, *The Seeking Heart* (Beaumont, Tex.: Seedsowers, 1992).

141. *Drummond:* Henry Drummond, *Natural Law in the Spiritual World* (London: Hodder and Stoughton, 1885), 365.

141. *"And having disarmed":* Colossians 2:15.

142. *Girard's disciple:* Gil Bailie, *Violence Unveiled* (New York: Crossroad, 1995), 21.

142. *O'Connor:* Flannery O'Connor, "A Good Man is Hard to Find," *Flannery O'Connor: The Complete Stories* (New York: Farrar, Straus and Giroux, 1973), 131.

142. *"It is better":* John 11:50.

143. *"Lord, show us":* John 14:8.

144. *"Don't you know me":* John 14:9.

144. *Bondi:* Roberta Bondi, *Memories of God* (Nashville: Abingdon, 1995), 43.

144. *"I no longer":* John 15:15.

145. *"Who, being in very nature":* Philippians 2:6.

145. *"This is my Son":* Matthew 3:17.

145. *Weil:* Simone Weil, *Gravity and Grace* (London: Routledge, 1995), 80.

146. *"Lord, show us":* John 14:8.

12. The Go-Between

147. *Thoreau:* Henry David Thoreau. From his *Journal,* quoted in Loren Eiseley, *The Star Thrower* (New York: Harcourt Brace Jovanovich, 1978), 246.

147–148. *Eco:* Umberto Eco, *Travels in Hyper Reality* (New York: Harcourt Brace Jovanovich, 1983), 53.

148. *"God is spirit":* John 4:24.

149. *Taylor:* John V. Taylor, *The Go-Between God,* op cit., 43.

149–150. *"The wind blows":* John 3:8.

150. *"It is for your good":* John 16:7.

150. *Merton:* Thomas Merton, *Ascent to Truth* (New York: Harcourt Brace Jovanovich, 1951), 280.

150. *378 passages:* Cited in Adolf Holl, *The Left Hand of God* (New York: Doubleday, 1997), 7.

150. *Nouwen:* Henri Nouwen, *Sabbatical Journey* (New York: Crossroad, 1998), 161.

151. *Moltmann:* Jürgen Moltmann, *The Spirit of Life* (Minneapolis: Fortress, 1971), 180.

151. *Queen Victoria:* in David Smith, *The Friendless American Male* (Ventura, Calif.: Regal, 1983), 72.

152. *Packer:* J. I. Packer, *Knowing God* (Downers Grove, Ill.: InterVarsity, 1973), 107.

152. *"We know that the whole":* Romans 8:22.

152. *"The Spirit helps us":* Romans 8:26.

155. *"Unless a kernel":* John 12:24.

155. *Peterson:* Eugene Peterson, *Reversed Thunder,* op. cit., 54.

156–156. *Taylor:* John V. Taylor, *The Christlike God* (London: SCM, 1992), 205.

156. *Hillesum:* Etty Hillesum, *An Interrupted Life: The Diaries of Etty Hillesum, 1941–1943* (New York: Random House, 1983), 151.

156. *Hopkins:* Gerard Manley Hopkins, *The Sermons,* op. cit., 100.

13. Makeover

161. *Kierkegaard:* Søren Kierkegaard, *The Prayers of Kierkegaard,* Perry LeFebre, ed. (Chicago: University of Chicago, 1956), 147.

162. *Arnold:* J. Heinrich Arnold, *Discipleship* (Farmington, Pa.: Plough, 1994), 28.

163. *Doren:* Mark van Doren. Quoted in Eugene Peterson, *Leap Over a Wall* (San Francisco: HarperSanFrancisco, 1997), 236.

163. *Rabbi Zusya:* in Kathleen Norris, *Cloister Walk* (New York: Putnam/Riverhead, 1996), 63.

163. *"No one ever hated":* Ephesians 5:29f.

164. *"How great is the love":* 1 John 3:1.

164. *"Dear friends,":* 1 John 3:2.

164. *"Our hearts":* 1 John 3:20.

164. *Phillips:* J. B. Phillips, *Ring of Truth* (Wheaton, Ill.: Shaw, 1967), 74.

166. *Nouwen:* Henri Nouwen, *Life of the Beloved* (New York: Crossroad, 1992), 62.

166. *Norris:* Kathleen Norris, *Amazing Grace,* op. cit., 151.

167. *"Don't you know":* 1 Corinthians 3:16.

167. *"Set his seal":* 2 Corinthians 1:22.

167–168. *Taylor:* John V. Taylor, *The Christlike God,* op. cit., 276.

168. *Taylor:* John V. Taylor, *The Go-Between God,* op. cit., 18.

168. *"Set your minds":* Colossians 3:2.

168–169. *"Whatever is true":* Philippians 4:8.

169. *Bonhoeffer:* Dietrich Bonhoeffer, *Meditating on the Word,* David McI. Gracie, ed. (Cambridge, Mass.: Cowley, 1986), 32.

169–170. *Bondi:* Roberta Bondi, *Memories,* op. cit., 201.

170. *"Be transformed":* Romans 12:2.

170. *Hammarskjöld:* Dag Hammarskjöld, *Markings,* trans. Leif Sjöberg and W. H. Auden (New York: Ballantine, 1993), 103.

170. *Eliot:* T.S. Eliot, *Four Quartets* (London: Faber and Faber, 1944), 33.

14. Out of Control

173. *Lonergan:* Bernard Lonergan. Quoted in Robert J. Wicks, *Touching the Holy* (Notre Dame: Ave Maria, 1992), 14.

174. *King:* Martin Luther King, Jr. Quoted in James Wm. McClendon, Jr., *Biography as Theology* (Philadelphia: Trinity Press, 1990), 83.

176. *"But the Counselor":* John 14:28.

176. *Psychiatrist's study:* Robert Jay Lifton, *Thought Reform and the Psychology of Totalism* (Chapel Hill, N.C.: University of North Carolina, 1961), 6f.

177. *"Take up your cross":* see Matthew 10:38.

177. *Crabb:* Larry Crabb, *Connecting* (Nashville: Word, 1997), 39.

179. *Eric Liddell:* from the movie *Chariots of Fire.*

179. *"I am not ashamed":* Romans 1:16.

180–181. *Mouw:* Richard Mouw, in *The Reformed Journal* (October 1990), 13.

181. *Lewis:* C. S. Lewis, *God in the Dock* (Grand Rapids: Eerdmans, 1970), 50.

184. *Unamuno:* Miguel de Unamuno. Quoted in James Houston, *In Pursuit of Happiness* (Colorado Springs: NavPress, 1996), 264.

15. Passion and the Desert

185. *Sulivan:* Jean Sulivan, *Morning Light* (New York: Paulist, 1976), 19.

185. *Lewis:* C. S. Lewis, *Screwtape Letters* (New York: Time, 1961), 5.

185–186. *Nouwen:* Henri Nouwen, *Sabbatical Journey,* op. cit., 5–6.

186. *Nouwen:* Henri Nouwen, *The Inner Voice of Love* (New York: Doubleday, 1996), xiv.

186–187. *A Kempis:* Thomas à Kempis, *The Imitation of Christ* (Nashville: Nelson, 1979), 188.

187. *Thérèse:* Thérèse of Liseux. Quoted in Ernest Kurtz and Katherine Ketcham, *The Spirituality of Imperfection* (New York: Bantam, 1992), 220.

187–188. *Jerome:* Saint Jerome, *Select Letters of Saint Jerome* (Cambridge, Mass.: Harvard University, 1933), 397.

188. *Moltmann:* Jürgen Moltmann, "The Passion of Life," in *Currents in Theology and Mission,* vol. 4, no. 1.

189. *"They turned their backs":* Jeremiah 32:33.

190. *"A man after God is":* Acts 13:22.

190. *"I will become":* II Samuel 6:22.

190. *Buechner:* Frederick Buechner, *Peculiar Treasures* (San Francisco: Harper & Row, 1979), 24.

191. *"I have sinned":* 2 Samuel 12:13.

192. *"Against you":* Psalm 51:4.

192. *"A broken spirit":* Psalm 51:17.

192. *"O God, you are":* Psalm 63:1 to 3.

192. *"For my sake":* 2 Kings 20:6.

192. *"I will make":* Isaiah 55:3.

194. *de Sales:* Francis de Sales, *The Art of Loving God* (Manchester, N.H.: Sophia Institute, 1998), 36.

195. *Nouwen:* Henri Nouwen, *Gracias* (Maryknoll, N.Y.: Orbis, 1993), 69.

195. *Merton:* Thomas Merton, *Thoughts in Solitude* (Garden City, N.Y.: Image/Doubleday, 1968), 81.

16. Spiritual Amnesia

197. *Voltaire:* Quoted in Leonard I. Sweet, *Strong in the Broken Places,* op cit., 1995, 181.

198. *Auden:* W. H. Auden, "Pascal," in *Collected Poetry of W. H. Auden* (New York: Random House, 1945), 88.

199. *Müller:* George Müller. Quoted in John Piper, *Desiring God* (Portland: Multnomah, 1986), 116.

199. *"Those who hope":* Isaiah 40:31.

200. *Claypool:* John Claypool, *Tracks of a Fellow Traveler* (Waco, Tex.: Word, 1974), 55.

201. *Donne:* John Donne. Quoted in Gene Edwards, *The Secret to the Christian Life* (Beaumont, Tex.: Seedsowers, 1991), flyleaf.

201. *Guardini:* Romano Guardini, *The Lord* (Chicago: Regnery Gateway, 1954), 38, 211.

201. *"Only be careful":* Deuteronomy 4:9.

201-202. *"Your heart will become proud":* Deuteronomy 8:14.

202. *"Does a maiden forget":* Jeremiah 2:32.

202. *"I am like a moth":* Hosea 5:12.

203. *Lewis:* C. S. Lewis, *Letters to Malcolm: Chiefly on Prayer* (New York: Harcourt Brace & World, 1963), 114.

203. *Merton:* Thomas Merton, *No Man is an Island*, op. cit., 230.

204-205. *Lawrence:* Brother Lawrence, *Practice of the Presence of God* (Nashville: Nelson, 1981), 51, 41-42, 88.

205-207. *Laubach:* Frank C. Laubach, *Man of Prayer* (Syracuse, New York: Laubach Literacy, 1990), passim.

17. Child

211. *Auden:* W. H. Auden, *The Age of Anxiety* (New York: Random House, 1947), 123.

213. *"Whoever is stealing":* Paraphrase of Ephesians 4:28.

214. *"I could not address":* 1 Corinthians 3:1.

214. *"Unless you change":* Matthew 18:3.

214-215. *Weiser:* Artur Weiser, *The Psalms* (Philadelphia: Westminster, 1962), 777.

215-216. *Packer:* J. I. Packer, *Knowing God*, op. cit., 223.

216. *"To the faithful":* Psalm 18:25.

216-217. *"Such regulations":* Colossians 2:23.

217. *"The entire law":* Galatians 5:14.

217. *"Lazarus is dead":* John 11:14.

217. *"Unless you change":* Matthew 18:3.

218. *Buechner:* Frederick Buechner, "The Breaking of Silence," in *The Magnificent Defeat* (New York: Seabury, 1966), 124.

219. *"Give us this day":* Matthew 6:11.

219. *"Abba, Father":* Mark 14:36.

219. *"Father, into your hands":* Luke 23:46.

219. *Norris:* Kathleen Norris, *Amazing Grace,* op. cit., 63.

219. Ibid., 66.

220–222. *Ciszek:* Walter Ciszek, *He Leadeth Me* (San Francisco: Ignatius, 1973), 38, 142, 175, 182, 57, 79.

222. *Buechner:* Frederick Buechner, *The Magnificent Defeat,* op. cit., 134.

18. Adult

223. *Epictetus: Discourses.* Quoted in Diogenes Allen, *The Traces of God* (n.pl.: Cowley, 1981), 31.

225. *"Not my will":* Luke 22:42 (KJV).

226. *Lewis:* C. S. Lewis, *Letters to Malcolm,* op. cit., 148.

228–229. *Langerak:* Edward Langerak, "The Possibility of Love," in *The Reformed Journal* (February 1976), 26–27.

229. *"If anyone love me":* John 14:23.

229. *Nouwen:* Henri Nouwen, *Inner Voice of Love,* op. cit., 70.

229. *Augustine:* Saint Augustine, *Day by Day* (New York: Catholic, 1986), 17.

231. *Benedict:* Saint Benedict. Quoted in Kathleen Norris, *Cloister Walk,* op. cit., 7.

231. *Chittister:* Joan Chittister, *Wisdom Distilled from the Daily* (San Francisco: HarperSanFrancisco, 1990), 7.

231–232. *Edwards:* Jonathan Edwards. Quoted in James M. Gordon, *Evangelical Spirituality* (London: SPCK, 1991), 43.

232. *"Train yourself":* 1 Timothy 4:7.

233. *Lewis:* C. S. Lewis, *Mere Christianity* (New York: MacMillan, 1952), 130.

19. Parent

235. *King:* Bishop King. Quoted in H. Wheeler Robinson, *Suffering, Human and Divine* (New York: MacMillan, 1939), 200.

236. *Vanier:* Jean Vanier, *Man and Woman He Made Them* (New York: Paulist Press, 1984), 84.

236. *"I no longer call":* John 15:15.

236. *"This is how we know":* 1 John 3:16.

237. *"Though I am free":* 1 Corinthians 9:19.

237. *Browning:* Robert Browning, "A Death in the Desert," *Dramatis Personae,* F. E. L. Priestly & I. Lancashire, eds. (Toronto: University of Toronto, 1997), n.p.

237–238. *Rolheiser:* Ronald Rolheiser, *Holy Longing* (New York: Doubleday, 1999), 192.

240. *"For even the Son":* Mark 10:45.

241. *Lewis:* C. S. Lewis, *The Screwtape Letters,* op. cit., 25.

241–242. *Nouwen:* Henri Nouwen, *The Living Reminder* (New York: Seabury Press, 1977), 45.

242. *"You have hidden":* Isaiah 64:7.

242. *"Why are you like":* Jeremiah 14:8.

242. *Hopkins:* Gerard Manley Hopkins. Robert Bridges and W. H. Gardner, eds., *Poems of Gerard Manley Hopkins* (New York: Oxford, 1948), 43.

243. *"My God, my God":* Matthew 27:46.

243. *Lewis:* C. Day Lewis, "Walking Away," in *The Complete Poems of C. Day Lewis* (London: Sinclair-Stevenson, 1992), 546.

244. *"Whoever loses his life":* Matthew 10:39.

245. *Buechner:* Frederick Buechner, *Wishful Thinking,* op. cit., 28.

20. Paradise Lost

251. *"And God saw":* Genesis 1:10.

252. *Lewis:* C. S. Lewis, *Screwtape,* op. cit., 27.

253. *May:* Gerald May. Interview in *The Wittenberg Door* (Sept./Oct. 1992), 7–10.

254. *Levi:* Primo Levi, *The Reawakening* (New York: Macmillan, 1965), 163.

254–255. *Van Gogh:* Vincent Van Gogh. Quoted in Cliff Edwards, *Van Gogh and God* (Chicago: Loyola University, 1989), 70.

255. *Robinson:* Marilynne Robinson, in Alfred Corn, ed., *Incarnation* (London: Viking Penguin, 1990), 310–311.

257. *"The creation itself will be":* Romans 8:21.

257. *Macarius:* Quoted in Kathleen Norris, *Cloister Walk,* op. cit., 125.

21. God's Irony

259. *Dell:* George Dell, *The Earth Abideth* (Columbus, Ohio: Ohio State University, 1986), 317.

260. *"Now we see":* 1 Corinthians 13:12.

261. *"Thorn in the flesh":* 2 Corinthians 12:7.

261. *"You intended to harm":* Genesis 50:20.

261. *O'Connor:* Flannery O'Connor, *Mystery and Manners* (New York: Farrar, Straus & Giroux, 1961), 118.

262. *de Chardin:* Teilhard de Chardin, *The Divine Milieu* (New York: Harper & Row, 1960), 86.

263. *"I have learned":* Philippians 4:11.

264. *"Your grief will":* John 16:20.

264. *Tertullian:* Quoted in Dallas Willard, *The Spirit of the Disciplines* (San Francisco: Harper & Row, 1988), 35.

264. *Tournier:* Paul Tournier, *The Person Reborn* (New York: Harper & Row, 1966), 80–81.

265. *Weatherhead:* Leslie D. Weatherhead, *The Will of God* (Nashville: Abingdon, 1972).

266. *Wolterstorff:* Nicholas Wolterstorff, *Lament for a Son* (Grand Rapids: Eerdmans, 1987), 96–97, 81.

266. *Nouwen:* Henri Nouwen, *Making All Things New: An Invitation to the Spiritual Life* (San Francisco: Harper & Row, 1981), 51–53.

22. An Arranged Marriage

269. *Chesterton:* G. K. Chesterton, *Collected Works, Vol. IV* (San Francisco: Ignatius, 197), 69.

272. *"If I must boast":* 2 Corinthians 11:30.

272–273. *Sayers:* Dorothy Sayers, *The Mind of the Maker* (London: Methuen, 1959), 152.

274. *"In all things":* Romans 8:28.

274–275. *O'Connor:* Flannery O'Connor, *Letters: Habit of Being,* op. cit., 163.

275. *"Not many of you":* 1 Corinthians 1:26.

275. *Norris:* Kathleen Norris, *Amazing Grace,* op. cit., 29.

276. *Kundera:* Milan Kundera, "A Life Like a Work of Art." In *The New Republic* (January 29, 1990), 16.

276. *Havel:* Vaclav Havel, "Faith in the World," *Civilization* (April/May 1998), 53.

277. *Masefield:* John Masefield, *The Everlasting Mercy and The Widow in the Bye Street* (New York: Macmillan, 1916), 221.

23. The Fruit of Friday's Toil

279. *Cahill:* Thomas Cahill, *Desire of the Everlasting Hills* (New York: Doubleday, 1999), 130.

279. *Willard:* Dallas Willard, *The Divine Conspiracy* (San Francisco: HarperSanFrancisco, 1998), 337.

280. *Wilson:* Bill Wilson in Kurtz, *Not-God,* op. cit., 61.

281. *Tournier:* Paul Tournier, *Creative Suffering,* op. cit., 29.

282–283. *Price:* Reynolds Price, *A Whole New Life* (New York: Atheneum, 1994), 179.

283. *"I am the way":* John 14:6.

284. *Milton:* John Milton, *Paradise Lost,* op. cit., 338.

285. *Augustine:* Saint Augustine, *Enchiridon,* 27, as quoted in John Chapin, ed., *The Book of Catholic Quotations* (New York: Farrar, Straus & Cudahy, 1956), 313.

285. *"And having disarmed":* Colossians 2:15.

285. *"If God is for us":* Romans 8:31.

286. *Wright:* N. T. Wright, *Following Jesus* (Grand Rapids: Eerdmans, 1994), 58.

288. *"For now we see":* 1 Corinthians 13:12 (KJV).

288. *Kavanaugh:* Patrick Kavanaugh. In Ford, *The Shape of Living,* op. cit., 185.

288. *Steiner:* George Steiner, *Real Presences* (Chicago: University of Chicago, 1989), 231–232.

The Jesus I Never Knew

Philip Yancey

What happens when a respected Christian journalist decides to put his preconceptions aside and take a long look at the Jesus described in the Gospels? How does the Jesus of the New Testament compare to the "new, rediscovered" Jesus—or even the Jesus we think we know so well? Best-selling author Philip Yancey says, "The Jesus I got to know in writing this book is very different from the Jesus I learned about in Sunday school. In some ways he is more comforting; in some ways more terrifying."

Yancey offers a new and different perspective on the life of Christ and his work—his teaching, his miracles, his death and resurrection—and ultimately, who he was and why he came. Relating the gospel events to the world we live in today, *The Jesus I Never Knew* gives a moving and refreshing portrait of the central figure of history. With a willingness to tackle difficult questions, Yancey looks at the radical words of this itinerant Jewish carpenter and asks whether we are taking him seriously enough in our own day and age.

From the manger in Bethlehem to the cross in Jerusalem, Yancey presents a complex character who generates questions as well as answers; a disturbing and exhilarating Jesus who wants to radically transform your life and stretch your faith.

Hardcover 0-310-38570-9

The Bible Jesus Read

Philip Yancey

With his candid, signature style, Yancey interacts with the Old Testament from the perspective of his own deeply personal journey. From Moses, the amazing prince of Egypt, to the psalmists' turbulent emotions and the prophets' oddball rantings, Yancey paints a picture of Israel's God—and ours—that fills in the blanks of a solely New Testament vision of the Almighty.

Probing some carefully selected Old Testament books—Job, Deuteronomy, Psalms, Ecclesiastes, and the Prophets—Yancey reveals how the Old Testament deals in astonishing depths and detail with the issues that trouble us most. The Old Testament in fact tackles what the New Testament often only skirts. But that shouldn't surprise us. It is, after all, the Bible Jesus read.

Join Philip Yancey as he explores these sometimes shocking, often cryptic, divine writings. You will come to know God more intimately, anticipate Jesus more fervently, and find a wonderful, wise companion for your faith journey.

Hardcover 0-310-22834-4

We want to hear from you. Please send your comments about this book to us in care of the address below. Thank you.

ZondervanPublishingHouse
Grand Rapids, Michigan 49530
http://www.zondervan.com